OLIVETTI

A STUDY OF THE CORPORATE MANAGEMENT OF DESIGN

SIBYLLE KICHERER

olivetti

TREFOIL PUBLICATIONS LTD, LONDON

Contents

Part 1 The Beginnings of the Company

1	The beginings of the company
10	Foundations of the design substance
37	Transition to a new era
49	The Status of design in the company from 1960 to 1978
51	The Organisation of Design Activities under Renzo Zorzi

Part 2 The Company under Carlo De Benedetti

59	The Company under Carlo De Benedetti
61	Central aspects of Olivetti's design management today
68	Principles of managing design in Olivetti

Part 3 Product Case Studies

125	Product Case Studies
128	Portable Typewriter ETP55
137	The Delphos office furniture system
150	Keyboard design for the DM 309 printer
164	Notes & bibliography

Published by Trefoil Publications Ltd.
7 Royal Parade, Dawes Rd. London SW6

First published 1990

Copyright © Sibylle Kicherer, 1990

All rights reserved: the material published in this book is copyright, and no part of it may be reproduced, stored in a retrieval system, copied or transmitted in any form or by any means, electronic, mechanical photocpying or otherwise, without the prior permission in writing of the publishers.

ISBN 0 86294 115 6

Typeset by Wandsworth Typesetting.

Printed and bound in Italy by Graphicom, Vicenza.

British Library Cataloguing in Publication Data.
Kicherer, Sybille.
 Olivetti: a study of the management of corporate design.
 1. Companies. Corporate identity.
I. Title
659.2'85.

Foreword

The most recent thorough account of design within Olivetti was published seven years ago by the company itself. Called *Design Process Olivetti 1908-1983* it was a historical account of the company's first seventy-five years, listing and illustrating in elegant detail product ranges, publicity material, and company architecture, with notes on the designers and architects involved.

The present book does not attempt to repeat or add to the earlier descriptive work, though it contains an analysis of design in Olivetti from its earliest days. Rather, the present book concentrates on the design management activity within Olivetti, looking at attitudes and systems rather than products. But a comparison with *Design Process Olivetti* is instructive. While *Design Process Olivetti* might be different in its aims and intentions, much about the book epitomises the Olivetti attitude to design that is the subject of the present book.

The front cover, for example, shows a twisted and truncated starshaped column, segmented into the years of Olivetti's history, and subdivided through its length into the different areas of Olivetti activity explored in the book (see illustration). Industrial, graphic and architectural design form the outer leading edges, with interior design, exhibition design and typography and identification systems as less exposed surfaces. At the centre sits cultural activities, interfacing with every other aspect. This central role of the cultural in the company's image of itself, and its conception of design philosophy as an ongoing, historical and cultural force within the company forms one of the main themes of this book.

Another aspect of *Design Process Olivetti* illuminates central Olivetti policy. The graphic design was commissioned from Perry King and Santiago Miranda, whose main responsibility is for keyboard design, as we shall see in Chapter 3 here. Neither is by first definition a book designer but they *are* Olivetti designers, that is to say part of the group of independent designers who have built up a special consultant relationship with Olivetti over a number of years, and so are imbued with the company's traditions and culture. Giving a job to someone whose ablity is proven, and who understands the company's history and attitudes, has been a hallmark of the Olivetti design management style, which we will also meet in the pages of this book. For at the heart of the Olivetti design philosophy has been the concept of the independent in-house designer, an apparent contradiction in terms, but a concept which put Olivetti at the forefront of international product design for decades.

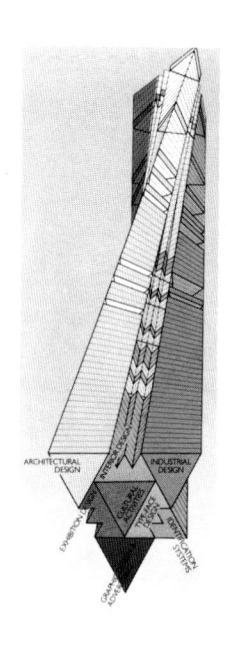

One of the problems in writing about design is that is is both relentless and a process, so that by the time a design reaches the retailer's shelves or the printed page of a book or magazine the thinking that led to it is already a year or more in th past. A book that claims to deal with current design practice can, in reality, rarely do any such thing, and so it is here. Work is probably already in hand to to replace or upgrade many of the products described here, but the process of designing them and the management of that process remains a valid and valuable example. Also, because design is a process, it is self-consuming. Few designers have the space or the vanity to keep every sketch, rough drawing or model for every project, and photography tends to be haphazard. Often, therefore, it is not possible to reconstruct the visual process of design in its entirety, even assuming such a visual record were a true parallel of the mental process of design.

There is a further difference between the books: the earlier book was published by Olivetti themselves, an appropriate act of company history. This book is an independent survey, its brief dictated by the requirements of the series into which it falls, which includes an earlier book on design management in Philips. The choice of Olivetti and Philips as the opening titles in the series was a deliberate one: the different product base and the differing design histories of the two companies were felt to complement each other. Further volumes in the series are planned. This is not to say that the generous access and advice given by Olivetti staff – especially Paolo Viti and Macchi Cassia – has not been essential in the preparation of this book. The publishers would like to add their thanks to those of the author for this willing and welcome help, while stressing that the opinions in the book are those of the author, not of the company.

Products are identified by the name of the principal designer or design office only, and the date given is the date of production, not necessarily of design.

Preface

Design has long been ignored in the history of economic and management theory; only very recently, since its decisive role as a means of differentation and profile identification in highly competitve markets has become obvious, and since industry urgently began looking for criteria on how to produce successful designs, has it been increasingly identified as an issue which should be dealt with by the management. More and more frequently, design is found not to be just another marketing function but a crossfunction running through the whole of the company structure. Design does not come into existence only through designers: design is a result of management employing designers, giving them information and room to move; design is the result of teamwork between marketing, engineering and design. This understanding and analysis of design is still undeveloped. There are very few people able to deal with the question of the requirements for management to produce and use design successfully in a company. The aim of this book is to contribute further to this debate.

Case studies of design management in contemporary situations play a vital role both for the development of a theoretical basis for study and for meeting practical gaps in knowledge. By introducing a series of studies of corporate design Trefoil is making a major contribution to the question of design management, which still needs to be established and developed as a specialised field within management theory.

In the history of industrial design Olivetti is one of the most famous as well as one of the most interesting cases. The company had developed a wide ranging concept of corporate design long before image, corporate identity and corporate design as terms or topics had been discovered. Almost no other company is known to have had design integrated so completely in its corporate strategy so early. By looking again at Olivetti, our intention is not just to cover the story of the objects designed by Olivetti, fascinating as that is. This book concentrates on one specific question, that of the conditions and activities which made possible the particular design performance of the company; the process and background behind this performance and behind the objects. The questions which in this context are of interest are : which goals, which priorities, which beliefs and principles and people determine the design proceedure? How is design integrated in the company structure and the company strategy? How is the process of design with its necessary multitudes of interactions with other departments – such as marketing, engineering, production – organised in Olivetti?

Olivetti has developed from a small owner-run company producing mechanical typewriters to a management-ruled global supplier of information technology ranking among the ten biggest worldwide in its market. Its particular design approach has to be seen in the context of the specific fields of the products, the specific management and the size of the company. For its first fifty years Olivetti was a medium-sized company in which the design function and organisation was totally personalised, centering on Adriano Olivetti. It was determined in every sense by his ideas and style of working. The uniqueness of Olivetti design is very much a result of the unique personality of Adriano Olivetti, who developed the basic guidelines of design criteria and organisation which still determine the company's approach to design. In my own opinion Adriano's understanding of industrial design in its broadest and most essential sense has had an immense effect on the company's development. Design to him was the visible, perceptible expression of quality in industrial activity: quality not only in economic terms but in terms of cultural values. In the specific field of production, design was meant to make a contribution of quality to office work, making technology an efficient means of dignifying human work, enhancing the progress and development of society at large. Design for office products for Adriano meant accepting responsibility for the working society and also for the development and application of technology in a human fashion. Olivetti's approach cannot be understood without this specific awareness and their attention to technology as a means of attention to design, as a necessity to guarantee the development of technology into a human culture: for technology can turn too easily into the antagonist of man.

For many reasons Olivetti is a case of particular interest in studying the concept of managing design, but it is by no means a case to use as a model, still less a programme. In fact the mixture of the unique person, building up a unique tradition and what can be called a particular Italian attitude makes Olivetti a case beyond imitation. When speaking about this book the former Director of Olivetti's Corporate Image, Paolo Viti, immediately saw the risk of misunderstanding Olivetti's design management and its operation if the present methods were isolated from their origins. He pointed out that today's management and use of design in the company is possible and comprehensible only by bearing in mind a long developed, carefully built infrastructure of knowledge and experience, of relations and co-operation in the world of international design. No other company can achieve comparable results with the same input today. The importance of this background is often underestimated, and for this reason many wonder how Olivetti achieves its design function with an investment which in comparison to other companies seems incredibly small. The case of Olivetti's design management needs in another sense to be looked at in terms of its background and cultural roots.

There is an element of the design process that is inaccessible to logical analysis, something always out of reach, that has left many surprised and unable to respond. During my studies it became more and more clear that this lack of access and understanding is due to cultural differences in thinking and acting. From a certain point on, the case of Olivetti became very much a confrontation with Italian social culture. Much of what seemed to be strange and mysterious turned out to be the normal way of acting and behaving in Italy, the results of typical values and attitudes. I was not unprepared for this phenomenon. The problem of cultural differences in management and design had been given special attention at Munich University with Professor Leitherer who especially cared about the background of management and design in economic theory. However, in spite of being aware of these differences, one's thoughts and emotions are still radically challenged. Understanding is not possible unless you are ready to forget about the concepts of the design process carried through your own culture. Design management in Olivetti provides a framework of given corporate philosophies, traditions and personalities which determine the design process. The process itself is only partly formalised and documented; more importantly it is the result of individual interpretations, interactions, and the commitment to design in general and in Olivetti in particular. This is only fully understandable by examining its roots in the company tradition and the Italian culture.

Olivetti's approach does not fit the concepts of management and organisation usually applied to design. I have found myself in the awkward position of striving to show the importance and details of the management of design function whilst having to point out that Olivetti is a case which in many aspects opposes the classic idea of management as a planned and stuctured activity. Instead of detailed decision making, general principles, attitudes and the values behind the actions are the driving forces. Although Italians dislike logical step by step decision making and actions, which they see as a limitation to individuality and personal freedom, it would nevertheless have been impossible to analyse the process in the classical way, for fitting it into a detailed grid would still necessitate abstraction and so would miss its very essence. Readers with management experience expecting the classic steps of analysis will be confronted instead – and I hope they will forgive me – with the more general world of the values and the behaviour that rules the process.

The success of Olivetti's approach through the years of extreme change inside and outside the company make it worthy of attention, despite the questions left open in this study. The fact that Olivetti follows principles that are not easy to put into the classic concept of organisation and planning makes it a case of particular interest. Its proceedings meet only the most recent management theory, that which steps back from fully fledged strategies to give greater flexibility. Who knows, maybe Olivetti's Italian culture based approach to design can give some input into the present discussion about new management for a future of extreme uncertainty and unknown possibilities and about the open questions and problems of the present development of Olivetti's design organisation.

This book is divided into three parts. The first part is dedicated to the history of Olivetti. It shows how the design 'substance' of Olivetti has been built up and developed through many years of continual care. It also shows that design is not an isolated function but a consequence of a specific corporate strategy deeply connected with the company's technological policy, personnel and management style. Apart from the period from 1960 to 1968 when Renzo Zorzi built up the department of Corporate Image, Olivetti's history is well documented and it is possible to trace facts of interest concerning the question of design management.

The second part deals with the present situation and details of design management in Olivetti. Apart from the general economic development of the company and some of De Benedetti's recent statements regarding corporate strategy, almost no documented information regarding the management of design is available. This chapter was the most difficult to write as it required an examination of the driving forces and opportunities in the Italian approach to management and design. Paolo Viti had given me full and open access to all levels of the company but I was confronted with another culture, a culture which put a higher value on individual freedom and responsibility together with individual privacy or at least expressed those values differently to the culture I was used to. Much of what was discussed to some degree had to be understood without words, so that it became necessary to understand the limits of analysing living persons as objects of research in this culture. In this instance, information was provided by involved managers, designers and engineers through interviews. An important discovery in this part of the book, which contributed to my understanding of Italian design, resulted from discussions with the designers and design managers. It became clear to me that the Olivetti philosophy of design as an activity with a cultural claim and the designer's function of defining and interpreting this cultural quality are more general phenomena characterising Italian industrial design from the early 1970's and having their roots in the educational and historical backgound of Italian designers as architects.

In the third part the process of design is described for three projects. The projects have been chosen to demonstrate the different approaches within the single Olivetti design offices and to explain the general principles of Olivetti management design in more detail. Some of the examples have been dealt with at length as they are particularly relevent to this point.

The open approach and great encouragement of Corporate Image's designers and management provided an invaluable experience for an understanding of Olivetti. The Olivetti attitude and spirit became a living perceivable element, beyond a purely work relationship. Paolo Viti and his operational design manager Antonio Macchi Cassia have been both patient and passionate in their understanding of the Olivetti phenomenon in a period of transition that was difficult to trace. I would also like to thank

Renzo Zorzi, Emilio Torri, Massimo Samaya, Vittorio Levi, James Hansen, Pierparide Vidari and all the other people at Olivetti with whom I spent many hours of discussion. Anna Galeazzi has been most charming, an incalculable help in organising the many meetings and discussions with busy designers, engineers and managers. Maria Vittoria Lodovichi was of great assistance in advising and organising much of the the Olivetti literature as well as the photographs.

Part of this book was written while I was working at Munich University where Professor Eugen Leitherer, the institute secretary Edda Frey, and my colleagues supported my work generously. My thanks also go to Christopher Lorenz of *The Financial Times* for help in smoothing my path. Last but not least I would like to thank Professor John Heskett for his support for the book and the stimulating hours of discussion and information exchange spent with him.

1. Camillo Olivetti, founder of the company.

PART 1
THE BEGINNINGS OF THE COMPANY

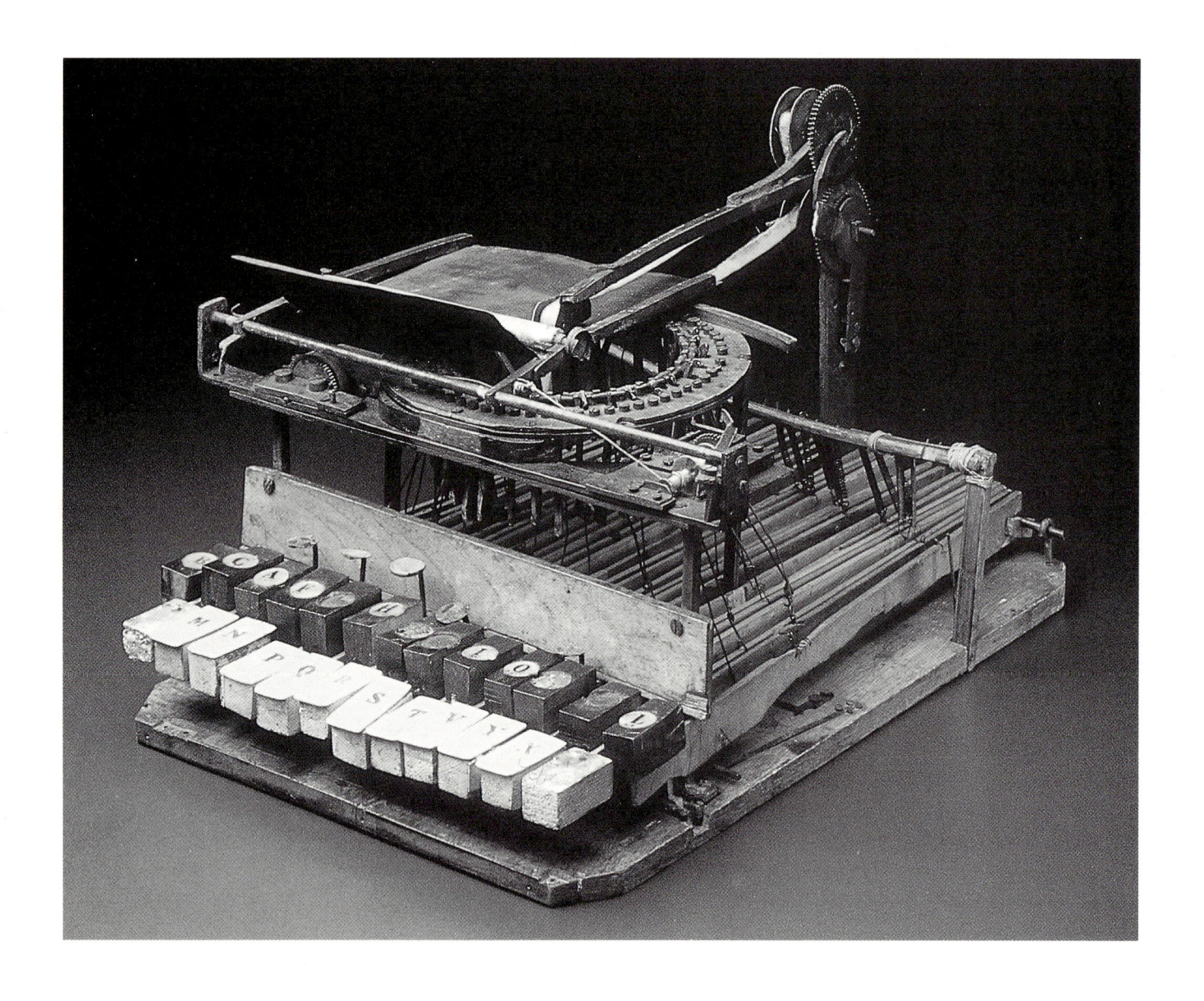

OLIVETTI

Beginnings of the company under Camillo Olivetti

When Camillo Olivetti founded the company 'Ing. C. Olivetti & Co., Prima Fabbrica Nazionale Macchine per Scrivere' in 1908, he was forty years old, and he already had a clear idea of what he wanted(fig. 1). After qualifying as an engineer at the Polytechnic in Turin – his specialization was electrical engineering, he followed his professor to America. Inspired by the ideas which were being introduced there for the mechanization and automation of work as well as by everyday conditions, he was to stay in the U.S.A. for two years. He worked partly as lecturer in electrical engineering at Stanford University, and also devoted a large part of his time researching new technical propositions and ideas for their application. When he returned to Italy he brought authorized sales rights for several American products with him, among others 'Victor' bicycles and 'Williams' typewriters. However, he was not satisfied with selling on its own. He decided to form his own company manufacturing precision instruments for electrical measuring equipment and computation. 'Centimetro Grammo Secondo' (C.G.S.) was founded in 1903 in Milan and later moved to Monza where the company today is still one of the most important of its kind in Italy. Camillo, however, was again not content with company management or the returns that came with it. Both were only an intermediate step on the way to his own real area of interest: the development and production of typewriters in Italy.

Although it was an Italian who designed and presented the basic model of the typewriter much earlier than anyone else, the real meaning and far-reaching implications of this discovery were not recognized in Italy: Giuseppe Ravizza unveiled his *Cembalo scrivano* (fig 2.) or writing piano in 1855 in Turin, but received no recognition or acknowledgement whatsoever. He wrote with resignation in 1876 'It is pure madness to hope that the world will one day write or sew with a machine.'[1]

In America, then a country of optimism and endeavour, many saw opportunities in the inventions of Shole (patented in 1868) and Remington (1873) which followed on from Ravizza's work. As Camillo was building his factory in 1908 there already existed in America a whole series of recognised manufacturers, such as Remington, Monarch, Oliver, Royal, Corona, Underwood and others who introduced their typewriters onto the Italian market with a great deal of advertising and a wide network of representatives. Nonetheless, it was an exceptionally appropriate point in time for starting domestic production of typewriters: for as to raw materials the iron and steel industries of Italy were just being built up; a whole series of large, and for Italy very important, companies were getting established in this phase. The conditions for starting and developing companies also were particularly favourable at this time. But, although the activities of the American manufacturers of typewriters also prepared the way from a marketing point of view, many economic experts regarded Olivetti's undertaking as over-ambitious to a degree and extremely risky. On the one hand there still existed a lot of skepticism about this new mode of writing in Italy, and on the other hand no opportunities whatsoever were going to be conceded to the Italian

2. Giuseppe Ravizza's Cembalo Scrivano.

OLIVETTI

3. The first factory at Ivrea.

newcomer since his American competitors were more advanced technically. So first of all credit must be given to Camillo Olivetti for the vision, shared by all industrial pioneers, for seeing future possibilities in new technologies and for his persistent willingness to take risks.

Within three years he succeeded with twenty co-workers in Ivrea (fig. 3) in developing the first Italian typewriter. The M1 (fig. 4) was presented at the international exhibition in Turin. The typewriter, designed by Camillo, was executed in detail under the direction of the engineering director Domenico Burzio at the factory in Ivrea. Camillo's enthusiasm and experience alone had a forceful and decisive effect. Gradually a systematic manufacturing process was built up, specialized branches were set up, such as OMO (Officine Mechaniche Olivetti) for the manufacturing and sales of machine tools. In 1920 the M20 (fig. 5) typewriter was introduced as a new product and it was followed in 1930 by the M40. In 1914 4 machines per day were manufactured with 110 employees, in 1922 2000 machines per year with a staff of 250, and in 1930 13000 machines per year with a staff of 700. The network of dealers formed at this early stage was remarkably international: outside Italy there were customers in Spain, Argentina, Holland, France and Belgium.[2] (fig. 6).

THE BEGINNINGS

5. The Olivetti M1 typewriter, 1911.

4. The Olivetti M40 typewriter, 1930.

OLIVETTI

6. Olivetti machines packed for export to Egypt and Buenos Aires.

Design

At first glance, in the initial phase up to 1932 the company's products did not suggest a special emphasis was being placed on industrial design nor did the presentation of the company even show any outstanding application of design. The graphic image of the company, the company architecture as well as its advertising do not show any special variety in comparison to the norm at that time. And yet when examined in detail there are clearly the first signs of a special interest and attention to design to be seen. These make it quite obvious that design played an important role for Olivetti from the very beginning. For example, in 1912 Camillo commented specifically on the question of design, taking as an example the M1 typewriter: 'particular attention was paid to aesthetic aspects. A typewriter cannot be understood as an object of dubious decorative worth; it must have an elegant and at the same time serious appearance. For this reason the question of aesthetics was handled with particular care. This concerns not only the shape, but also the nickel-plating and varnishing of the surface. In order to attain a good result the manufacturer has installed the best available equipment for the galvanizing and firing process.'[3]

The new path Olivetti was then searching for in industrial design may become clearer if we make some comparisons and are aware of some details. At the beginning of the 20th century industrial production in engineering was still in its initial phase. In contrast to the increasing confidence shown in dealing with purely technical and production engineering possibilities and problems, there was a marked lack of confidence regarding design. Historical design concepts offered one refuge, though the imitation of craftmanslike design qualities stood in crass opposition to engineering production ideals and frequently also to the products themselves. But it was a time of historicism, a time for ornamental overloading and decoration on even the most technical machine tools. The luxuries of ornamentation and decoration which had only been accessible to the upper classes were made available, through industrialization, to a wider public eager to have access to these status symbols from which they had been deprived for so long. This industrial aesthetic overglazing indeed not only led often to enormous extra costs but was frequently also deceptive, being quite unsatisfactory in the functional quality of the machine. Increasingly, critics attacked such unnecessarily high costs and also began to give expression to the notion that too little attention was being paid to design. Such an idea became a fundamental belief for many, including the architects, designers, craftsmen and companies who formed the "Deutsche Werkbund" in 1907.

7. Advertisement for the M1, by Wolf-Ferrari, 1912.

8 Advertisement for the M20, by Pirovano, about 1920.

OLIVETTI

9. The drawing office in the factory at Ivrea.

11. Publicity for the Olivetti Lettera 22.

12.(facing) Cover of *Storia della scrittura*, published by Olivetti in 1937.

Their ideas and demands for a new up-to-date design concept supporting the industrial conditions of production and its positive realization, met with little approval and eventually failed because of internal disagreements. Thus it was that these ideals were first realized and developed further by the Bauhaus.

Camillo Olivetti attempted with his M1, M20 and M40 to find an aesthetic formula based on the technical functions and requirements of typewriters. His basic belief was that the aesthetics of engineering products was based on first-class technical engineering. He consciously avoided every kind of the 'superimposed' decoration which was very popular at that time. With the M1 the first attempt to organize the technically necessary elements and to bring them into an integral design was made. If we compare this typewriter with a contemporary model, for instance with the Underwood designed in 1898, the effort to make a clear, unified shape is apparent. But the M1 was also the first example of using design as a means of market strategy. It was intended to differentiate Olivetti and meet the needs of a market segment which had not been covered by the competitors. The machine was designed with particular care for use in state Ministeries and official services. It was the only one to be designed to fit the four line pattern of the documents and forms used by the Italian civil service. Its functional and technical design allowed office work to be done more quickly. An advantage which the advertising argumentation and visualisation emphasised: in the poster for the M1 (fig. 7) the train was meant to symbolise the new speed.

With the M40 the casing is completely closed and an obvious unity reigns. The technical innovations were so far advanced that the casing could be treated as one unit detached from the details of the mechanical mechanism. The way was thereby open for a unified presentation of Olivetti products in shining black varnished casings.

Apart from the actual steps taken in the region of industrial design Camillo shaped the company's appreciation of design on a completely different level. He was concerned from an ethical-philosophical point of view, with the company and the company's achievements. Products for writing should be seen in the context of writing as a cultural achievement and task. Companies themselves had social and political responsibilities. This thinking formed the essential basis for the overall cultural point of view of the company's activities as this was then further developed by Adriano Olivetti. Camillo also wished to be considered an international entrepreneur, with global openmindedness, not only in aspects of engineering, or of markets but also in terms of cultural development.

THE BEGINNINGS

10. Adriano Olivetti, son of the founder Camillo.

Setting up the design structure under Adriano Olivetti (1924-1960)

Adriano Olivetti (fig. 10) started working for the company as soon as he had completed his engineering degree in 1924. At first he worked in the factories as an ordinary worker and apprentice, before going on a six month trip to America with the engineering director Domenico Burzio. The special purpose of this trip was to study new organizational methods and new production and engineering processes. We can assume that Camillo Olivetti wanted to give his son the chance to widen his horizons by allowing him to go on this trip: it was indeed to be just such an experience, which he documented

7

OLIVETTI

13. The Olivetti MP1 typewriter, designed by Aldo and Alberto Magnelli, 1932, the first machine produced under Adriano Olivetti's direction.

vividly in his *Lettres Americaines* (fig.11). It is important that we understand the significance of such a trip, travelling from remote Ivrea in a hardly industrialized part of Italy at the foot of the Alps, to the centre of technological and economic progress, the country of unlimited opportunities. Adriano's major employment first began after this trip when he began to put this newly acquired knowledge to work, adapting everything he had seen to the actual situation in Ivrea. This does not mean that he tried to reproduce an American model and to take over American methods and organizational theories without modification. On the one hand he looked for a combination of increased economic efficiency and improved manufacturing technology, while on the other hand his method was marked to a considerable extent by the culturally and socially orientated philosophy of the company. With respect to the former, his experience in the USA provided numerous starting points. One reason for the very real importance given to the latter by Adriano may be found in his criticism of the thinking in American economics that solely vaunted achievement and profit maximization, overlooking all the disadvantages for the quality of life on a human level of such an approach. His effort to combine the purely economically rationalistic thinking of the company with an ethical and social company function, and his personal beliefs and ideals relating to this, have characterized the entire further development of the company. The latter aspect is thereby decisive for the company's identity and the company's culture, for which Olivetti is still so much envied. How the enormous potential of a company of this kind could be built up, is not only interesting today at the management level of the company itself, but also as evidence for an actual trend generally, being researched under the title of 'company culture' at American and European universities.

The following chapter can contribute something to this from an empirically historical viewpoint. It is clear at once that Olivetti's competence in design is inseparably connected with a specific understanding of entrepreneurial industrial activity and an corresponding consistent application in all areas of the company. Seen from this point of view design develops not as an isolated area of business, but within the entire context of the company philosophy and company politics.

THE BEGINNINGS

Initial situation and its development

When Adriano returned in 1926 from the USA the company had about 300 employees and produced about 8,000 appliances per year (fig. 14). Although in a subordinate position – Adriano was now officially the assistant to the engineering director Domenico Burzio – he managed to introduce in 1927 far-reaching changes to the entire organization of the company which were of great significance for its further development. His reorganization measures were an important step, for thereby the company could make the most of the advantageous conditions of the Fascist politics of economic self-sufficiency in Italy at that time and paradoxically also of the world economic crisis of 1929[4]. The devaluation of the lire meant that the prices of foreign suppliers in comparison to domestic producers were not competitive. The world economic crisis forced the two major importing countries, America and Germany, to reduce production by as much as seventy percent. Imports to Italy sank away from a minimum number of 12,000 articles before 1929 – this was only a little more than the annual production of the Olivetti typewriter M20 – to 4,000 machines per year. The result was that Olivetti could expand his domestic portion of the market from 40.6% in 1929 to 50.8% in 1933 and thereby win a dominating position in the market. Olivetti was only one of several suppliers in Italy, alongside such companies as Inzadi, Stiatti and Lagomarsino.[5]

An expansion of this size would not have been possible without re-organizing production methods from semi-manual to mass-production for the larger series, and securing appropriate engineering and political measures in the programme.

The new direction which the company took was first and foremost made clear to outsiders by advertising, before the products and their design took over a central image-forming function. The formative and intellectual demands of the advertising as well as the unusual procedure of employing famous artists for the communications policies aroused a considerable sensation, and not only in Italy. The same approach was begun with the typewriter Studio 42 then, also continued for other product lines. The designs of the sculptor Nizzoli brought Olivetti international acclaim and exceptional economic results even before the outbreak of World War Two. A decisive step for the growth of the company within this context was the expansion of the programme for calculating machines and later for accounting machines, a region which was planned to develop into a major seller

14. The Ivrea factory in the 1920s.

up to the mid-1960s.

Although Olivetti profited economically from Fascism, Camillo and Adriano Olivetti had entirely conflicting opinions regarding politics and company management. Adriano went to go into political exile several times – in London in 1927 because of his commitment to the socialist leader Turati, and in Switzerland in 1943 because of his anti-Fascist petitions[6]. He used his forced absence from the company for setting down his theories and thoughts on the function and organization of industrial companies[7], as well as for social, political, and regional planning[8] (figs. 15-17). The effect of his ideas on the public, at the time considered highly unconventional and pioneering, have certainly contributed to the fact that Adriano managed to get the most interesting intellectuals, artists and designers to take part in his projects. Olivetti's theoretical and practical preparatory work for a new view of the company and its social orientation was fully developed after 1945. At this time it was no longer only the concern of an intellectual and artistic minority to build up a new, more democratic society geared towards progress in Italy. A definite atmosphere of freedom of experimentation for a new beginning in politics, society and industry began after the war and the *Modello Olivetti* provided important orientation points, in particular offering appropriately motivated people extraordinary chances to experiment and realize new ideas. Olivetti was transferred to a new location, to a small multi-disciplinary centre for new industrial design concepts which were not only discussed, but also applied. The result of this was advertising campaigns which interested the international specialized field, for products which not only won design prizes in Italy, but were also exhibited in museums as the new industrial style, industrial architecture which time and again enriched the architectural scene with significant new events.

What the actual conditions and measures behind this development were, is the subject of the following points in 'Foundations of the design substance'.

Foundations of the design substance

Principles of reorganization: engineering and personnel policies.

When Adriano went to America in 1925 it was then the most advanced country regarding industry and engineering. Adriano visited 105 companies, accumulated the entire specialized literature at that time – around fifty books – and quickly realized that the success of the American companies did not rest on the talents of the staff, but was the result of organizational structures and methods[9]. For Adriano, the most impressive visit was to the Henry Ford factory which 'he considered to be a wonder of organization which kept everything moving, tidy and clear without bureaucracy.'

His conclusions for improving the company in Ivrea relate essentially to two major points[10]. First came the improvement of production by introducing a standard speed for the conveyor belts and production line. A work speed should be reached which lies below the maximum limit and therefore guarantees the required quality of the product without physically exhausting the workforce. This is instead of the pace of the individual as a measure, and which therefore could be maintained by a large proportion of the well-trained workforce[11].

Secondly, it was necessary to have improved, more specialized management structures and an efficient personnel policy. In detail he saw here a decentralization of the personnel with function orientated management positions, instead of the previous centralized management using unspecialized official channels. This involved cutting down the power of the management personnel, which had worked its way up from below, in favour of experts with the appropriate training. The entire company structure should be dependent on highly qualified people, who would bring with them the latest stages of research.

Adriano maintained that to achieve motivation and efficiency, it was important to give employees the freedom to take up contacts within and outside the company and to give each individual some insight into the purposes and aims of the company. Only if the task of the individual is seen in the context of the whole can the responsibility of each person be understood correctly and taken on voluntarily in the interest of the company.

These proposals which Adriano gave to his father meant complete change, especially with responsibilities and skills. It was thought essential to replace long-standing department managers and employers with well-trained expert personnel. After his initial objections Camillo finally let himself be persuaded. His condition for the reorganization was that the introduction of new methods would not lead to dismissals[12]. Simultaneous to the reorganization, an expansion of the field of activity had to be undertaken which allowed the existing team and the new personnel to be fully occupied.

In 1927 Adriano, accompanied by his father, explained the new plans to the entire team before they were put into practice. The changes were begun in the production engineering region, where with the first application of the new standard tempo the production time per typewriter could be reduced from 12 to 4.5 hours. The productivity index doubled between 1924 and 1929. By using the most modern technology, the conversion from semi-manual production to mass- production was made.

Programme foundations

It was already clear from 1919 with Camillo's M1 typewriter that Olivetti was looking for a strategic line in its product and sales policy. In contrast to other suppliers, Camillo had developed a typewriter that was clearly aimed at the specific demands of an exact target group: the new clerical worker and in particular the secretary. The advantage of this first Olivetti typewriter was that its shape concentrated on special features[13] which could make office paperwork easier and therefore more efficient[14]. Appropriately the focal point of the design of the typewriter took into account new speeds made possible for the secretary. Its initial success was

15. *Tecnica ed Organizzazione*, the magazine founded by Adriano Olivetti in 1937.

OLIVETTI

16. *Communità*, published by Adriano Olivetti, 1948: Communità was the name of his publishing house founded in 1946.

due to the consistent directing of product design and communication to an exactly defined market sector, with the later expansion of the programme to cover every aspect of office work.

In the years of reorganization, Olivetti could expand far more than the average company because of the favourable economic and political climate, together with the intended expansion measures in combination with an acceleration of the sales. In the area of professional typewriters, the internal sales network was built up considerably; branches and vendors multiplied.

The foreign market was selectively ripe for development and the first foreign branch was founded in Barcelona in 1929. Marketing channels were added to with the help of contract dealers, so that a new form of market presence was created through the internal sales network, appealing directly to potential consumers. The careful consideration of the shop fittings and presentation of goods in the company's own showroom developed into its own communications medium and attracted IBM chairman Thomas J. Watson to Olivetti design.

In 1932 Olivetti expanded his programme offer with the MP1 portable typewriters approaching the market sector of private office work. The advertising aimed to make the typewriter known to a wider sector of the population as a general writing medium. Industrial designers tried to reduce the size of the machine as much as possible to make it easier to use and more attractive (see also the product design section). Another addition to the programme followed in 1936 with the first *Synthesis* card-file boxes, creating a new realm of demands for office furniture from Olivetti. This was followed in 1940 by the acceptance of calculating machines, in 1952 accounting machines, in 1958 teleprinters and in 1959 the first large computer. As time passed technology was changed in these office appliances to fit new office requirements; the technological development in the office appliance sector led to changes in the requirements which the companies attempted to adapt to with a corresponding programme policy. While in the initial phase until 1940 typewriters were the significant profit and growth carrier, calculating machines determined the economic success until the middle of the 1960s. Olivetti calculating machines had an exceptionally high degree of circulation in government and industrial administration, because of their selective design and targeting for public administration. This market share created a solid financial basis for the cost intensive research work and experiments geared towards the future in the field of electronic data processing. In order to realize new and unusual technical and informative solutions, Olivetti started his own machine tool production (OMO,

THE BEGINNINGS

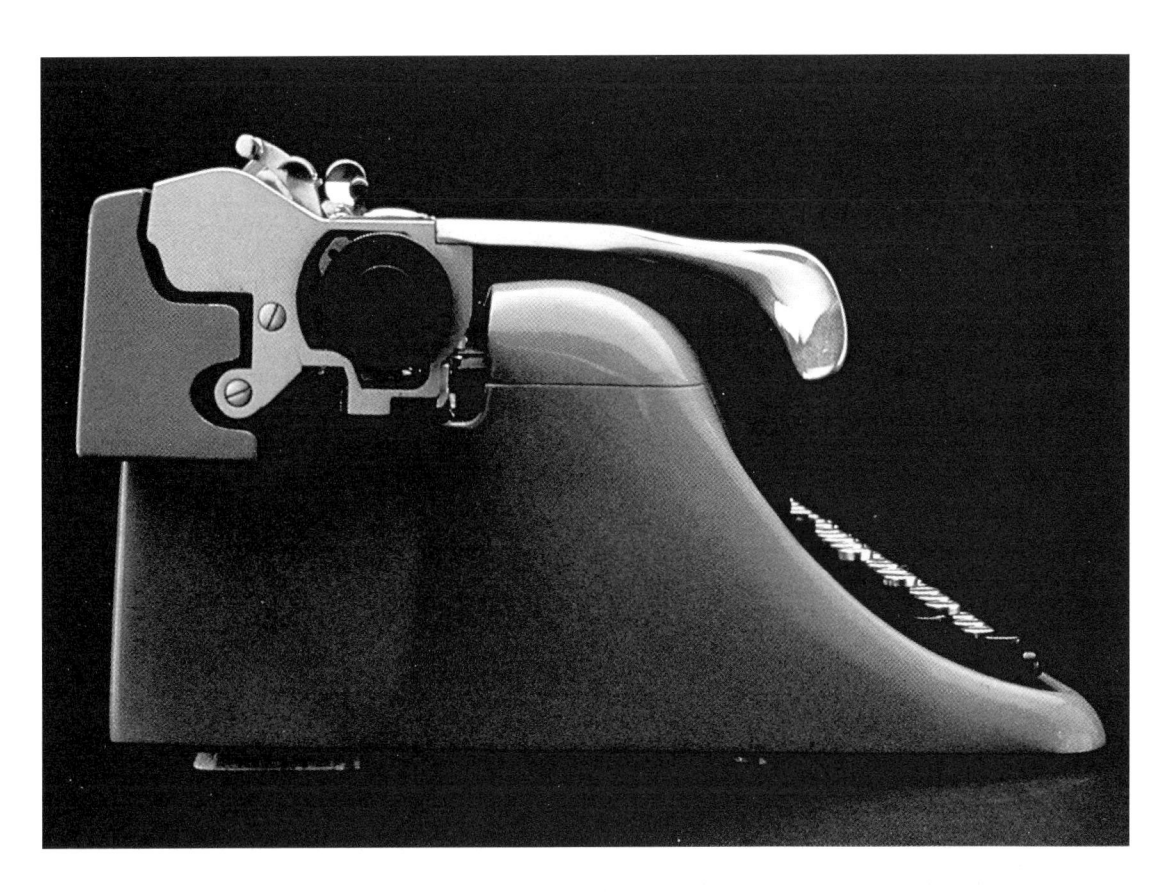

17. The Lexicon 80 typewriter, designed by Nizzoli, 1948.

18. The MC 4S Summa calculator, designed by Nizzoli, 1940.

Officina Meccanica Olivetti) in 1929, not only for its own needs, but also for the market.

The programme policy consistently tried to offer a comprehensive programme specializing in office equipment. Adriano Olivetti saw office work not only from a economic perspective and here Olivetti differs from all other suppliers. More important were his social and political thoughts on the question of office and industrial work, with production and design involving entirely different criteria than the purely commercial.

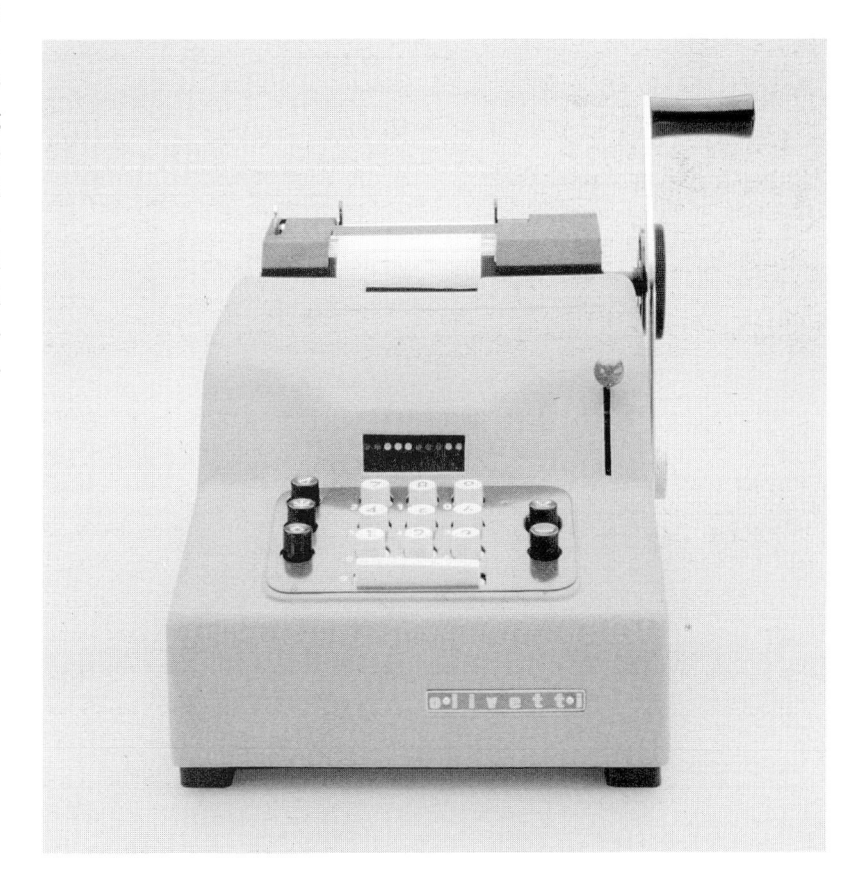

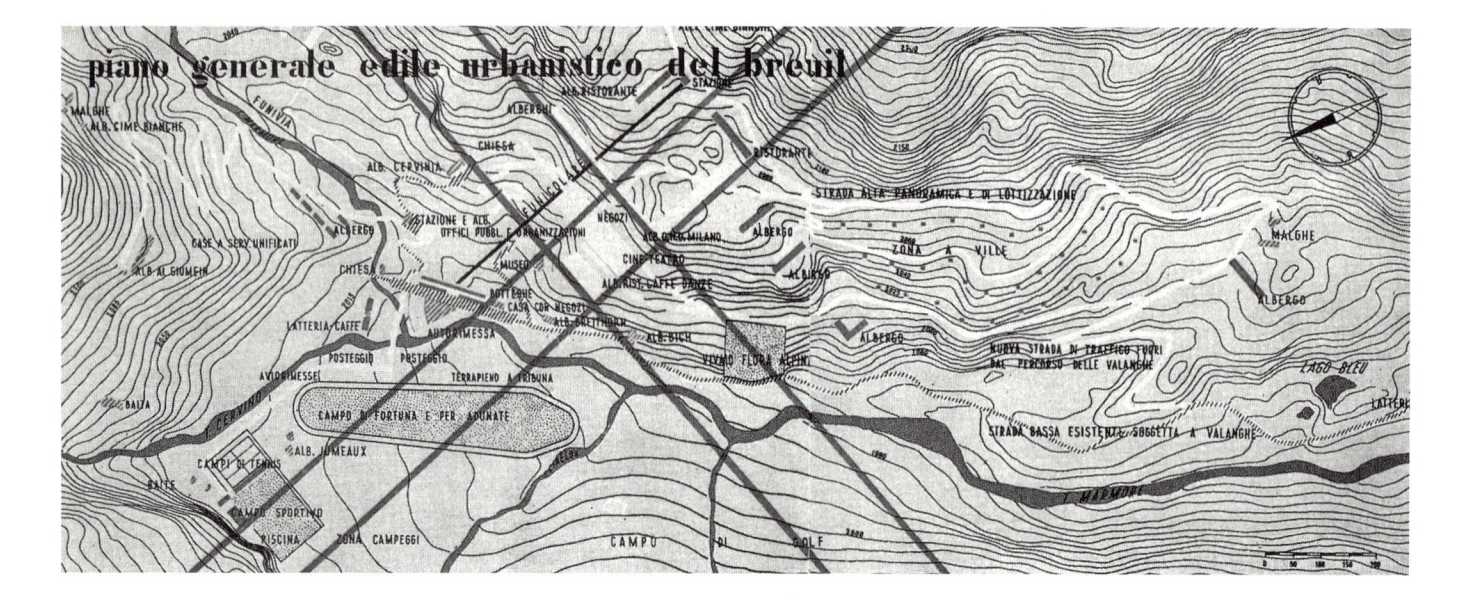

19, 20. Regional development plan for the Valle d'Aosta and Ivrea, produced at Adriano Olivetti's request by a group of architects including Figini and Pollini and others, and (facing page) a map of Ivrea showing developments there during Adriano Olivetti's lifetime.

The company's philosophy of business

Olivetti's then revolutionary and still exemplary concept of image – the 'Olivetti style' – will though much discussed remain inexplicable and even secret unless the sources, the common point of departure behind visible appearances and measures, are taken into consideration and recognized with regard to their innovative significance. With these sources we are not dealing with aims and plans as described in the field programme or organizational policy documents, but with attitudes and ideas of a philosophical type which from the first steer the economic transactions of a company in a specific direction. They cannot be justified on a purely economic level; they contain a far more a subjective attitude to life, to which the entire business in a company is orientated and for which it is equipped[14].

Fundamental political philosophy

The fundamental and central attitude of Olivetti is a democratic one, which at that time stood in contrast to both the prevailing Fascist politics in Italy and an American-influenced capitalism within industry in general. Although Camillo and Adriano Olivetti shared the same general outlook in this respect Adriano took his own initiative in these matters, not always meeting with his father's approval and sometimes causing problems.

As to the basic philosophy of work and free enterprise, for Adriano the philosophical trends concerning life and work in an industrial society were connected inseparably with the task of the company. Theoretician and politician that he was, he devoted himself first of all with enormous energy to numerous essays and papers[15] and to discussions with leading representatives in all areas, who in some way or other could contribute to the question of the quality of life and work in industrial societies. He believed in scientific and technical progress and its cultivation for cultural and social development. As the company owner, he discounted the purely mechanistic viewpoint, with methods aimed solely towards achievement and success maximization, as not being the solid foundation needed for a responsibility-conscious management.

His studies in the USA helped him to understand the company as an entire complex of human work and mechanized systems, as a place of human endeavour and of cultural generation. Motivation of the co-workers is therefore not purely a question of financial incentive systems, but of communicating the idea of self-realization to people in an industrial system. In this sense people are not there for the company, but the company is to be created for the people. The aim is the *Fabbrica Felice*, the company as place of work governed by progress, directed by justice and enlightened by beauty[16].

Adriano saw one of the basic problems of combining work and life in the fact that people and technology are hostile to one another: 'The scientific study of the organization showed me that people and machines were two hostile camps which have to be reconciled with one another. I understood the terrible monotony of the repetition of the same movement and knew that it was necessary to protect the people from this kind of slavery. But the path there was dreadfully long and difficult'[17]. This led Adriano first to critically analyze the conditions for work and the working area. The work station and area should be designed in spite of the most modern technology. He saw the answer in new design shapes, bringing people and technology together and contributing to the further development of civilization. Inspired by writings of Le Corbusier[18] and the industrial buildings of Le Corbusier[19] and Gropius, industrial architecture became for Olivetti the first impressive medium which later transformed Adriano's ideas into reality. Through continual conversations with Adriano, architects like Figini and Pollini developed an entire symbolical building, made up of many parts of his work and philosophy of life (see below on Architecture). The essential component of industrial architecture was not factory and administration buildings, but numerous social establishments like sick bays, kindergartens, canteens, libraries, rooms for cultural events and sports facilities. In contrast to other socially conscious companies like Zeiss or Bosch, Adriano did not restrict himself to the limits of his company. Starting from the narrow integration of industry and the surrounding regional social structure, he asked for an industrial development plan which took into consideration the effects on the social and cultural structure. He spent much time and money on the design of a regional plan for the area of Ivrea, to support an economic development of the area and at the same time keep and promote the natural and cultural quality of life.[20] It was a pioneering project for that time, with no equivalent in Italy or Europe, triggering extensive discussions in magazines and among intellectuals. In many respects problems were touched on that still require solutions today. In spite of several attempts, it was politically impossible to carry through the plan.

Basic philosophy regarding design and aesthetics

Adriano saw design as both an expression and medium for obtaining unity between living and working life and as a reconciliation between people and technology. He gave priority to contemporary design, which to a large extent placed engineering achievements at the service of people and thereby made work easier. A design which was furthermore enjoyable inspired people's intellectual and artistic values. In this respect it had not only a functional value in a technical sense, but had specific progress and culture promoting functions to fulfill, as well as communicating symbolically the individual company's demand. This can be seen as the basic philosophy and point of departure of the entire design activities, valid for architecture as well as for product design. Design and aesthetics are in this sense communication media, a symbol and personification of a philosophical opinion.

Only a few institutions and establishments – like the Deutsche Werkbund, the AEG under Walter Rathenau, which commissioned Peter Behrens as structural consultant, and the Bauhaus – were concerned with the question of up-to-date industrial design. Either overloaded historical references dominated or there was a tendency towards monumental design which did not take industrial problems into consideration. The Bauhaus gave Adriano significant ideas and encouraged him in the path he had chosen, especially regarding his opinion towards all design activities of a company ranging from the interior furnishings and factory premises to the product itself as a holistic activity, and of company communications as a unit and a synthesis for artwork. This is particularly true of the modern rational design style, with its geometric, clear lines.

Basic principles of the management style

Adriano's management style was marked by the idea that companies as social organizations are only harmonious and efficient if the employers have the opportunity of making social relationships and contacts which enrich their working life.[21] If some insight is given regarding the purposes and intentions and the sense of entirety, responsibility can be communicated without giving rigid rules, curtailing motivation, creativity or the required flexibility. Adriano's ideal was to develop a 'technique' which inspired the co-workers and allowed them to continually improve their ideas and performances. His task would then be to act as a stimulus, like the theatre or film director who relies on an intelligent well-rehearsed team.[22] In this way Adriano built up a sense of responsibility, ability and independence of the individual, whilst demonstrating the advantages of interdisciplinary teamwork.

Furthermore, he believed that company business which wants to contribute to a modern civilization requires collaboration with other cultures other than just from the engineering and economic point of view. Attracting artists for industrial projects like product design, designing the work environment and advertising was not simply a way of avoiding experienced people in the field of design, since a training in industrial design did not exist until then. Instead, it consciously attempted not only with artists, painters, sculptors but also with poets, writers, psychologists and social workers, among others, to introduce new perspectives and ideas which could contribute to the question of work and quality of life in industrial societies.

His managing principles included the requirement of high scientific qualifications for the co-workers, who were always required to be informed of the latest research. This implied that jobs should not only be dealt with specifically by subject. The co-operation of an extremely well-trained technically and economically specialist workforce, with persons of different specialities in interdisciplinary teams, was obviously for Adriano a decisive criteria for the company directorship. They guaranteed not only the required cultural scope for the work done in the company, but also released various creative and motivational processes. The problem of bringing completely different circles of people onto the same wavelength for fruitful collaboration presented no difficulties for Adriano. His achievement as a director was in the end not just based on an exceptional, much admired ability to combine outsiders and traditionalists to a unity, rather 'he brought people of totally different opinions, cultural backgrounds and different characters to work together towards the same aim,' in Nivola's words.

A further decisive leading quality stems from his ability to recognize in people talents they may not have been aware of. He entrusted people with large and important tasks for which they did not have any specific experience. Many young, unknown people were set up and developed in this way. Sculptors like Marcello Nizzoli began to develop and artists and architects like Ettore Sottsass produced epoch-making examples of modern industrial design. Many examples of this unconventional high risk commissioning of work can be found in Olivetti's history.

Adriano deliberately attempted to win the most interesting personalities from art, architecture, engineering and science, as well as from the intellectual scene. Olivetti became a kind of cultural centre and experimental workshop, similar to the Bauhaus. The first step in this direction was undertaken by Adriano from his offices in Milan. In 1931 he opened the 'Ufficio di tecnica e organizzazione', which he managed personally, and in 1934 the office for advertising under the management of Renato Zveteremich. Milan offered a better access to the design world than the more provincial Ivrea and Adriano felt he could build up contacts, make an impression and personally set up and develop a new kind of advertising and product development from there.

During the time of Fascism between the two World Wars, Olivetti attempted a new industrial concept with a sense of responsibility, a kind of model character for a cultural-social revision, continuing into the newly oriented post-war Italy. Adriano's publishing activities, alongside his theoretical and political views, played a decisive role here. In the early 1930s he founded the magazine *Tecnica ed Organizzazione* and in 1937 *Communità* on both magazines he was the leading figure. In 1937 he also conducted the area planning project for Ivrea. Adriano deliberately worked against the ideas and configurations of Fascism, supporting

21. Cover of *Notizie Olivetti*, launched in November 1952.

instead modern, social and democratically orientated movements in art, politics and science. He consulted representatives of these movements for his publications and industrial projects, giving them the opportunity to experiment, not only to discuss but also to apply ideas in reality and to produce examples. In view of the historical background, the positive effect that Olivetti gradually had over a modern, openminded public and potential employees is understandable. The cycle was complete: a cultural and social sense of responsibility for the basic direction of the company, good working conditions and appropriately designated and trained co-workers. Results were visible in advertising, architecture and product design, with a corresponding company image providing an invaluable attraction for potential employees who brought with them new impetus. The building up of the image thus has been conducted from inside to outside. It began with the new design of internal working structures and conditions through industrial architecture.

Fields of activity within Adriano's concept of design

Adriano Olivetti had a special talent for different modes of communication. He realized at an early stage that messages are not only communicated through oral or written means, but also through a number of more emphatic and subtle means like pictures, graphics and sculptures. The all-embracing concept of design represented by the Bauhaus led him to look at all the activities of the company with regard to their design and communication potential and to use this network of varied media to communicate a single message. This should not only influence the employer's thinking, but should have a corresponding effect on the market and public. He was particularly concerned with developing a unique company 'trademark'. What he actually thought on this topic can only be judged by his actions in the various fields of design but what is remarkable is the extent to which he saw the design potential of the company and his clear-thinking regarding the message he wished to communicate in the respective design fields.

Between 1927 and 1960 an entire concept of a corporate identity and a corporate image was built up, long before this concept was introduced into economic terminology. In contrast to another pioneer in this field, the AEG company in Germany, Olivetti did not rely on a single designer and his particular style, but on a number of people with quite different approaches, setting into motion a dynamic development of the company from all aspects.

Company architecture

22,23. The headquarters at Ivrea, designed by Bernasconi, Fiocchi and Nizzoli, completed 1962.

Still under the influence of Camillo Olivetti, the first housing estates for employers were built, in the Swiss country-house style. In 1930, social facilities like canteens, sick bays, a library, a nursery and sports facilities were added. A significant development for Olivetti's concept of the company was introduced when Adriano brought a new generation of architects into the company and with them their ideas on modern architecture. In 1933 he had seen at the Triennale in Milan the work *Villa-Studio for an Artist*, by the architects Figini and Pollini. They belonged to the Gruppe 7 and to MIAR (Movimento Italiano per l'Architettura Razionale). At this time the Italian architectural scene and the building industry was dominated in the wake of Fascism by the rhetorically monumental style *à la Picentini*. Only a few outsiders merged into groups like the MIAR to make way for the modern movement in Italy.

What fascinated Adriano mostly about these young architects[23] was their commitment to contemporary design, their desire for truth and logical order. They followed the ideas of Le Cor-

24. Glass facade of the Ivrea factory.

25-27. (facing) The Pozzuoli development, 1955, showing the relationship of factory and offices to the surrounding landscape, and the housing also built by Luigi Cosenza for Olivetti workers.

busier and Rationalism and yet searched for a form of expression suited to the Mediterranean temperament and culture. It was typical of Adriano not to try and recruit the great architect himself[24], but instead young Italian architects who devoted themselves energetically to the project. In fact Adriano did not meet Le Corbusier until 1936 in Ivrea. Although Corbusier was interested in rebuilding the factory plants there, no working liaison followed because of Corbusier's refusal to adopt to the demands and ideas of Adriano. (It was not until 25 years later that Corbusier worked at the instigation of Roberto Olivetti on the *Città elettronica*.) They were prepared to a certain extent to comply with Adriano's basic ideas and to adopt certain regional and cultural strategies in Italy, to interpret them and to transform them, something which Corbusier would hardly have done himself. Instead of simply adopting the Bauhaus ideas, an individual concept was collectively developed.

Adriano had several disagreements with his father when working with Figini and Pollini, generally about the new movement in architecture. 1933 in Ivrea must have seemed like a revolutionary year to him. Adriano asserted himself in the face of all these disagreements, made his company philosophy clear to Figini and Pollini in long discussions and persuaded them to make an appropriate design. In four phases[25] the factory plants of the parent company in Ivrea were fully extended and modernized. The result of this liaison lasting twenty-six years is one of the most comprehensive examples of Italian Rationalism.

The dominating feature is the glass front. It allows the old factory plants made of red brick to be casually juxtaposed to modern architecture, it resolves the tension between the surroundings and the buildings and allows those working inside the buildings to have a view of the world outside. Adriano's aim was to create a symbol

THE BEGINNINGS

OLIVETTI

28. The Olivetti showroom in New York, 1954, designed by Belgioso, Peressuti and Rogers.

with this new architecture, representing his notion of the ideal factory which at the same time was a public street with the appropriate service facilities. It was he who encouraged both architects to think and go further in the new direction created by Gropius, in spite of structural engineering problems. He put them in contact with engineers from Ivrea who could make important contributions towards solving the problems of statistics and isolation for what was then the longest glass front architecture. The new notion of company architecture meant that buildings were not isolated but living of a town, a complex to which not only the factory plants and office buildings belong, but also public streets, shops and social facilities like a library, a canteen, a nursery, sports facilities and housing estates for the employees.

The combination of this ideal programme with the new architectural language marked a decisive and significant turning point for Italian architecture.

Later, in Canton Vesco near Ivrea, housing estates and social facilities by architects like Sissa, Lauro, Fiocchi, and Nizzoli were built.

A prime example of Olivetti's understanding of architecture and its function for companies are Adriano's own words on the factory in Pozzuoli, built by Luigi Cosenza in 1955: 'Located opposite the most extraordinary gulf in the world, this factory rises gracefully, in accordance with Olivetti's ideas on beautiful surroundings, in such a way so that the beauty should encourage inspiration in work each day. We wanted nature to accompany factory life. The danger arose that nature would be violated

THE BEGINNINGS

by too large a building in which the closed walls, air conditioning and artificial light would have transformed people day by day from what they were when they entered. The factory was therefore created according to the proportions of the individual so that he would have freedom in the workplace, instead of making him an object of dejection. We wanted lower windows and open courtyards with birds in order to exclude the impression of a forced and hostile confinement. The factory was also supposed to be a valuable example for our future work in the North'[27], in Adriano's words.

The design of shops and showrooms followed, providing a stronger, more market-orientated image promotion. Long before companies made use of this means of communication, Adriano offered shops in central locations presenting

29. The Olivetti showroom in Paris, 1958, designed by Albini and Helg.

30. The Olivetti showroom in Venice, 1958, designed by Carlo Scarpa.

23

OLIVETTI

31. The Olivetti showroom in Venice, 1958, designed by Carlo Scarpa.

Olivetti products, initially in Milan in 1935 and later in cities like Brussels, Bologna, New York, Chicago, Venice, and Paris[28]. In contrast to advertising for instance, the products themselves could present a physically accessible picture of Olivetti, with the help of architecture and interior design. Unusual and interesting architects and artists were called in to develop the image into a 3-dimensional picture of a new, more user-friendly attitude towards office work and a modern company. In the shop in Milan the shop windows were rearranged every fourteen days, by Bianchetta and Pea. They soon became an attraction and topic of conversation. The New York showroom become world famous, with its refined, artistic design, the precise playing-off of products, interior furnishings, architecture, and the detail in the design like the presentation stands inviting the customer to come into contact with the equipment. It interested IBM Chairman Thomas J. Watson as well as the New York public. Carlo Scarpa's shop design in Venice became a much cited example in contemporary architecture. It introduced a large, culture-zealous public in Venice to Olivetti, and attracted a wider public through a number of newspapers and magazines. These and other experiments in architecture, often the making of a young architect's reputation, gave Olivetti a major role in modern architectural patronage.

Product design

Olivetti's image revolution started in Milan and from this point on the modern world was brought into the company. Adriano moved to Milan between 1931 and 1934 and thus was to have direct access to the centre of Italy's cultural movement. In accordance with his principles for the improvement of the organization, he first created internal organizational structures and then recruited the best personnel. In 1931 founded the *Ufficio Sviluppo e Pubblicità*, the office for publicity and advertising. He gradually gathered together a group of talented people including painters, graphic designers and poets, intentionally looking for people involved in the latest ideas in art and design with a large network of contacts which could be beneficial to the company. Through freelance contracts was able get these people to work together without taking them away from the art scene. This procedure consequently proved to be an important instrument for bringing the contemporary cultural trend actively into the company and enabling the company itself to make a contribution. One of the early central figures was Renato Zveteremisch who Adriano appointed as manager of the new department. He had many contacts and brought people like Schawinsky, Persico, Nizzoli, Munari, Veronesi and others into contact with Olivetti.

The first project of this office was almost exclusively started for developing an advertising strategy (see below on Advertising). Indeed, Adriano's great personal engagement in this department was not only regarded as a new style of communication, but also in particular as a search for new symbolic shapes in the field of product design. They aimed to create a unique company style, with machines becoming an emblem of the company[29].

For this purpose he commissioned artists who worked in advertising in the Milan office to be involved with the product design. The basic idea for advertising and products was the same. It involved developing and presenting a new type of office environment and a new concept for paperwork at home, bearing in mind the progress of civilization and dignity of humanity. All available knowledge and artistic qualities were to be used for this project too.

Adriano's first attempt in the field of product design was the MP1, Olivetti's first portable typewriter, manufactured in 1932 (fig. 32). It was designed by the engineer Aldo Magnelli in accordance with Adriano's ideas. Its speciality in comparison to a competitive product like a Minerva was that here for the first time a deviation was made from the distinctive outline of the typewriter, from the vertical outline of the tall box to a flat horizontal outline. Likewise the characteristic colour black was replaced by a light coloured varnish. According to Gregotti[30] the design was radically new from the beginning, as Magnelli designed the casing as an autonomous and separate element, perfectly suited to the inner mechanism. As Olivetti wanted to establish typewriters as the general writing medium, it was also attempted with the MP1 and ensuing products to reduce the size as much as possible, to make it easier to use and to give it a more attractive, friendlier appearance.

With his office in Milan, Adriano had a tremendous design potential. For the next typewriter, the Studio 42 manufactured in 1935 (fig. 33), he employed for the first time artists and architects, namely Schawinsky[31], Figini and Pollini for the industrial design. Together with the engineers from Ivrea, he developed a clearly

32. The Olivetti MP1 typewriter, designed by Aldo and Alberto Magnelli, 1932.

OLIVETTI

33. The Studio 42 typewriter, designed by Schawinsky, Figini and Pollini, 1935.

34. The MC 4S Summa calculator, designed by Nizzoli, 1940.

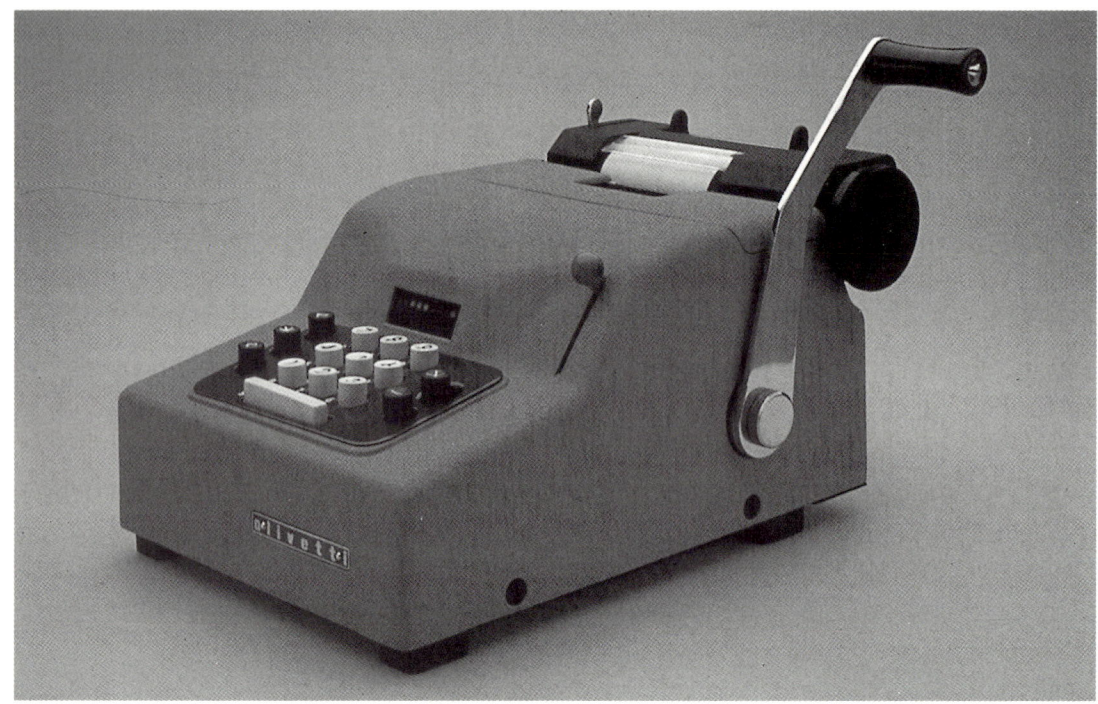

35. (facing) The Lexikon 80 typewriter designed by Nizzoli, 1948.

36. (facing) The Divisumma 14 calculator, designed by Nizzoli, 1948.

defined outer structure which had the character of an architectonic work.

In the history of Olivetti this typewriter was of fundamental significance because it marked the beginning of a new vision of industrial design. Shortly after its introduction Adriano commissioned the painter Pintori with the design of a tool machine and the sculptor and graphic designer Nizzoli with the design of the calculator MC4S Summa (fig. 34). As a result Nizzoli's work contributed quite significantly to the success of the company and the formation of its overall image.

An examination of his particular liaison with Olivetti and his personal comments gives some insight into Olivetti's understanding of product design and the type of working liaison between designers and companies. The artists and designers worked as freelancers together with permanently employed, experienced engineers and

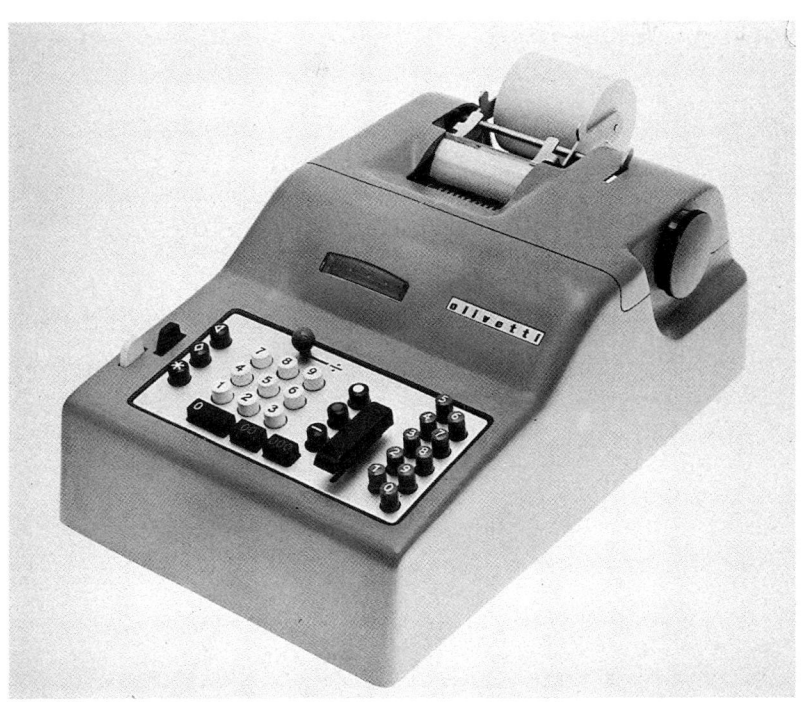

OLIVETTI

37. The Lettera 22 typewriter, designed by Nizzoli, 1950.

38. The Divisumma 24 calculator, designed by Nizzoli, 1956.

39. (facing) The Diaspron typewriter, designed by Nizzoli, 1959.

40. (facing) The Electrosumma 20 calculator, designed by Nizzoli, 1963.

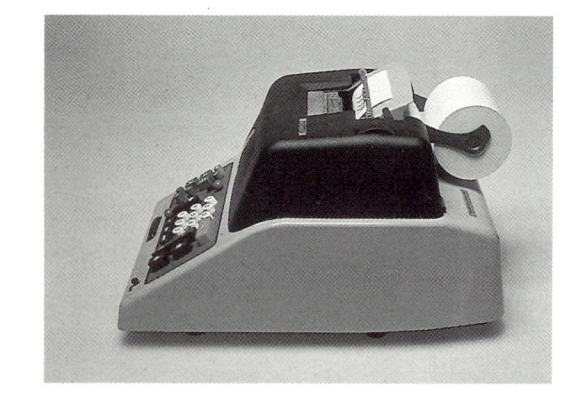

technicians[32]. It involved extremely close and intimate collaboration between designers and technicians, out of whose relationship and engagement a joint product gradually evolved. Nizzoli found unprecedented support from the technicians, who followed his ideas without imposing any ambitions concerning their own professional field. Adriano provided everything required for experiments and allowed sufficient time for the planning.

It also became necessary to find a design formula for technical, industrially manufactured products, to define the relationship between technology and aesthetics. Although they form a unit in the end, Adriano and his designers saw them as two independent design processes with their own degree of freedom. From Nizzoli's point of view, the task of an industrial designer was first and foremost to study the mechanical-engineering demands and conditions of the products and to discuss them in detail in close co-operation with the engineers. Then it was a question of developing the largest number of alternative basic shapes, to design them in detail under the given schemes and to compare to assess the best design. The shape found by agradual process of improvement and further development[33]. The task of the designer begins frequently with a given engineering structure. He has to investigate it again in detail with the co-operation of the engineers. If the designer attempts to skip this stage and to develop a purely aesthetic solution, the product becomes a concept of taste, without consideration for its suitability for the engineering cquipment and the user's application of it[34].

For an artist Nizzoli represents a remarkably functionalist attitude to design, which coincided exactly with Adriano's thoughts that the design criteria should be first and foremost its functional and being user-friendly. From this stage a sensible starting point for the equally important symbolic-artistic quality was created. The extraordinary success of Nizzoli is mostly due to the consistent application of these ideas. This applies in particular to calculating machines. His most pioneering designs were the Lexikon 80 in 1948 (figs. 35-37), the Divisumma 14 in 1948 – the first calculating machine which

28

THE BEGINNINGS

could carry out four operations and with remarkable technical innovations that made it the quickest in the world – and the Lettera 22 in 1950 (fig. 38). Seen from an aesthetic point of view, Nizzoli's work had a sculptural outline, which did not follow the formalism of the Bauhaus in graphic design and architecture. He first referred back to the geometric style with the Diaspron in 1959 (fig. 39).

The development of a new design concept for products was far more difficult than, for instance, in the field of advertising. For the designer there was no training for technical problems and furthermore it was not a matter of finding a technical-artistic solution, but a symbiosis of engineering and form (figs. 40-42). Engineering alone created its own conditions and difficulties. Corporate images and models as in the field of architecture and graphic design did not exist at this time for industrial engineering special-purpose products. Here a massive

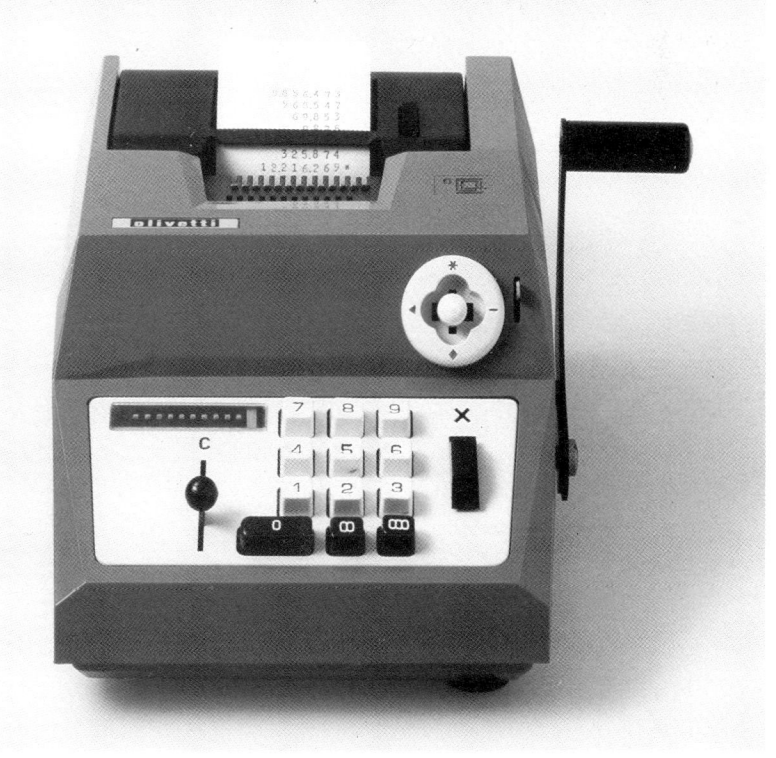

29

OLIVETTI

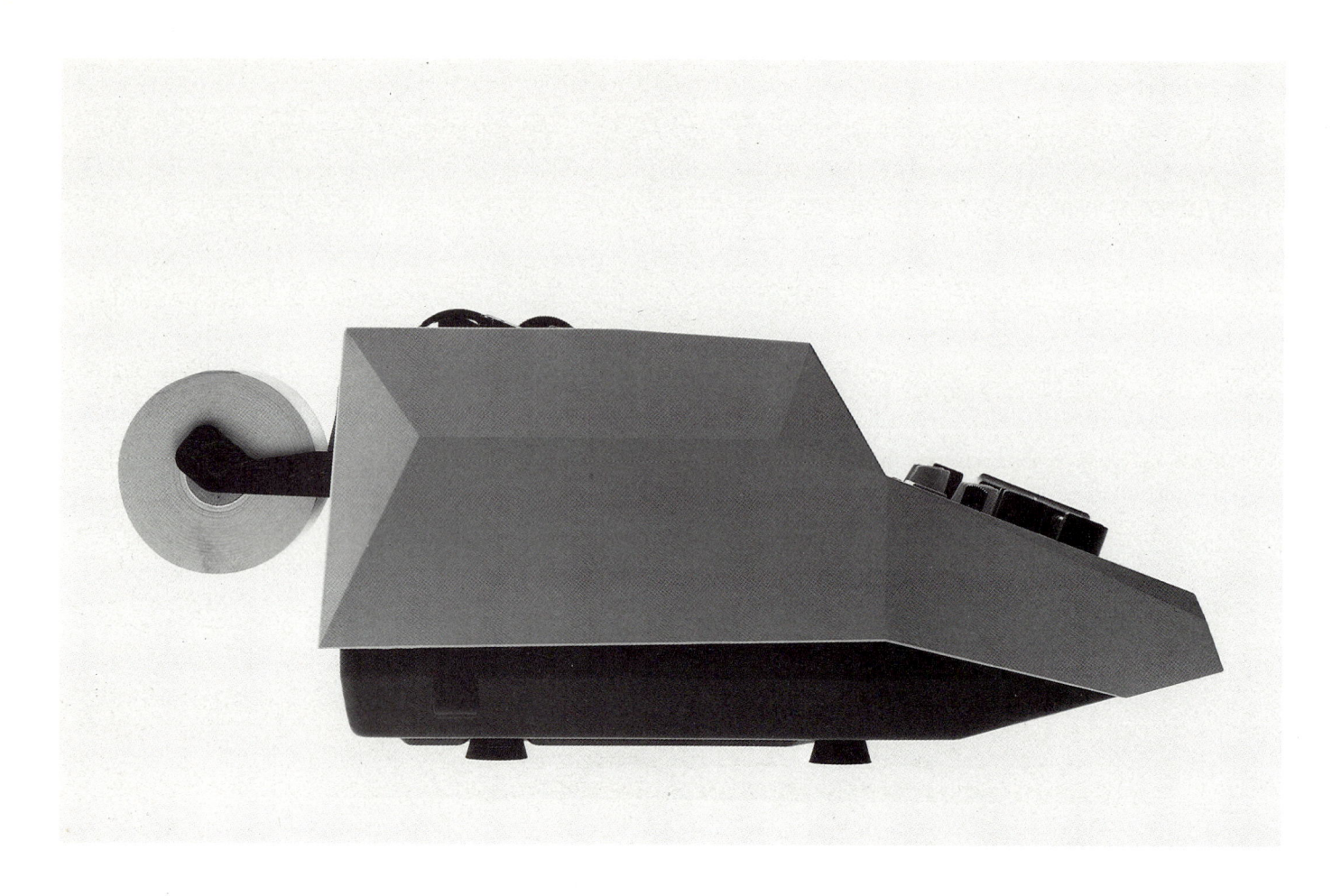

41. A side view of the
Electrosumma 20, showing
the kinds of sculptural forms
Nizzoli could create.

42. A drawing for the Lettera
22 by Nizzoli.

interpretation and development project had to be carried out. For this reason Olivetti's contribution in this respect cannot be estimated highly enough. Important beginnings for the pioneering of industrial design were created for industrial special purpose products, and not only in Italy.

Through the recognition and acknowledgement which this work found worldwide[35], the appeal of Olivetti as a studio and theatre of industrial design increased and it soon became easy to get the best people to work together.

30

Advertising

Adriano's studies of companies in the USA certainly brought him into contact with advertising and its significance in American business. After America had overcome the problems of industrial manufacture in its first phase, it now had the problems of marketing the new mass-produced goods and motivating the potential consumer to buy. Consequently America developed professional advertising and independent advertising offices which offered their services to companies[36]. The purpose and content of American advertising was solely commercial, purely to increase sales.

By starting an office for development and advertising, Adriano introduced advertising policies in Italy as an independent area within companies. However, he did not go along with the American model, but tried to introduce a new style of communication, which should be far more than a simple sales device. Starting with his basic attitude to the purpose of the product and the function of the company (see above), he had a message that ultimately dealt with modern civilization, its development by means of technical progress and the corresponding products and methods. These products were for Adriano only a means to a higher goal, he was not only concerned with bringing products to mankind, but with opening up the horizons of a modern, industrial society.

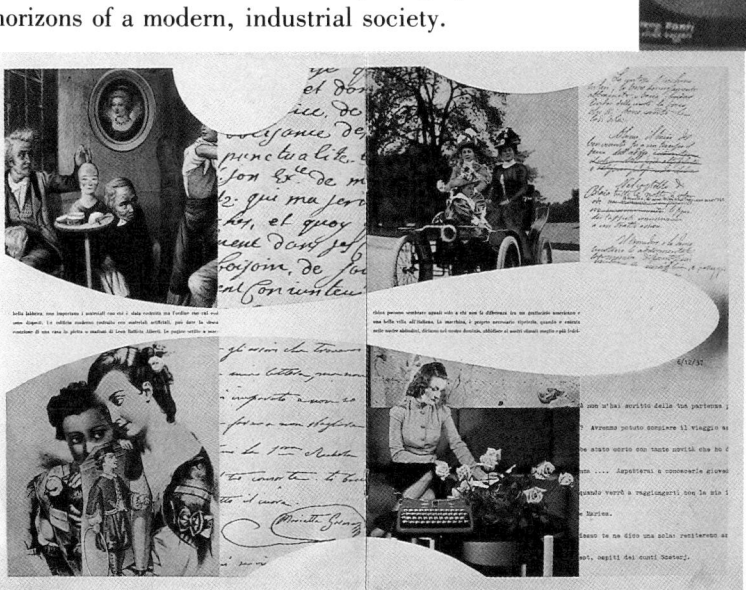

43. Advertisement for the MP1 by Xanti Schawinsky, 1935.

44. Magazine advertisement by Schawinsky, 1930s.

45. Advertisement by Pintori for the Lexikon 80.

The task of advertising was to communicate this demand by content and graphic design. Many artists and intellectuals commissioned by Adriano worked on it with idealism and great engagement. Their work not only helped the stagnating art scene[37], it also contributed to establishing advertising graphics as an independent field apart from art. The new beginnings of the Bauhaus came later to Italy and were taken up by only a few people, including the engineer Olivetti. He brought in Alexander Schawinsky, a direct adherent of the Bauhaus, as head graphic designer for his advertising office and attempted to make the principle thoughts of the Bauhaus feasible for the enterprising advertising business, with help from Schawinsky and Zvetermich. In this respect one can speak of a genuine enrichment of the Italian culture. The names of many men who worked for Olivetti belonged to the avant garde of Italy, Switzerland, France and Germany. Under the direction of Adriano a new advertising style was created, characterized by geometric figures, photography and collages, with the most careful design of the typography and texts. A connection between product, graphics and text was sought to playfully extend and enrich the onlooker's image of the product (figs. 43,44).

This was not simply a case of a pure aestheticism or philosophical demand. Adriano was too much of a business man and knew the state of the market and the commercial organization too well. His procedure shows how decisively he strived for a combination of economic and cultural demands. Advertising was not an isolated instrument but part of a comprehensive design concept, with areas like architecture, product design, advertising and shop design following a common direction. Adriano's basic philosophical position and his *dirigismo estetico*[38] were a predecessor of the much discussed theories and practice of company image concept.

After the opening of the Milan office, a short transitional phase was clearly recognizable. One of Schawinsky's first works for the MP1 was for the new female workforce in the office, a theme already applied by Dudovich. The transformation followed with a much more modern technique. In this phase the reworking of the

THE BEGINNINGS

graphic image of Olivetti took place. Instead of the former typography, a new letterform was now used. A clear change in direction can be seen with the brochure *Storia della Scrittura* (fig. 12), on the history of writing. Here not only did the new graphic line from Schawinsky and Nivola manifest itself, but there was also a new contextual beginning. The poet, mathematician, painter and graphic artist Sinisgalli was responsible for the text. In 1938 he and Pintori entered the Olivetti advertising office and took over its management after Schawinsky's emigration to the USA. The phase of graphics by Sinisgallis, Pintori and Nivola created a world reputation for Olivetti. Pintori, who had been to the famous school of Persico, Pagano and Nizzoli in Monza, was one of those personalities who introduced Razionalismo to Milan between 1928 and 1935, a new and inspired movement of architects, painters and intellectuals from the other side of the Alps who were clearly opposed to the Monumentalisti and the Piacentiniani of the Fascist regime.

Pintori was famous for bringing his extraordinary talent for poetic forms of expression to the design of Olivetti advertising posters and materials. Examples include the posters for Studio 42 between 1938 and 1939 and for the Lettera 22 in 1953 and the poster for the Lexikon 80 (figs. 45, 48). He remained attached to Olivetti for thirty-one years and is known today as one of the world's most extraordinary graphic artists.

Several interesting pieces of work in the new style are also those posters with which Nizzoli worked as both product and advertising designer, the poster for the Lexikon 80 and the Diaspron poster (figs 46, 47). If one compares Schawinsky's poster for the MP1 with Pintori's work for instance it can be seen how rapidly the design expertise in this area of Olivetti was evolving.

46. Advertisement for the Lexicon 80 by Nizzoli.

47. Advertisement for the Diaspron 82 by Nizzoli.

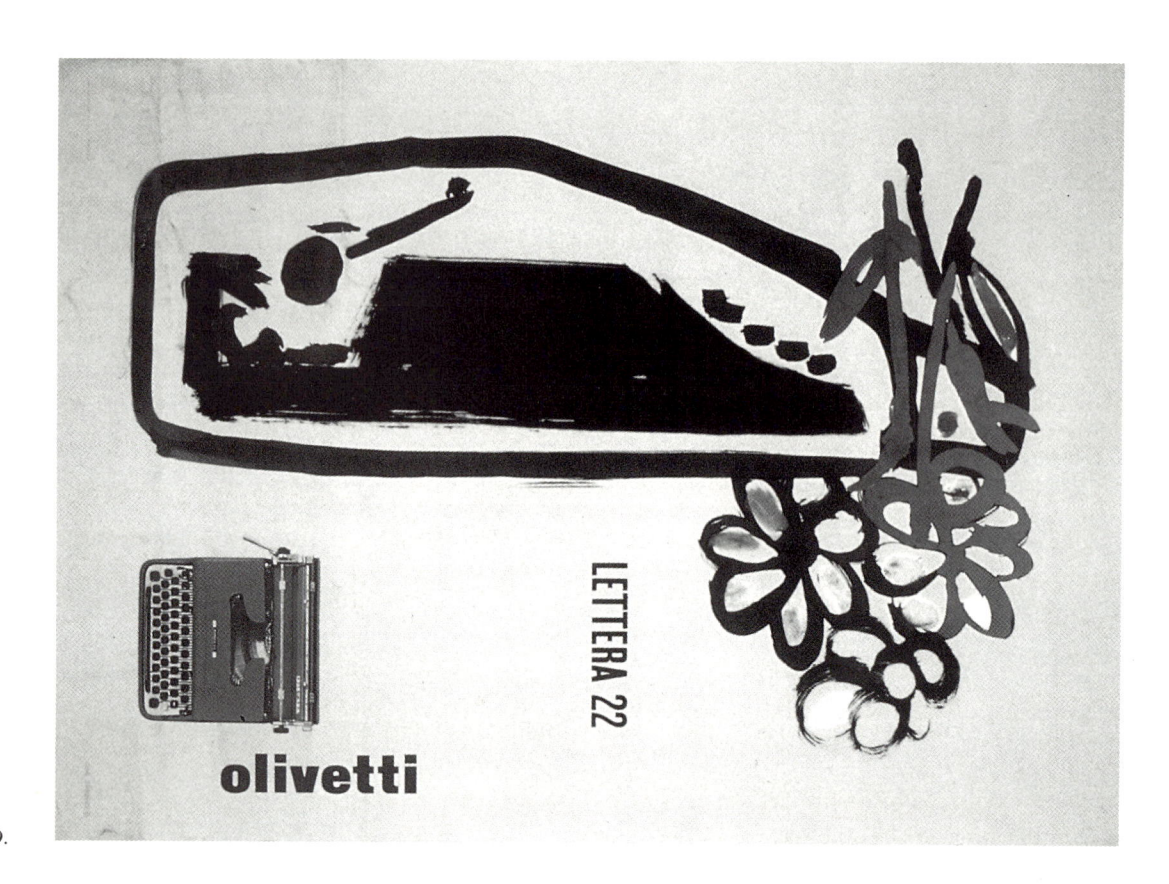

OLIVETTI

48. Advertisement for the
Lettera 22 by Pintori, 1949.

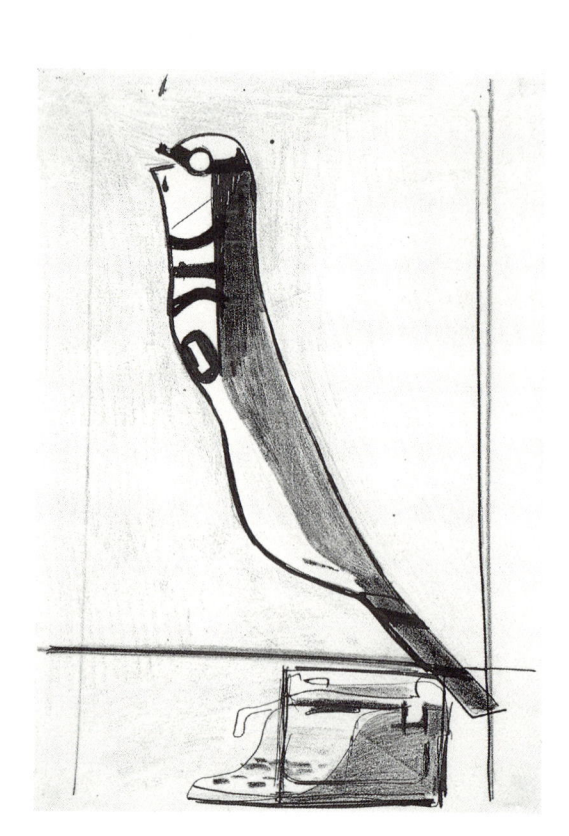

49. Original design by
Nizzoli for an Olivetti poster.

Further image building activities under Adriano

Adriano started also a field of activities which later by Zorzi was to be established and continued systematically as "cultural activities". With *Notizie Olivetti* (fig. 21) Adriano created a highly qualified cultural magazine for Olivetti staff. He asked the writer Libero Bigiaretti to edit it. Adriano's foundation of the publishing house Communità in 1946 made Olivetti a publisher of a number of periodicals and books. Famous became the cultural magazine Zodiac – it only recently has been restarted with Zorzi as editor – and the art review SeleArte. It "played a considerable part in the circulation of news and criticism of the figurative arts at a time when art books were still very expensive and not available to the general public".[36] Olivetti publications encompass also catalogues of Olivetti organised exhibitions, re-editions of rare books and publications in the public interest like in ecological problems.

Another part of cultural activities is gift design, calendars and agendas illustrated and dedicated to one painter which were to become collectors pieces and drew international attention to young and less well-known artists.

Typeface design

In the late Fifties Adriano established an in-house office for typeface design under direction of Arturo Rolfo. It was to develop special alphabets for Olivetti writing and calculating machines all over the world, also in small and developing countries where type design had rearely before been considered. Olivetti is the only company in the field which does this kind of basic research for developing alphabets to use in mechanical and electronic writing systems. Olivetti has made a considerable contribution to the establishment of new standards and to making writing systems accessible to what may seem numerically minor cultures.

50. French keyboard for the Praxis 48 typewriter designed by Sottsass.

OLIVETTI

51. The tape readers on the
Elea 903 computer system.

Transition to a new era

The introduction of new electronics

When in 1938 calculators (fig.51) were included in the programme, no-one had any idea of the significance this would have for the development of the company. Informed on the situation in America, Adriano Olivetti became involved, in accordance with his principle of keeping up to date with the latest stage of engineering, and developing it for the company with electronics. At this time such methods were still not recognised in Europe.

A delegation from the University of Pisa, under the direction of Professor Anselmi, interested Adriano when it proposed a collaboration between science and industry for the development of the first electronic calculator plant in Italy. The suggestion was made on the advice of the physicist and Nobel prizewinner Enrico Fermi, who was involved with the building of an Italian research centre for electronics, which would guarantee the international, especially the American, development in this field. The University of Pisa was particularly well-suited for this because of their personal and financial resources. In 1955 a group from the Institute of Physics at the University of Pisa took up the project with co-workers from Olivetti. Shortly afterwards Olivetti equipped his first electronics laboratory in the town of Barbaricino near Pisa[37]. It was directed until his death in 1962 by the very capable Mario Tschou from China.

Adriano handed over the entire responsibility for the setting up of the electronics field to his son Roberto. As with other questions concerning the company, he relied on the management principle that the correct organizational establishment and the best available personnel enable the greatest development. The laboratory in Barbaricino soon proved to be too small and a new, larger building was set up in Borgolombardo some miles from Milan. Physicists and researchers from all over the world were recruited. They worked in the most unconventional way, according to their own working rhythm and overcame national barriers within the team. Due to the new and therefore unfamiliar technology, the different working style and the unusual team, it was sensible at first not to integrate the electronics laboratory with the normal office business. When a further extension was needed, one was found in Rho near Milan, which guaranteed the neighbourhood as the production and commercial centre of electronics in Italy and at the same time lay on the connecting route to Olivetti's parent company in Ivrea. The electronic activities could be removed from the daily routine and other development plans could be supported whilst gradually making a connection with the co-workers in Ivrea. Adriano saw the greatest challenge, the management problem, in integrating the new electronics with the former activities of the company, to find the correct time to introduce electronics onto the market and to overcome the far-reaching organizational and financial questions, in order to create a bridge to the original area of production for mechanics and electromechanics.

Open to every modern development, Adriano was fascinated by electronics and the perspectives thereby opened up. He saw the new electronics as a necessary complement to the former technology, which could allow growth in new directions and prevent the risk of becoming out of date technologically (figs 52-53). The long-term security and continuous development of the company was for him directly dependent on Olivetti's ability to adapt from an early stage to new engineering and economic conditions, and to design for them. On the occasion of the presentation of the ELEA before the Italian President Gronchi in 1959 he said[38]: 'Electronics lead people to a new stage of freedom and conquest, releasing man from the most tiring routine and equipping him with the instruments of

OLIVETTI

52, 53. Two views of the Elea as installed.

planning, calculation and control for each technological, production engineering or scientific activity, which was previously unthinkable. The development of the calculating plant of ELEA did not only present a general contribution to the technical development and to the instrumental organizational equipping of our state administration, but also contributes to the social and humane progress in our country. With the ELEA the company expands its activities not only in a new field of business, but also touches the highest aim, for which a company should strive; not to work alone for establishing a name, but for general progress of an economic, social and ethical kind, of the collective whole.' The extent to which he believed in electronics, from a social-political point of view can be seen by the fact that he planned to commission Le Corbusier, who personified the town of the future for him, to design the new electronics laboratory in Rho. This building was supposed to be a symbol of both renewal and of future society.

The bridge between the original field of mechanical and electro-mechanical typewriters and calculating machines was not easy to build. The possibilities were difficult to view clearly due to the young physicists' and researchers' different mentalities and working methods. Additional problems were expected from the speed with which the new technology would be applicable for the company and the entire in-

38

dustry. The workers in the parent company regarded the new technology with suspicion and worried about their own jobs and existence. In addition Olivetti's own business situation at that time made an approach more difficult. It was a question of producing and selling mechanical calculating and accounting-machines in large numbers to new overseas markets, competing against such rivals as Underwoods in America, whose project was from an organizational and financial point of view extremely lavishly planned.

The first working result of the electronics laboratory was the electronic data processing computer ELEA, the first mainframe computer exclusively designed and manufactured in Italy. It was intended for use by the Ministry of Organization and Administration[39] and its characteristic functions were based on the economic and technical requirements of large organizations, such as ministries, banks and public companies. Some months later the laboratory delivered the first in-service manufactured computer to head office. In the opinion of Olivetti staff, the function and technology of this computer were perfectly on a par with the machines made by IBM at that time. But what made this computer totally unique and incomparable was the fact that, for the first time, electronics were given a new appearance through design (figs. 54, 55). New technology and a new product language went hand in hand. The de-

OLIVETTI

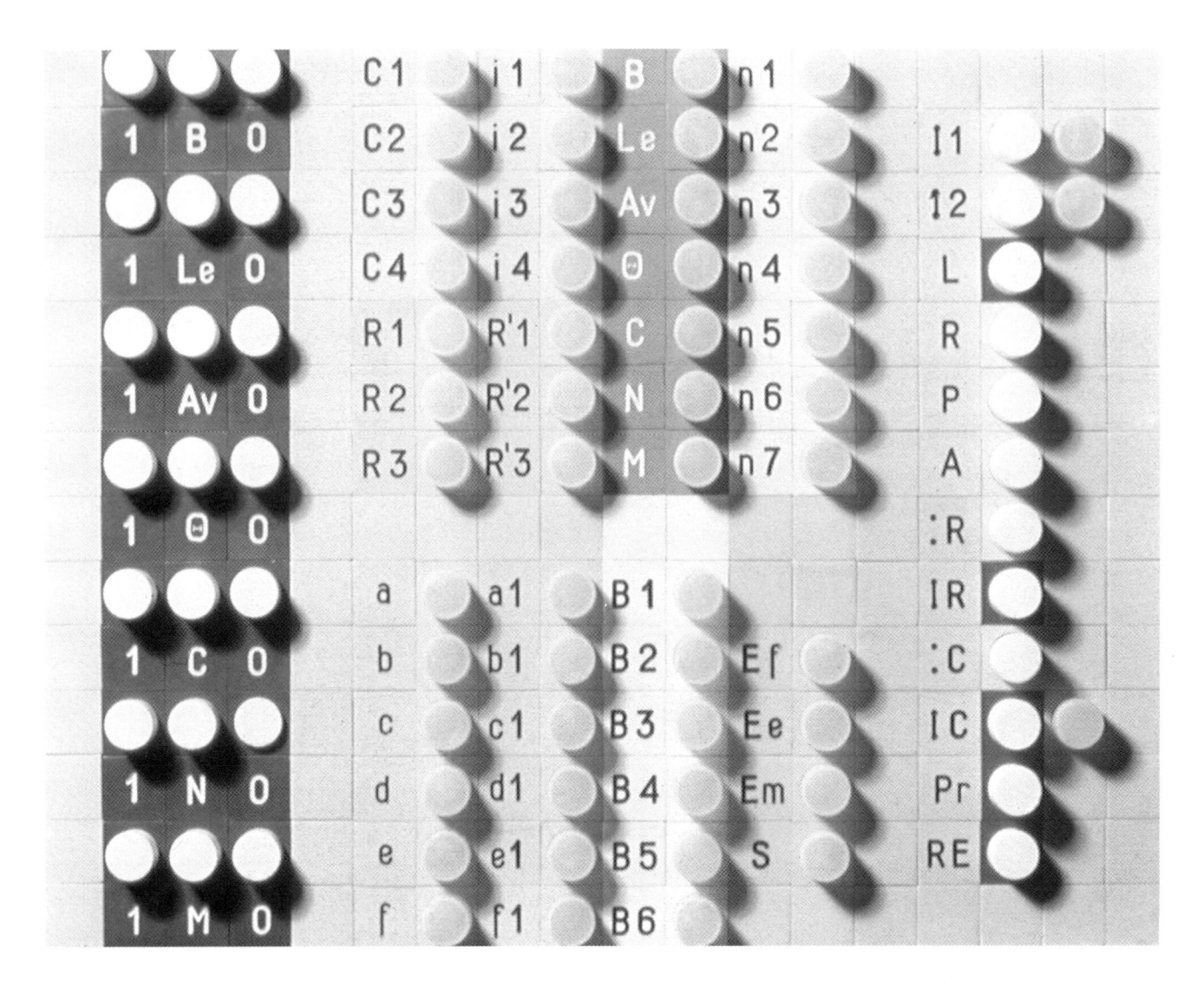

54, 55. Two designs by Nizzoli for the T2 series, late 1940s.

sign fully satisfied Adriano's stipulations (see his *Philosophical Principles*), regarding the function of new and improved technologies, defined by better handling, dignified working conditions and culturally sophisticated form. As with the Divisumma and, later on, with the Programma 101, the quest for unifying technical innovation, quality and design became apparent, one enhancing the other (fig.68). Adriano considered this unifying process to be at the heart of the quality design within his own field of technical purpose products for work processes. Technological development is now the most decisive and primary determining factor of new design concepts. Fully aware of these correlations, Adriano promoted the co-operation of technicians and designers and he saw the necessity to look for new design concepts as early as the laboratory stage in electronics, concepts which were to ensure human dignity and ease of work which he expected from applying the new technology. The ideas promulgated by the pioneers of the Bauhaus in Germany provided the pointer for the design issues of a new electronic era. Looking for designers who were familiar with, and versed in, this design philosophy, Adriano eventually found Ettore Sottsass.

It was Soavi, Adriano's brother-in-law, who introduced Sottsass to Olivetti. He was the 'headhunter' of the company, looking for young designers and architects. He spotted Sottsass because the latter had made a name for himself in his writings about art and architecture. Ettore Sottsass was the only son of a well-known architect of the Italian Razionalismo. It was through

40

his father that Ettore was quite early on confronted with the Bauhaus ideas, having read everything that had been written about that era and having analyzed intensively the artistic and social ideas of that movement. Although he had never been there himself, he was well acquainted with the Bauhaus concepts through his contacts with the Italian movement. This specific constellation allowed him to view the Bauhaus concept with the necessary critical distance and to find his own Italian approach to it. His ideas, first tentatively voiced in his writings, were eventually implemented in concrete product design. Perhaps Adriano had intuitively recognized the capabilities of this young architect, because he gave priority to a youthful approach owing everything to Italian culture (as he had done with Figini and Pollini in industrial architecture instead of adopting the original Bauhaus concept through Bauhaus masters). When Sottsass took up work with Olivetti, electronics was to him a totally new and extremely complex and involved field, as it was to all the other non-experts. He said later that he 'was totally lost' for several months, without any guidance or orientation as to how to approach the ELEA design. His writings show that he was primarily looking for a conceptual and structural approach. He began to deal intensively with the particular characteristics of electronics in relation to people working with it: its effects on the working method and the necessary changes and problems as a result of its use and handling.

Compared with the conventional calculating machines office staff were used to, the new elec-

56. Designs by Sottsass for the Tekne series, 1960s.

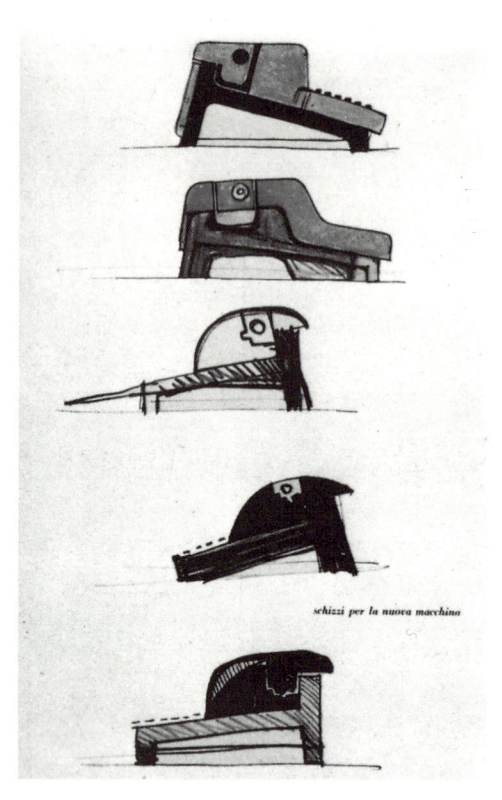

tronic computer displayed some remarkable differences. Its sheer size and its number of operating elements made it a gigantic machine which gave the immediate impression of being utterly uncontrollable and complicated. Whereas office staff had been used to starting a calculating function at the push of a button and getting a direct reaction to the operation, they now had to cope with a new functional relationship to the new computer. Interim steps and processing operations took place inside the machine which were now invisible and rather incomprehensible to the user.

Sottsass started from the assumption that the design of the new electronic appliances could no longer be restricted to single machines, but that these machines had to be considered as part of an entire organism in which they represented just one interim stage. Whole machine complexes and entire landscapes had to be developed, a kind of architecture within work rooms, as it were. His task also involved designing reproducible elements capable of standardization and also capable of being combined in a variety of forms, as well as to develop basic outline dimensions which would allow unusual and unscheduled structures to be designed[40].

Owing to the technical complexity of the new computers it was no longer possible to convey or explain the technical properties through design. As Sottsass put it: 'A new form had to be found which, by its nature, had to be more symbolic and less descriptive.' The symbolism was to create an immediate emotional relationship, satisfying the overall spectrum of working people not only physically but also culturally and psychologically. This means that the symbolism also had to be capable of overcoming fear and distrust in the new technology and, above all, to facilitate the complex operation by means of colour and form symbols. This also implied that a totally new approach had to be found, instead of simply continuing with the design principles involved in conventional computers. Sottsass felt that imitating the older principle would most likely be more confusing than making a clean break, and therefore tried to accelerate the acceptance of the new designs on the part of the user. The issue was therefore to find a new and intrinsic 'language' of electronics. In this context Sottsass also referred to cultural aspects and to the negative effects of the unmethodical design of machines which, after all, take more and more space in the work place of the future. Without a design concept for a growing number of appliances a similar situation was to be expected in the field of work as already existed in the suburban sprawl near big cities: soulless living quarters, contemptuous of people and of culture.

Instead of following the American development (where new computers were given a similar appearance to radio and television sets in order to create an atmosphere of familiarity with known objects), Sottsass called for a new and characteristic language of electronics which would still be valid and appropriate as the technology, and civilization's familiarity with it, developed. In comparison with the American approach, this method posed a much greater risk for Olivetti. But at the same time, this approach fully reflected Adriano's design philosophy and standards. Although Adriano must have had problems in visualizing the realization of the new design concept, he allowed Sottsass a free hand, with the outcome that Sottsass tackled his

THE BEGINNINGS

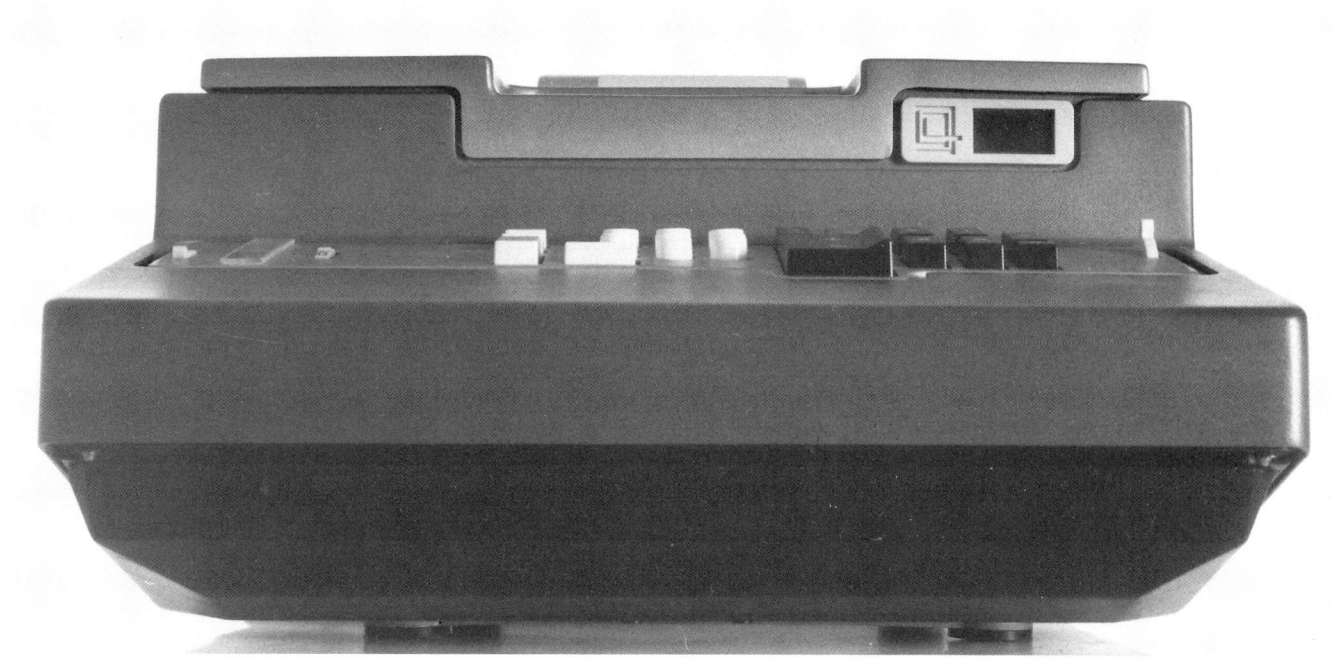

57, 58. Two views of the Logos 27 designed by Sottsass.

tasks with the utmost commitment and a very pronounced sense of responsibility.

The collaboration between Olivetti and Sottsass proved to be as fruitful for the further advancement of the company's design competence and design image as the relationship with Nizzoli. While Nizzoli pioneered new designs of typewriters and calculators with the characteristic company image, Sottsass' work initiated a new view with regard to the design of electronic machinery – and not only at Olivetti. In contrast to Nizzoli's rather sculptural designs, Sottsass emphasized the creation of a conceptual frame of reference and structural design. He succeeded in bringing into a primarily technological field considerations for a more humane and culturally more ambitious relationship between man and machine. Up to this point there had been no discussion of the theoretical or practical aspects of electronic machine design worth mentioning. Sottsass therefore followed a course which provided Olivetti with an invaluable advantage in product design and an unrivalled position among its competitors, both of which contributed to a pronounced image creation in questions of design among experts and among the educated public. But Sottsass'

59,60. Two sketches by Sottsass for typewriters.

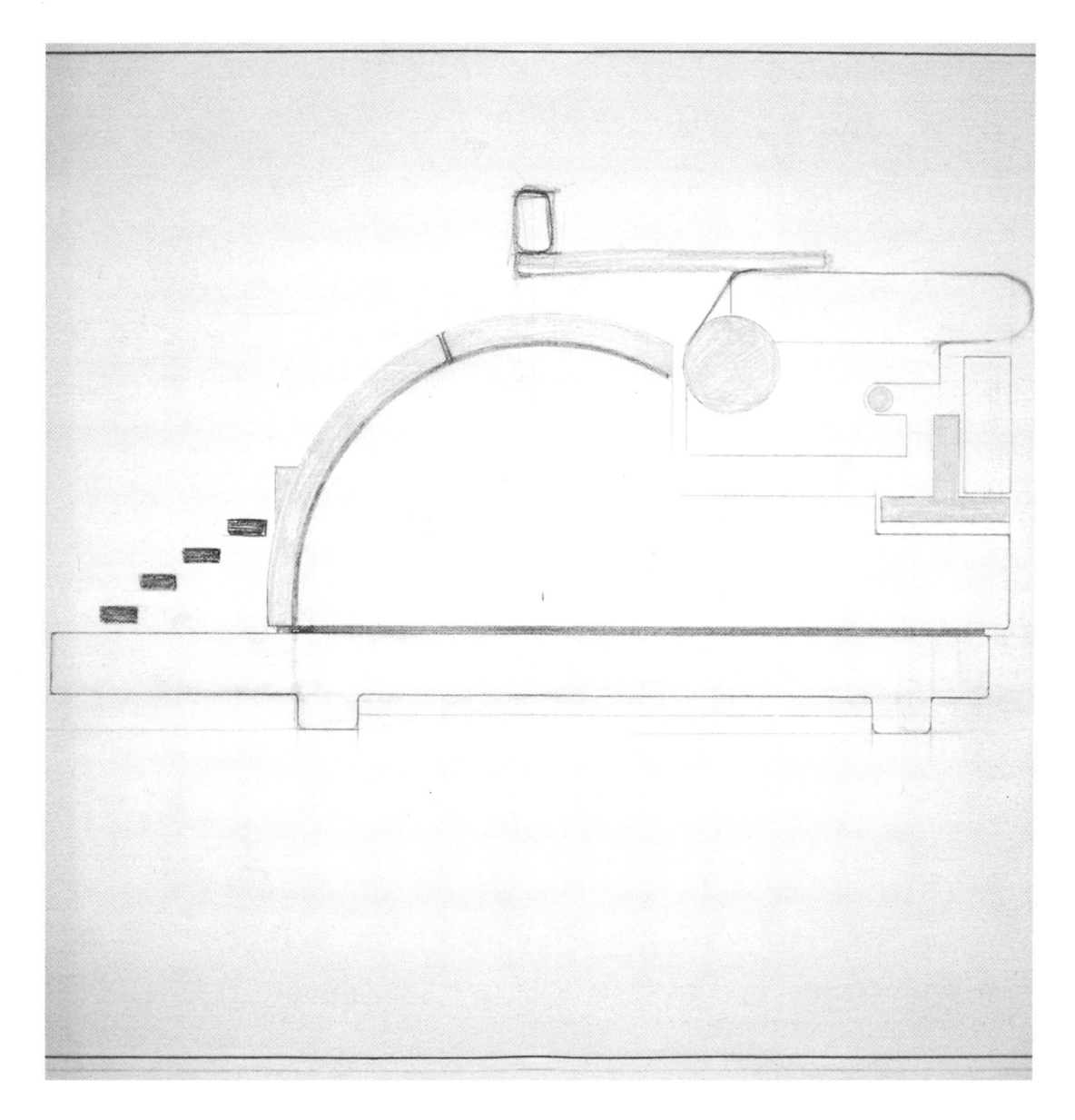

work, now spanning almost thirty years, proved to be extremely fruitful for Olivetti from other points of view, too. On the strength of his activities outside Olivetti, Sottsass became something of a cult figure and philosopher of the new design. Hardly any other designer of the post-war period was more exposed to the limelight of publicity, and the influence he and his Memphis Group brought to bear on the discussion and the practice of design during the eighties was tremendous. His name and his work meant an additional design image for Olivetti and the rise of a whole generation of young, enthusiastic and committed designers, who were introduced by him 'like a father' to culturally and socially responsible design work. His flair for finding good young talent and team members and his charisma are renowned, together with his writings resulting in the highest possible degree of motivation. His 'school' saw designers such as Hans von Klier, Perry King, George Sowden and Michele De Lucchi, all of whom are engaged today in important design work for Olivetti. Sottsass' skill in picking the right people and his motivating force alone are invaluable factors in a company which always wants to stay one step ahead of the rest.

THE BEGINNINGS

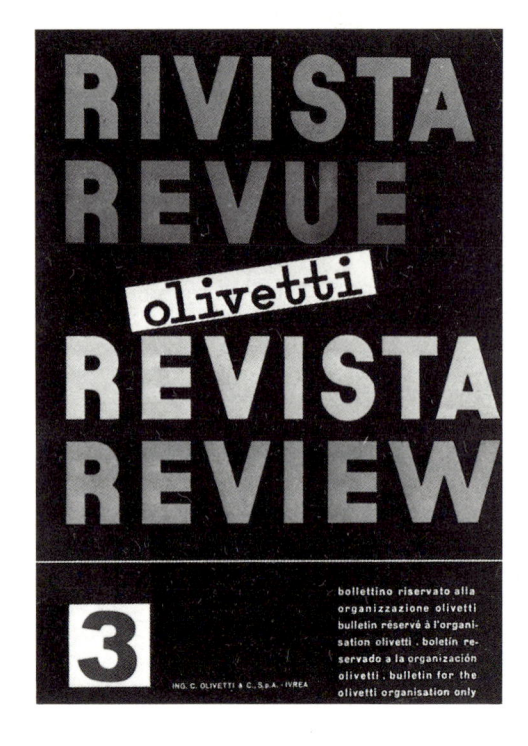

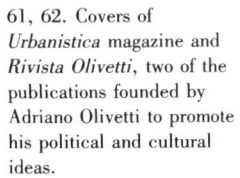

OLIVETTI

61, 62. Covers of *Urbanistica* magazine and *Rivista Olivetti*, two of the publications founded by Adriano Olivetti to promote his political and cultural ideas.

46

Adriano Olivetti's Legacy

By the time of his early death in 1960 Adriano made the company into a promising and many-faceted economic unit, with the public taking a keen interest in it. His theoretical work provided the company with a clear direction which was well-known both internally and, owing to his public and political activities, externally. Thanks to these activities the company succeeded in attracting high calibre staff and motivating them beyond purely monetary terms. Adriano created an enterprise which corresponded to his business concept, which allowed him to employ sensibly the type of scientifically trained staff who he felt would realize the kind of interdisciplinary team work necessary to provide new impulses.

His efforts to create an independent company team operating with relative freedom provided a good basis for continuing the work, even after his death. He had set up a body of permanent, loyal and committed staff which included people like Pollini, Nizzoli and Pintori. His writings, which provided them with a kind of written legacy, enabled them to continue his ideas. For many of them, Adriano's personal involvement in the initial stages, his creative dynamism, represented a deeply formative factor for many years. Although he could no longer actively engage in all business activities as the company grew, he still maintained a close personal contact with all staff and sections with key positions within the company, such as product design, PR and architecture.

His programmatic ideas, his support for a highly topical and technological basis within the company and finally his comprehensive view of entrepreneurial design tasks came to fruition towards the end of his life. The media, museums[41] and hence a wider public, including intellectuals and culturally interested people, began to take an interest in the philosophy and the design work of the company. At the same time the highly innovative Divisumma calculators brought about an unexpectedly powerful economic breakthrough in the post-war period.

Despite these positive perspectives Adriano's legacy brought a few problems with it. He had not exactly lavished his care and attention on finance. In contrast to his successor De Benedetti he never claimed to be a financial wizard. When Adriano realized the importance of electronic technology in about 1950, he set up the appropriate laboratory and research facilities in order to utilize the new technology for the product sector of the company. While investing heavily in electronics, he also emphasized improvements in electromechanical engineering. Thus despite a rather favourable sales development Olivetti ran into some serious financial difficulties when they acquired the majority of shares in Underwood, an American company. Almost overnight Olivetti made the headlines in the international financial press. A relatively small Italian company buying the biggest manufacturer of typewriters in the USA and investing one million dollars in the process was quite a sensation. But in this attempt to open up the American market Olivetti let its heart rule its head: it proved disastrous[42]. What Olivetti did not find out until after the take-over was that Underwood, which Adriano had seen in the twenties on the occasion of his visit to the USA as a flourishing and very progressive company, had meanwhile slumped into insignificance, with totally obsolete production facilities, a huge stock of obsolete and unsalable goods and an equally obsolete and useless sales network. After a few weeks the company was close to bankruptcy. Instead of getting out, Olivetti decided to ride out the storm. Adriano wanted to achieve a mode of commitment and interest on the part of Ivrea which would not exceed reasonable liability limits. He installed a new Italian management, reorganized the product range and sales and he finally managed to increase sales considerably by placing Divisumma on the market. Luckily, the door to the American market did open after all, but experts noted that all this could have been achieved with much less effort. Redimensioning was one of Adriano's last worries. A few hours before his death he gave the instruction to reduce the excess of the Underwood production lines.

OLIVETTI

63. View of the Sao Paolo factory designed by Marco Zanuso, 1959.

The Status of Design in the Company from 1960 to 1978
The Economic Background and Company Policy

After the death of Adriano Olivetti, the choice of successors for the business proved very difficult as the family disagreed about the appointments and the competence of the personnel. When Roberto finally took over the position of chairman of the board in 1962, he was only partially able to fill the vacuum left by his father. Different parties and diverging interests established themselves within the company, and no clear company policy was formed. One reason for this was the precarious financial situation which originated from the Underwood venture mentioned above, and from Adriano's substantial investments in electronic research. Moreover, the general economic recession in 1962 led to a considerable drop in demand for Olivetti's best-selling products. As Adriano's rationalization plans concerning Underwood were not followed up after his death and the range of products extended instead, the initial hard-won positive results soon changed to increased costs for the head office in Ivrea. By 1964, Olivetti were so heavily in debt that the company had to be rescued by a syndicate consisting of state-owned companies and private industries such as Fiat. Bruno Visentini, a lawyer, who had worked for several years for the Ministry of Finance and who was its chancellor from 1974 to 1976, was appointed chairman of the board of directors. One of the conditions of the take-over which the syndicate insisted on was the abandonment of the new electronics branch which, at that stage, had absolutely no hope of recouping the enormous costs so far incurred. The loss of Adriano Olivetti and Mario Tschou, the two key figures of the electronics research policy, had also led to concept failures between 1961 and 1964. With the subsequent sale of the research and development sectors to General Electric, the company abandoned its most important investment in the technology of the future at precisely the time when competitors began to plough all their resources into those technologies.

The new management first of all followed a short-term policy of reorganization, for example, by promoting the conventional best-selling products. However, they failed to recognize that technological progress would negative this sales potential in the long run, since the change-over from mechanical to electronic office equipment was imminent. What was started in the interest of security and stability of the company soon led to a difficult situation. Within two years the technology of Olivetti's products was outdated, overtaken especially by Japanese manufacturers who concentrated heavily on the electronics sector. Although Olivetti decided as far back as the mid-sixties to introduce electronics into the conventional range of calculators and typewriters, the technical change-over was slow and sporadic because Olivetti's engineers were specialists and perfectionists in the field of mechanical engineering. They even tried, through time-consuming experiments, to increase the efficiency of mechanics and electro-mechanics[43], thus wasting valuable time and resources. They did, however, succeed in leading the field and producing some world firsts which went down in history, such as the first desk-top computer Programma 101 of 1965, or the first fully electronic typewriter ET 101 of 1978. As will later be seen, design played a key role in these technical innovations.

The Application of Design During the Transitional Stage from 1960 to 1964.

After Adriano's death, his son, Roberto, assumed responsibility for design and tried to continue his father's design policy. This meant that design management involved looking after and selecting designers, as well as allowing maximum freedom in suitably equipped studios both inside and outside the company. Under Adriano's management, a number of employees had been appointed for graphics, advertising, sales promotion and product design, amongst others, over a period of time. Their duties partly overlapped, as Adriano, following the principle of flexibility, entrusted them with different duties at different times. Without his forceful personality, the tasks lacked co-ordination and clarity. One may talk here of a rather disorganized phase in design management, as the parameters which allowed Adriano virtually unlimited freedom of action and decisions, were to some extent withheld from Roberto. Increased financial pressure and disagreement between the family and the shareholders over the management of the company made it impossible to establish a comparable leadership or to follow a clear company policy.

One change which had great significance for design was an increasing separation of product and programme planning competence on one hand, and design competence on the other hand. Discussions about an appropriate product policy were aggravated by the uncertainty prevailing in electronics and pressure to increase turnover. The outcome was that, from 1960 to 1964, hardly any significant improvements or developments were made to the range of products. Therefore, design lacked the foundation which had initiated and given incentives to exceptional efforts and successes in the past. However, despite these difficulties, Roberto succeeded in maintaining and defending the position of design within the company. He laid the foundations for a continuity in design policy, which was later to prove to be the cornerstone in the success of the company. Long-term co-operation with leading designers played a vital role here. Despite weaknesses in management and economic problems, the quality of design could be maintained and developed, keeping Olivetti in the headlines. With the designers Pintori, responsible for graphics and advertising, and Nizzoli, responsible for mechanical products, Roberto Olivetti had a team with over twenty years' experience of working together. After working on the ELEA, Sottsass also had sufficient experience and knowledge of the company to be given responsibility for the development of a new generation of calculators and typewriters. He was eventually entrusted with the design of this range in his own design studio in Milan. Mario Bellini joined the team as a newcomer in 1962. He was 'discovered' by Roberto at the Compasso d'Oro, where he won first prize for a table, and he was instructed to design a new magnetic encoder, for which he subsequently also won the Compasso d'Oro in 1963. The 'new' designers Sottsass and Bellini took over from Nizzoli in the mid-sixties. Like Nizzoli, they also became long-term guarantors of the company's high quality of design and made an invaluable contribution towards the company's ventures into the electronic era.

The Organization of Design Activities Under

Renzo Zorzi Establishment of Design Responsibility Within the Company

The assumption of the company management by a syndicate in 1964 also had certain effects on design management. The separation of competence between product and programme planning and design was vigorously pursued and implemented. Owing to the size and the complexity of the company, the new chairman of the board, Visentini, was unable to deal in person with design matters. After the management of the company changed from the owner to the board, the responsibility for decisions passed to the directors of each individual company division. Adriano's centralized leadership was now replaced by a more complex management structure. Roberto Olivetti secured the position of design on the highest management level and represented the design interests of the company.

As a consequence of the far-reaching devolution into individual boards of management, it was felt necessary to establish an organization and a separate division for design. Decisions had to be taken as to which positions and which members of staff could be integrated into one suitable design section and which position this section would take up within the overall organizational structure of the company, especially in relation to product development, marketing and sales. It was Renzo Zorzi who, with Robert Olivetti's backing, did the decisive and basic spadework to ensure the continuity of the design policy in the new company management (fig. 64).

Zorzi and Adriano Olivetti met for the first time in 1948. As an intellectual, Zorzi identified himself closely with Adriano's ideas. He began work on Adriano's magazine *Communità,* became its chief editor and, after 1960, took over the directorship of the entire publishing house. He, like no other, dealt with Adriano's philosophy and theories intensively and completely, like no other he understood how to formulate these ideas clearly and to present Adriano's attitudes and concepts with great personal conviction.[44] Zorzi must have seen that Olivetti could keep its 'soul' under a neutral management only if he succeeded in establishing an institution right at the centre of the company which would serve precisely to maintain and publicize this 'soul', that is, the company philosophy. In the following years he succeeded in establishing a central authority at the highest level which not only presented a unified and comprehensive image of the company to the outside world but, above all, conveyed the specific ideas and the basic attitudes regarding quality of work, products and social and cultural functions of the company to the workers and staff within Olivetti, motivating them correspondingly. Zorzi not only set up the appropriate organizational structure for this division, he also created the theoretical and abstract foundations for defining the purpose and necessity of a corporate image policy in a modern company.

64. Renzo Zorzi.

OLIVETTI

65. The P603 Minicomputer
by E. Sottsass and P.A.
King, 1972.

Establishment of the Corporate Image Department

Zorzi's first consideration was to concentrate in one department all the activities which the company employed to express its physical and tangible essence. This meant integrating all those sectors under one management which Adriano in his time had specifically used to publicize and convey his company philosophy: the architecture of production facilities and offices, product design, graphics design, the interior decoration of showrooms and sales points, etc. As already envisaged by Adriano, these activities were intended to determine the attitude and the actions internally and to convey the overall image of the company to the outside world. The idea behind centralizing these activities under one management was to keep alive the individual line or 'culture' of the company, established by Adriano, and to continue it under new premises. In contrast to widely accepted concepts of corporate image and corporate identity Olivetti did not primarily and exclusively concern themselves with presenting a unified and concise appearance in form and in style in order to obtain an additional profile factor on the market, but rather a company philosophy which determined activities in internal and external relationships. For Zorzi, this was no mere 'add-on', but an essential and vitally important factor for the company. It served to maintain and develop common ethics and a mental attitude within the company, in other words, an essence which exerts an attractive force and motivation on members of staff and outsiders alike, a force which, after all, is the secret of extraordinary achievements.

During the transition from owner to board management it was the corporate image department which, more than any other department, assumed a life-preserving function. It replaced, as it were, the previous leader personality, devoted its efforts to the continuation of the corporate spirit and formed the corporate backbone for the transition from the mechanical to the electronic era. One most important preconditions for fulfilling this function was that management (above all, the chairman of the board, Visentini) gave its unequivocal support to the fundamental tasks of the Corporate Image Department and placing it in a commensurate position within the company hierarchy. By virtue of the fact that the head of the Corporate Image department was not subordinate to any product or other function department, the company ensured that its long-term interests were not subordinated to any short-term interests of individual product fields or of the marketing departments.

During the establishment of the department, important technical and economic changes took place which made new demands on the organization and the structure of the individual corporate image activities. In particular, the gradual change from mechanical engineering to electronics represented a great upheaval for the company. Until the middle of the sixties, Olivetti's success was based on the most advanced and ergonomic quality of mechanical calculators and typewriters. In this field, Olivetti's designers and engineers had achieved true pioneering work, giving the company a worldwide reputation as the leading manufacturer of mechanical office machines. With the changeover to electronics Olivetti had to change their image as manufacturers of mechanical machines to specialists for electronic information processing.

However, the transition was anything but smooth and was fraught with great difficulties.

66. The TCV 250 terminal designed by Bellini, 1969.

OLIVETTI

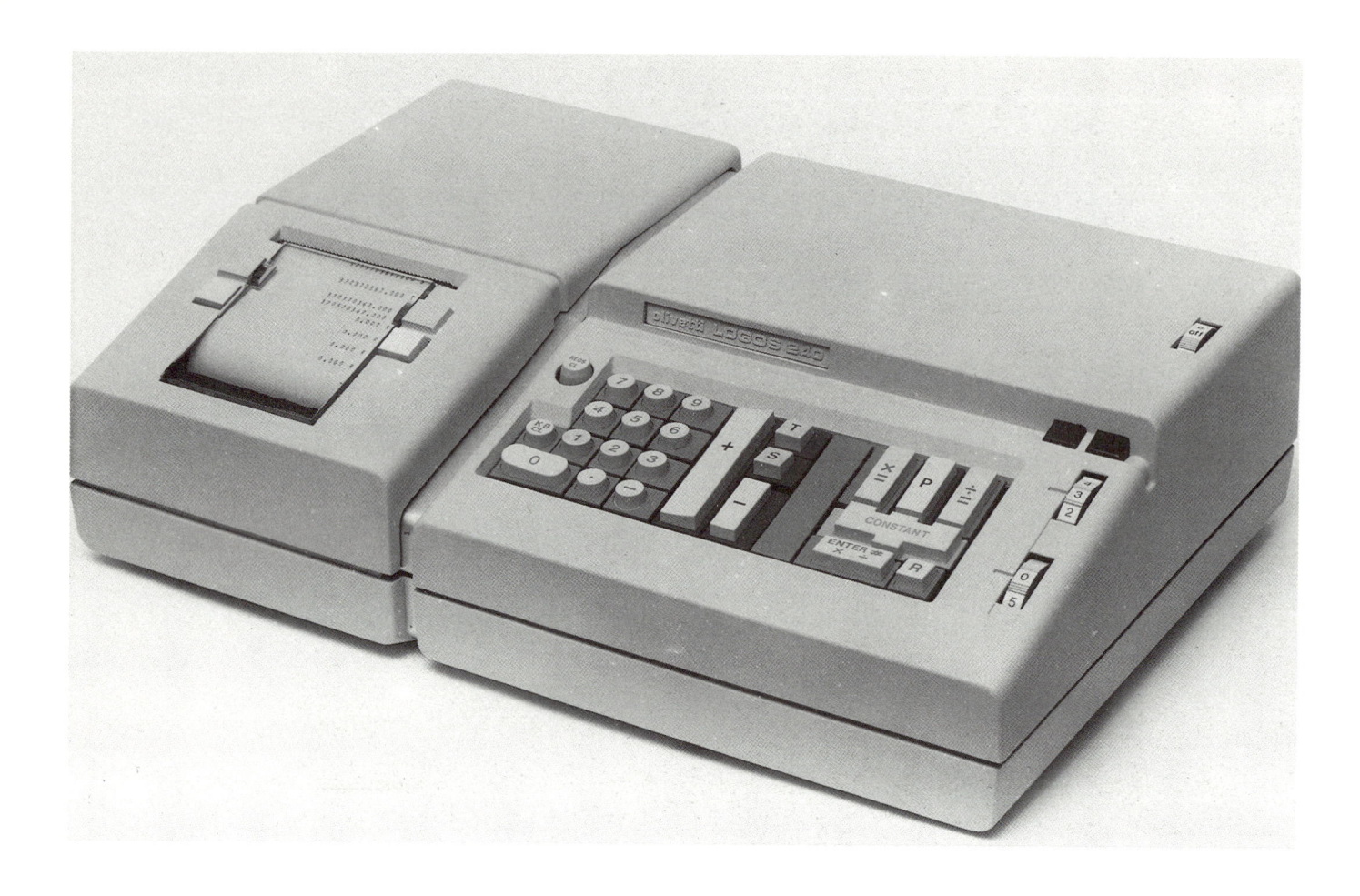

67. The Logos 240 computer designed by Bellini and Sylvio Pasqui, 1970 and (facing) the Summa 19 designed by Sottsass and Hans Von Klier.

Although the new management decided to make a fresh start after giving up the large electronic appliances by using electronic equipment on the conventional production line, electronics were not supposed to be confined to display units only (as already successfully implemented by other competitors), but were to determine the entire product structure to an ever-increasing degree. The change-over still proceeded slowly and hesitantly. Financial problems apart, management faced some difficulties in preparing the field for production, sales and personnel policies. In this context, the Corporate Image department saw itself confronted with the task of creating a new company image without being able to fall back on a correspondingly consistent company policy.

Despite these problems, the Corporate Image department in these years made quite a decisive contribution towards the modification and the restructuring of the corporate image. Outstanding work was done by product design. Through their product design the designers succeeded in regaining the lead Olivetti had lost for technical reasons. After the technological groundwork had been done, the designers were capable of showing their true strength. They began to tackle the problem which Sottsass had already formulated in 1959 with regard to research for an electronic mainframe computer: the development of a new design concept which helps the user to come to terms with the peculiarities of electronic technology. The designers approached precisely that aspect of product quality which was consistently ignored by their competitors. With the design of products like Programma 101, the first desk top computer, the Logos 270 (1970, (fig. 68)) or Divisumma 18 (1973, fig. 70)), Olivetti pioneered the electronic design concept for office machines. The other central figure in this field besides Sottsass was Bellini. Their work gained worldwide reputation and awards galore.

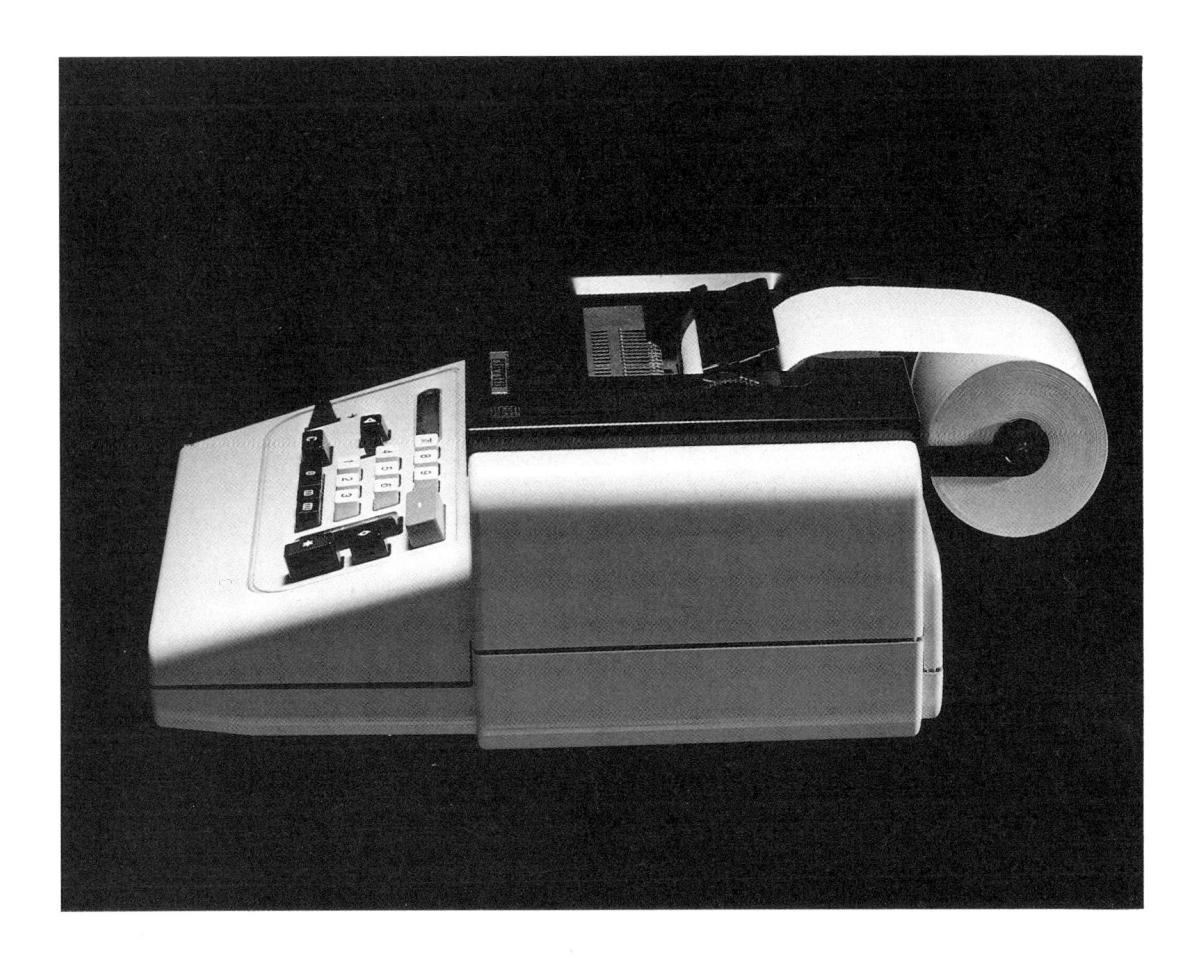

It was design which had made Olivetti's technological innovations famous and which led the company image in a new direction following a rather uncritical phase.

The important part which design was allowed to play was solely due to management and especially to the corporate image department. They ensured that designers were given the necessary freedom and a strong position in relation to engineers and marketing. This approach guaranteed that design concepts were realized which had their own specific standards, instead of following low-risk solutions just to please the market.

The basic structure of the Corporate Image department comprised the following areas: product or industrial design, type face design, corporate identity, cultural activities, advertising and graphic design, architecture, PR.

Industrial design was again subdivided into 'system design' (E. Sottsass) for larger calculators and typing systems for purely professional office use, a department 'office design' (M. Bellini) for conventional types of office machines for home and private use, and a department for the design of Olivetti's own tool machine production (R. Bonetto). The heads of each of these departments were external designers who enjoyed a relatively free hand regarding the organization and personnel of their departments. Sottsass' system design department, for instance, was set up in its own studio in Milan. Bellini, on the other hand, established his department in Ivrea, drawing engineers, model builders and graphic artists from other departments of the company and creating an integrated group with all the necessary facilities on one site. In the mid-seventies management decided to relocate Bellini's department to Milan. The Olivetti Design Office, accommodating Sottsass' and Bellini's departments, was set up in the Corso Venezia. The departments established in Ivrea

OLIVETTI

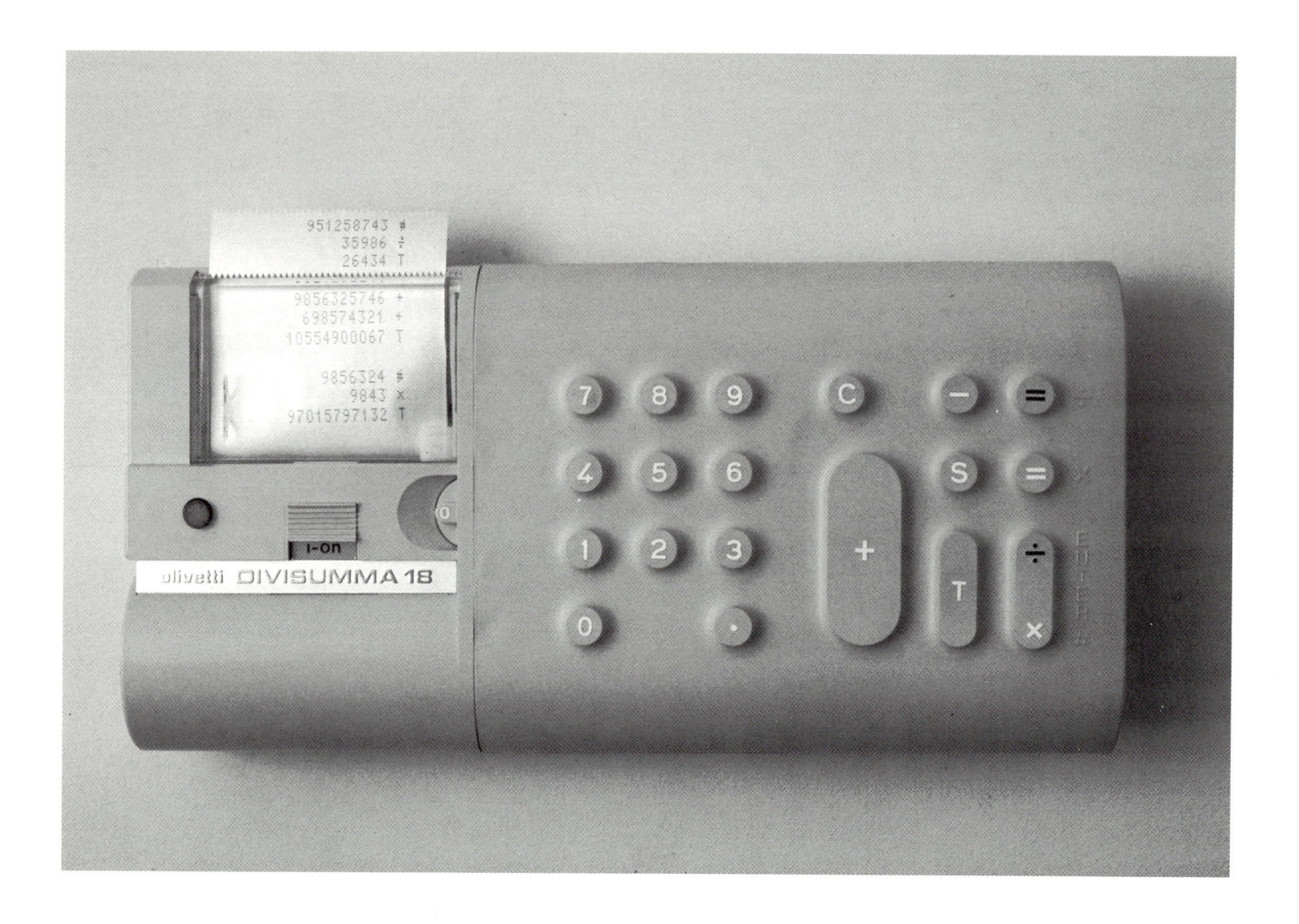

(model building, technical design) were enlarged to be accessible to all design departments for centralized use. Despite sharing the same location, Sottsass' and Bellini's departments have managed to maintain their very own style of work up to this day. The department of machine tool design is also to this day located in Milan, integrated into Bonetto's private offices.

Over and above the positions for industrial design, graphic design, architecture and exhibition design created by Adriano, Zorzi established typeface design, corporate identity and cultural activities as new and independent departments. As to typeface, Olivetti's thorough and comprehensive understanding of design and quality issues is shown by the establishment of an independent typeface department. Almost all Olivetti products (typewriters, calculators and the entire spectrum of electronic text and information processing machines) provide the user with results in written, mostly printed form. The progress in printing technology, from golf ball or daisy wheel typewriters to electronic jet printers, demanded a constant development of new and better typefaces and numerological systems which provide the user with the highest possible degree of readability in both functional and aesthetic aspects. The transition from mechanical engineering to electronics required extensive studies of electronic type characters and their ergonomic qualities, which are still far from being concluded. In contrast to all the other competitors in this field Olivetti conduct their own basic research, thus not only contributing towards further development of typeface quality in their own production, but

56

also establishing new standards for computer type characters which are of benefit to the entire area. Developing machine readable characters for traditional alphabets like Cyrillic, Arabic, Greek, Japanese or for neglected minor languages such as Senegalese, Nepalese or Algonquin was not only in the interests of the company's export activities, but also fulfilled the self-imposed duty to promote and develop cultural and civilizing activities. The long-term research investments into alphabets and characters proved to be an invaluable potential for present and future electronic information processing, a design of symbols and characters within modern electronic information processing which respects the cultural codes of mankind – comparable also to the question of communication between man and machine as research object of 'interface design', which is still very much at the initial stages.

With the encouragement of Zorzi and Roberto Olivetti, Hans von Klier, who had previously worked in Sottsass' office for seven years, devoted himself to the question of corporate identity in 1968. At that time Olivetti's foreign business activities had grown to a considerable extent (through branches, agents in markets or holding companies). As each branch, each office and each distribution partner attached great importance to their own, individual presentation and communication work, the design of a common and unique company image proved more and more difficult. The variety of appearances of Olivetti's individual departments and branches became increasingly more confusing, with a common approach hardly recognizable. Von Klier conducted a study on how Olivetti presented itself worldwide and he submitted

68. The Divisumma 18 (facing) and the Logos 18 calculators, by Bellini with De Gregotti, De Vries, Macchi Cassia, Pasini and Pasqui, 1973.

proposals for a co-ordinated company image. The first and most essential step in this direction was the establishment of a central department which was to work out mandatory design elements for the appearance projected by all departments of the company. Thus, the corporate identity department was eventually set up under von Klier's management, initially working out a modicum of basic elements for image formation, e.g. logo, company colours, characters, as well as a framework for a large variety of conceivable applications, such as letterheads, packages, company vehicles, buildings, etc. In the course of time and in the interest of a unified company image, the duties of the department were extended to include the design of trade fairs, commercial exhibitions, interior design for industrial and commercial buildings and design concepts for special events.

The cultural activities sector included any activity not only directed towards Olivetti's clients and staff, but primarily addressing a wider public: a special section, for instance, for gifts and calendars, one for cultural publications such as art prints, art posters, books – for several years Olivetti even published their own art and culture magazine. But at the centre of these activities are the art exhibitions. In the beginning, these were more or less offered to the company from external sources and eventually integrated into a consistent exhibition policy. They began in the fifties and sixties with sporadic enquiries by museums interested in Olivetti's design and company image as potential exhibits. The decisive turn came in 1968, when the Italian government asked Olivetti to support an exhibition which was intended to draw attention to Italy's endangered cultural heritage. The immediate reason was the damage caused to part of frescoes of the exhibition *From Giotto to Pontormo* following the floods in Florence in 1965. Olivetti not only provided financial support, but also promoted the presentation of this exhibition in various museums and cities and offered their advice on questions of exhibition design, the publication of catalogues and the preparation of posters. This was the beginning of the company's exhibition activities, now spanning over two decades, with the aim of drawing public attention to important cultural objects: paintings, sculptures, arts and crafts, as well as the Italian and European cultural tradition.

Another field of the company's exhibition policy dealt with noteworthy cultural achievements of the present, with the emphasis placed more on industrial culture than on art. Especially the topics 'design' and 'form' were very competently presented by Olivetti, for instance on the occasion of the exhibition *Concept & Form* in 1969.

From the seventies to the mid-eighties the company's art and culture orientated exhibition activities took up an important position within its corporate image policy. One may even be forgiven for believing that, in view of a rather vague and uncertain future of the 'electronic society', the company harks back to cultural values of the past in order to compensate for the lack of future perspectives. The exhibition activities, so vigorously pursued by the corporate image department, may even be considered as a substitute for a clear company policy. What was created rather haphazardly and intuitively now proves to be an essential component of the company's image, even more so since electronic products for office use are increasingly interchangeable and short-lived. In this atmosphere of uncertainty regarding technological developments, other aspects apart from the purely technical product quality or its commercial viability, which could be capable of creating an emotional tie between the user and the manufacturer have grown in importance. On the strength of their far-reaching involvement in cultural and other corporate image activities, practiced continually over the last years, Olivetti have accumulated an image potential which was applied credibly and with purpose.

69. Carlo De Benedetti.

PART 2
THE COMPANY UNDER CARLO DE BENEDETTI

Central aspects of Olivetti's design management today

The company under Carlo De Benedetti

Olivetti under De Benedetti is involved in a process of continual adaptation to new economic and technological requirements. Although it may appear rather hidden behind his spectacular financial activities, De Benedetti seems to be pursuing a clear industrial strategy for Olivetti. This strategy is, however, difficult to identify as it exists as a process developing with extreme speed and completely new dimensions and for this reason the role of design has to be seen from a long-term perspective. This first section tries to give some insight into the economic and strategic orientation of Olivetti under De Benedetti, as well as a backward look at the position and contribution of design in Olivetti's most fundamental change, that from a mechanical to an electronic company. It will also show that the design function or rather the Corporate Image department traditionally has been a quite autonomous unit. By maintaining this central position over many years it has been come to stand for a well-practiced and very specific approach to design management which follows some basic principles. Without some understanding of these long-term principles, today's design management in Olivetti would be difficult to comprehend. The next section is dedicated exclusively to this question. The last section of this chapter tries to outline some details of present design management at different levels of the company and in some design departments, which can only be interpreted correctly by bearing in mind the overall framework of the company and the special long-term principles of management.

The change from a mechanical to an electronic company

When De Benedetti took over in 1978, Olivetti was in crisis, under-capitalized and making heavy losses. New finance and new confidence in management were needed for the difficult transition from the mechanical to the electronic age of the company. De Benedetti's achievement in the following years was not only to make a striking improvement in the company's finances, but also to give a clear strategic orientation to the completion of the change that saw the company move from being a producer of mechanical office machines to becoming a global data processing company, playing the role of protagonist on the world market. Within five years of the publication of an analysis in *Time* magazine, De Benedetti had made Olivetti the leading West European manufacturer of office automation and data processing equipment. The product line had been completely renewed, with an electronic range covering all fields of business and private office work, and priority was given to technological innovation and updating, as well as to the decisive enlargement and improvement of the sales organization.

Design played a major role in this period of electronic renewal. Had the designers not succeeded in developing a new visual concept for electronic technology, Olivetti's entry into the new field would have been uneventful[1]. The striking new interpretation, in terms of both

70. The M24 personal computer: note the flat keyboard developed by Sottsass.

shape and user-friendliness soon made Olivetti a major figure in the world electronic field, although in terms of both technological standard and cost, Olivetti had strong competitors such as IBM and the new American and Japanese electronic companies.

In 1973 Olivetti introduced the world's first fully electronic typewriter with the ET series and a design which was to set a benchmark for the new generation of electronic typewriters in all markets. Mario Bellini's so-called wedge shape paid particular attention to easy use and ergonomic efficiency. It communicated both dynamic speed and technological refinement by emphasizing the flatness of the keyboard. Bellini followed the same concept with desktop printing calculators, such as the Logos EC 162 and 182. The 1981 Logos 9 was the world's smallest printing calculator, reminiscent of a cigarette packet in its size and shape. The new lines of cash registers from the CR and Mercator series were made adaptable to all kinds of customer types and requirements, by means of a design that communicates the new technology and meets all ergonomic and user requirements from both the operator and customer.

Sottsass's designs for the office included a complete new range of powerful mini computers. These were designed with all the necessary components including keyboard, printer, video display for wide ranging multi-purpose and multi-programmable data processing systems. These took into account office furnishing and so could form whole work stations. It was in particular the flat, easy to use keyboard, the first of its kind, which was in 1980 to establish a new standard for keyboard ergonomics, followed by a whole selection of user-friendly solutions, such as retractable arms which finally allowed the operator to change his position whilst still facing the screen. These integrated solutions, which also met individual requirements for new technology work stations, attracted very much interest and further success for Olivetti technology. The Sottsass design office has a particularly broad viewpoint over electronic equipment as its responsibility in Olivetti covers also the furnishing of office space: the Sottsass office has followed electronic developments in detail from the beginnings of the *Elea* in 1959 (see Chapter 1).

In 1982, Olivetti introduced its first personal computer, the M20, but it was the M24, its follower in 1984, which received the most interest due to its design (fig. 70). This model had a smaller electronic box, a thinner, detachable keyboard together with improved software and an IBM compatible operating system[2].

71. Designs for the Open Systems Architecture screens.

Corporate Strategy

Since 1985, Olivetti has developed from a relatively marginal position to an electronic company of major importance in the international market. It is now the main European manufacturer of personal computers, the leading producer of electronic typewriters and video-typing products and the main European manufacturer of printers, as well as being one of the world's leading information technology companies. In 1987, the new dimension of De Benedetti's strategy for Olivetti was presented to the public on the occasion of the market introduction of the new series of mini computers LSX 3000. They are part of a new offering called 'Open System Architecture' (OSA) (fig. 71), which De Benedetti announced as a new strategy and even a new Olivetti, 'the Olivetti of the mini computer age'[3]. This is a new strategic orientation of Olivetti from personal computers for single use to mini computers intended for a new, globally integrated information technology. Instead of offering stand-alone computers and other single information processing machines and components, Olivetti will, in the future, be able to offer a global service of an optimum mix of equipment and software, together with the ability to respond to changing user requirements. This continues the development of the personal computer which moved from a specialist product at first to a mass product, of which about 50 million units had already been installed in 1987. Making consumers familiar with information technology helped them to appreciate systems for wider usage and multiplied the need for interconnectivity and the demand for services.

OSA is conceived as 'a new way of configuring and interconnecting computer products, networks and services to create an optimum solution for any application'. In the words of Elserino Piol, it is a "comprehensive framework embracing all hardware and software components and providing connectivity in existing multi-vendor environments. It is also open to future advance in technologies and applications, and, in particular, to the new dev-

63

OLIVETTI

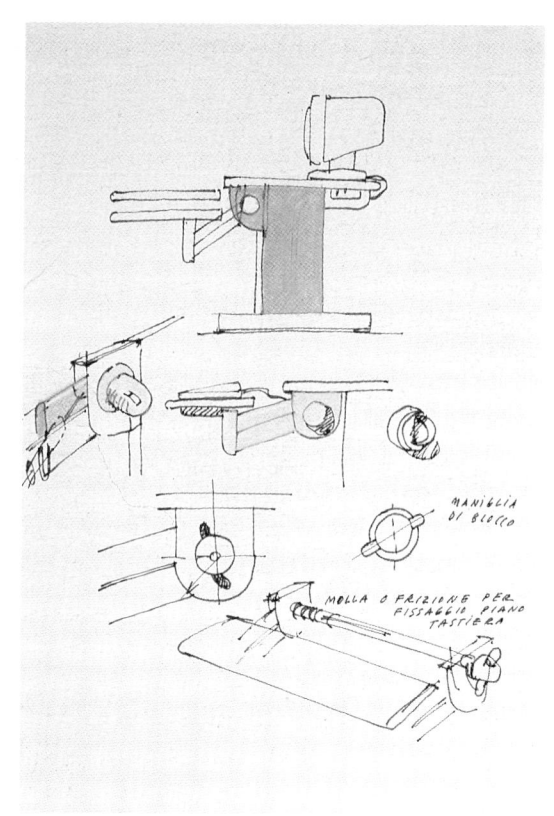

72-74. Designs by Michele De Lucchi for housings for OSA computers and terminals.

elopments already emerging in standards.'[4]

For De Benedetti, the ability to work with all compatible networks of information technology on a global scale meant that apart from developing the necessary hardware and software, there must also be a considerable increase in service and consultancy, to allow for building personalized, individual information networks. A comprehensive network development not only has to be capable of operating in its own right but also use other complementary hardware elements which Olivetti does not offer or from other producers, with whom the client prefers to deal. Furthermore, compatibility requires that

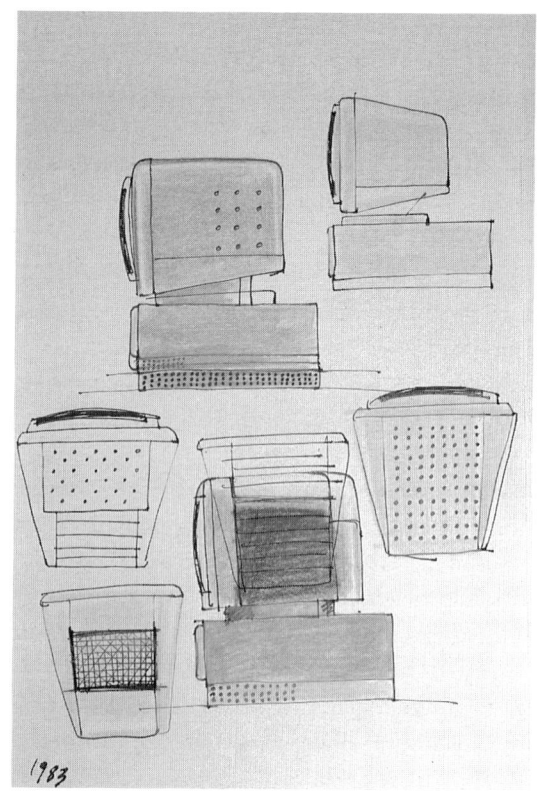

75. The current Olivetti product range in OSA.

all information technology producers and users worldwide will have to adopt and work to common standards, in order to enter a new dimension of information networks. De Benedetti's own words regarding this subject are: 'Standards are today one of the main driving forces for change. Users are now requiring – even demanding – communications and systems standards with an open approach. Standards favour integration and communication between computers of different levels and from different manufacturing origins....'[5]

To meet the requirements of developing new global networks and the requirements of the new economic situation, De Benedetti concludes with the necessity of 'strategic alliances' in the field of information technology: 'Companies operating in this global market are faced with a dual constraint, related to the speed of technological progress, the costs of researching, developing and launching a product are rising, while product life continues to diminish. We all know that certain products in our field have a life of from six months to a year. Increasingly large volumes have to be produced more rapidly. In my opinion, an important consequence is that, with the exception of IBM, the day of the traditional multinational is over: we have moved into the age of alliances.

By this concept of alliances – also recently proposed as a general need of future economic by the progressive management writer Tom Peters[6] – De Benedetti is working through partnerships, co-operations and agreements towards achieving the best and most advanced technological knowledge, for example knowledge for specialized markets such as education, as well as towards access to local markets and sales organizations. Looking back, many of De Benedetti's financial operations can be identified as strategical alliances necessary for Olivetti's new business role. Such operations would include Olivetti's participation in projects with AT&T, giving Olivetti access to research at Bell Laboratories and to the American market, the agreement with Toshiba which offered insights into technological advances and also helped in promoting common standards, and the joint venture with Acorn which gave access to specialized know-how for the education market, while the takeover of the majority of Triumph Adler put into Olivetti's hands a wide local distribution system.

Olivetti has been strengthening its worldwide distribution and service network over the last few years in order to further the new strategy's aims of achieving the highest possible market presence and of delivering quality. Today, with more than twenty thousand people employed, this network is an 'asset which very few other computer companies possess' and which can be seen as 'a guarantee of continuity and quality in relations with users', as De Benedetti wrote in *Olivetti News* in December, 1987.

Another factor of major importance for the new strategy is service for users. For this reason a new company, called Olivetti Information Services, has been created. It supplies a complete range of software and computer services: software products, business services, new telephone and voice-data services, facilities management, education and training.

In the future, progress in information technology will occur with more speed than ever before and with unforeseeable possibilities and consequences for the role of work and the organization of society. De Benedetti expects 'a secular change in the way society is organized....driven by an acceleration in technological innovation.' Producers of information technology 'must acquire a new sense of responsibility. Only then can we achieve a balanced transition towards a new social organization without paying too high a price. We are facing a whole series of challenges – in technology, in the market and in social progress.'[7]

De Benedetti developed this theme of the social aspects of technology practically by strengthening Olivetti's basic research in the field, which today is carried out by the Olivetti Research Division (ORD), consisting of a number of laboratories and co-ordinating offices. In contrast to the Applied Research Division, the ORD deals with questions of general overall importance for the new strategy such as software productivity, the man-machine interface and artificial intelligence. His second response to the new challenges of technology and marketplace can be seen in his strategy for the organization of the company and in his management style.

Corporate Organization

Since the De Benedetti take-over there has been a continual re-organization of the company, which the employees and associates of the company have come to see as a characteristic of his management. The basic direction of the change is a 'cautious but continual decentralization and delegation by product-market areas'[8]. In 1987 he started a series of reorganizations through which this move became more obvious. This series began with the creation of Independent Business Units which in 1989 were to become independent product companies under a central holding company. The new organizational policy was in response to the shift of products on offer, and to a shift in demand from the end user, marking a change in the traditional product-based classification of information technology towards a subdivision by channel. Because of this fragmentation of the market, the aim was to make full use of the potential in each segment, by creating organizational units to cover the entire range of relevant activities, with the industrial and distribution substructures working together to meet specialized customer requirements: an organisation structured towards the needs of the consumer, not the product list.

This book discusses the company structure of end of the 1980s. As the diagram shows (fig. 76), in 1988 Olivetti consisted of the parent company Ing. C. Olivetti, which as a holding company controls three independent 'product' companies and a company for group technological activities. The parent company represents and underwrites the unitary nature of the Group, formulates strategy, co-ordinates top level management and handles group image and external relations. The three main areas of supply are 'Olivetti Office', 'Olivetti Systems and Networks' and 'Olivetti Information Services'. The unit for office products is a supplier of mass consumer personal and business products for text, data and image management, serving a mass market through indirect channels. The unit for systems and networks deals with application systems as well as integrated systems. It serves a market of large professional

Olivetti Corporate Structure, 1988

- **ING. C. OLIVETTI & CO.**
  President — Carlo De Benedetti
  - Managing Director — Vittorio Cassoni
    - Secretary General
    - Press
    - Corporate Image
    - Quality control
    - Legal affairs
    - Other central functions
  - **Olivetti Office.** Franco Tatò.
  - **Olivetti Systems & Networks.** Luigi Mercurio.
  - **Olivetti Information Services.** Franco De Benedetti.
  - **Technological Activities.** Ettore Marezzi.

76. Olivetti Corporate Structure, 1988.

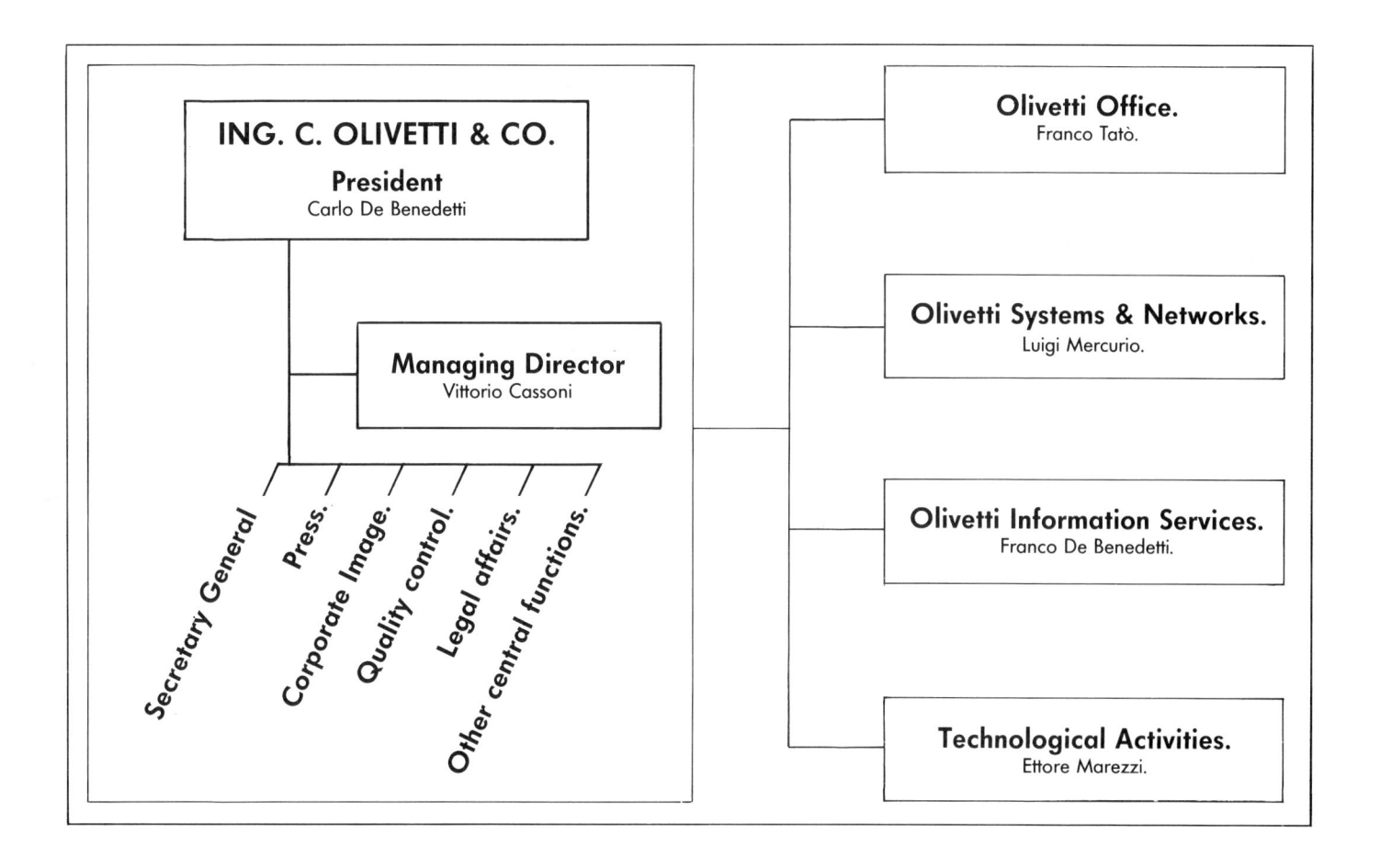

customers such as banks, state institutions and companies, mainly by direct channels. The third unit, for 'Information Services', consists of systems integrators and service suppliers. The user is approached directly with proposal for a complete business service, and the aim is to acquire thereby exclusive control of contacts with the user. Each of these units has been developed in order to serve separate market segments, which require different types of strategic and competitive approaches as regards pricing, quality, responsiveness, production volume and customer support[9].

Whereas product planning, production, marketing and sales are controlled by company, the function of design occupies a central position, under the title of the Corporate Image department. Its position in the company is the same as it was over twenty years ago — a central service department to the product units. As the diagram shows, the typical Olivetti concept of a holistic approach to all image-building activities has been kept together with the original personnel. The only visible changes are in the direction of the corporate image and in the responsibility for advertising. Regarding the first Renzo Zorzi, the intellectual and organizational builder of the Corporate Image (Ch. 1) was succeeded by his former representative and director of design, Paolo Viti.

Responsibility for advertising, apart from corporate advertising, now lies with the product companies. Corporate Image is divided into a substructure of two offices for product design; one serving the company for office products, the other responsible for product 'systems and networks' and office furniture. It also includes the offices for Corporate Identity, Graphic Design, Typeface Design, Ergonomics and Cultural Activities, together with consultants for signs and keyboard research and colour systems, all serving the other design offices.

De Benedetti's organization and management style is dedicated to the primary aim of quick and efficient adaptation to new situations. Continual change of organizational structures can only be interpreted as part of a continuous, flexible process. De Benedetti stresses the importance of involving the staff in the problems of the company. He follows what can be described as an 'entrepreneurial approach of emphasizing the personal responsibility and self-organization of the staff'. The main points of this concept are achieving clear objectives by the board, establishing direct and personal relations between board and management, as well as between the different management functions. Individuals are made to feel involved through the flow of information about all aspects of the company and any problems and through financial participation in terms of profit percentage schemes for management. This concept contributes to a broad knowledge of the company's situation internally and externally and to the development of a strong feeling of responsibility for the work of the individual and for the company as a whole. Giving responsibility to staff with a broad, open view of work, is what De Benedetti calls his Italian side of management. It takes advantage of the need for personal autonomy in combination with a 'family' shaped loyalty for the whole community – typical for individual behaviour in Italian culture (as we will discuss later in this chapter).

The second side of his management is the enforcement of effective accountability in order to achieve the most up-to-date view of the company's financial and economic position. This could can be described as management by responsibility for cost and profit.

De Benedetti's approach seems to be a step away from traditional, hierarchical concepts of management towards motivating individual responsibility and creativity, as well as creating company commitment. It is an approach which progressive management theory also endorses for today's uncertainty and change[10]. Within Olivetti this attitude towards management was already traditional, as it was very much Adriano Olivetti's personal style which he developed in the 1930s. Although completely different in personality and ethical approach, both Adriano Olivetti and later Carlo De Benedetti were developing advanced American ideas for business administration and technology. Both equally emphasized the Italian mentality and respected it. The bedrock, for which Olivetti was renowned, and which enabled the company to survive many difficulties was its investment in technological expertise and the potential of highly self-organized, independent minded people with great commitment to the company. Adriano had created a company identity and image, which was act as a bond within the company and allow it to develop after his time and despite ever changing structures and leadership.

Principles of managing design in Olivetti

The concept of continuity and change in the context of a humanistic understanding of design.

The most striking point in Olivetti's long-lasting design tradition is the specific commitment to continuity of design which at the same time means continual change. This goes back to an understanding of design as an element of a continually developing civilization with a history that is deeply connected with cultural factors. It is not only technological developments which require continual changes in design, but also changes of attitudes towards the quality of life and cultural values. Adriano Olivetti, from a humanitarian point of view, defined the company philosophy and aim as being the achievement of a worthwhile contribution to the culture of its time, and this also defines the function and value of design. Design for office products, therefore, has to make technology a medium for a human working life with high cultural standards (Ch. 1). During Adriano Olivetti's lifetime, this understanding of the company's role continued to determine the company's activities. As it asked for a high degree of participation in the development of all fields of civilization, the

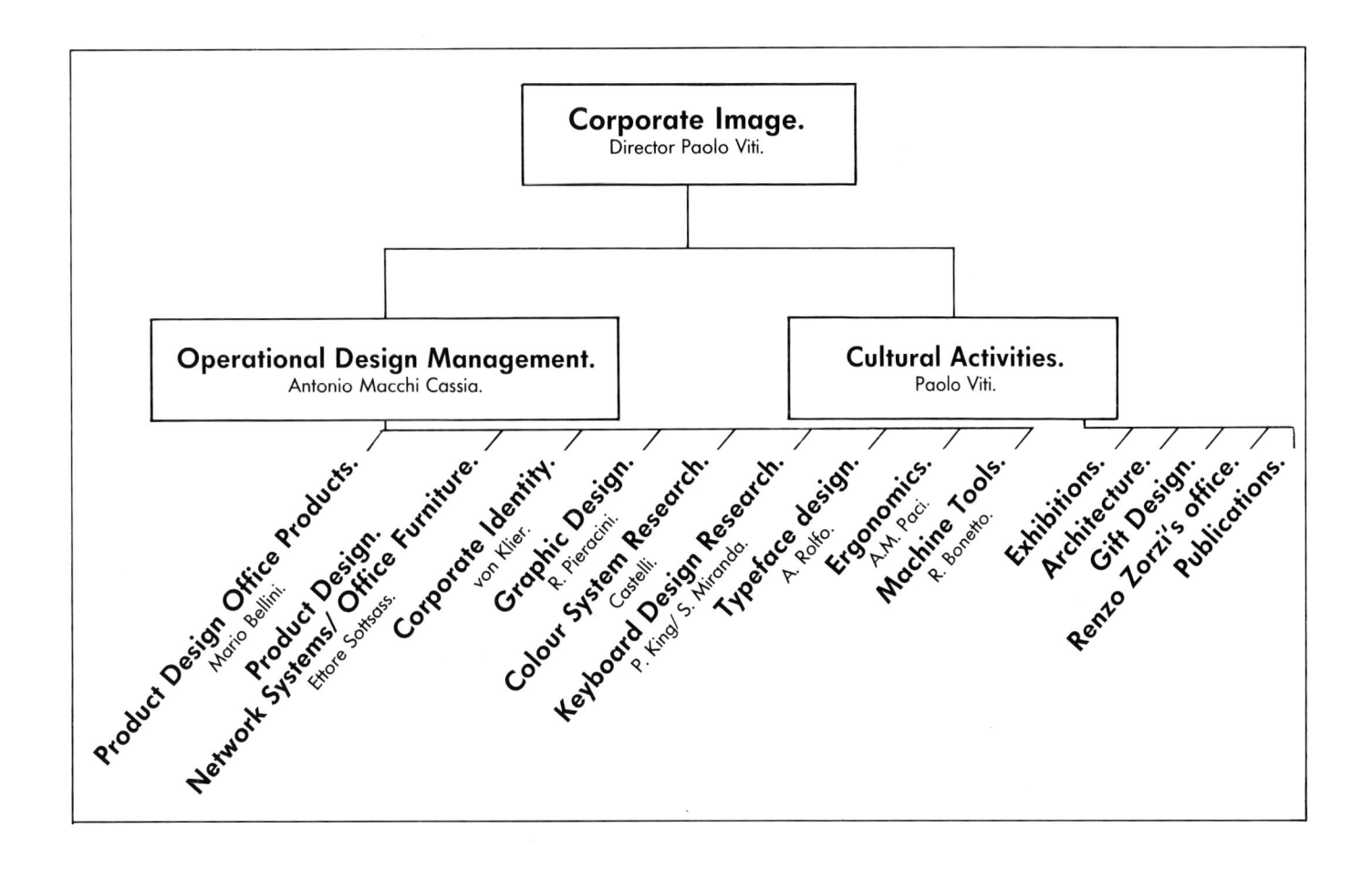

```
                    ┌─────────────────────┐
                    │  Corporate Image.   │
                    │ Director Paolo Viti.│
                    └──────────┬──────────┘
              ┌────────────────┴────────────────┐
    ┌─────────────────────────┐       ┌──────────────────┐
    │Operational Design Mgmt. │       │Cultural Activities│
    │  Antonio Macchi Cassia. │       │   Paolo Viti.    │
    └─────────────────────────┘       └──────────────────┘
```

Branches: *Product Design Office Products.* Mario Bellini. / *Product Design.* / *Network Systems/Office Furniture.* Ettore Sottsass. / *Corporate Identity.* von Klier. / *Graphic Design.* R. Pieracini. / *Colour System Research.* Castelli. / *Keyboard Design Research.* P. King/ S. Miranda. / *Typeface design.* A. Rolfo. / *Ergonomics.* A.M. Paci. / *Machine Tools.* R. Bonetto. / *Exhibitions.* / *Architecture.* / *Gift Design.* / *Renzo Zorzi's office.* / *Publications.*

77. Organization of Corporate Image under Paolo Viti.

aim was to develop the highest cultural design commitment, especially among development engineers and production workers, and to create a design organization that was open to cultural change and capable of interpreting the company philosophy with regard to contemporary changes in an independent, self-organizing way (as we shall see, the same attitude coloured the use of outside, independent designers). Continuity in Olivetti design until today covers continuity of staff, of design approach and of design organization.

Continuity of staff and continuity of design approach

Olivetti has a tradition of working with its main designers on a continual, sometimes on a lifelong basis. For this reason the central figures of Olivetti design are very few, although they do include such well-known designers as Nizzoli in the era of Adriano Olivetti, and Sottsass and Bellini from the time of Adriano's death until today. We could ask how it was possible to undergo such a striking change from a mechanical to an electronic company with the same designers. The best answer is to look at the development of Olivetti's product design which clearly shows the importance of the contribution of design to technological change. Olivetti's approach to product design has developed continually over the years, yet always reverting to previous concepts so as to give the user a chance to adapt to more complex technology. One of the most basic principles of all major Olivetti designers is their commitment to Olivetti's design history and their aim of continuing on a given line. A result of this is a continuity of personal style, clearly seen for example in the typewriters and calculators designed by Nizzoli between 1930 and 1960 and the electronic typewriters and calculators by Bellini since 1978. Formal continuity reverting to preceding design concepts can also be seen in other areas, as for example in keyboard research and in office furniture as described in Chapter three.

The long-term service and relationship with the company of the main Olivetti designers – that is, the directors of the Olivetti design offices – is the mechanism that enables a younger generation of designers to be educated into the same approach. The most striking example of this is the case of Ettore Sottsass, who is regarded as a kind of father and teacher by younger designers. He represents the intellectual and cultural approach to design first claimed by Adriano Olivetti and he has the charisma and idealism to communicate and realize it. His work and ideas have attracted and inspired many young designers who are now directors of Olivetti design offices.

Personal continuity benefits both designers and design managers. Adriano Olivetti reworked all of the design and image-building activities with only the support of his son Roberto. After his death Renzo Zorzi became the central figure for more than twenty years until his retirement at the end of 1987. Zorzi represented and continued the Olivetti philosophy by building the institutional structure of design and by having management responsibility for the whole field, to which his intellectual input through publications also contributed. Throughout the internal and external changes in Olivetti, he maintained the prominent position of design within the company. His follower as director of Corporate Image was Paolo Viti, who had been developing and working with Zorzi for twenty years as his assistant and director for design. In this way the Olivetti philosophy and culture was carried on by personality and personal rule.

Since its institutionalization as the department of Corporate Identity (see Ch.1), design has been always kept in the same position, just below top management and more or less in the same functional substructure (compare figs. 77, 78). This in combination with strong personalities in the direction of the design department allowed design to develop a strong base position inside the company which in the past to a certain degree has been independent from company reorganizations.

Central approach to a pluralistic and personalistic company style

Taken together, continuity and change may at first appear to be contradictory, both central and pluralistic, as we have seen. The reconciliation of what appear to be contraries characterizes Olivetti's approach. It is a phenomenon that can be seen throughout Olivetti's design history and that continues to appear in the most unexpected contexts.

The central approach to company style in terms of institutionalization goes back to Renzo Zorzi, as described in Chapter one. His concept was to put all activities relating to creating and building the image and identity of the company under a single head, and in a central position in the company. His aim was to replace Adriano Olivetti's former methods, which centred on personal contacts, with a formal structure that would be able to continue along the lines laid down and in the same spirit. Although the intention was to achieve an institution that would be independent of personality effects, the department of Corporate Image created for this purpose by Zorzi was in fact personality driven, since for more than twenty years he was to be the central figure in the development of Olivetti's corporate philosophy and image. Without his presence and intellectual input the developed identities of a multitude of different offices would be difficult to understand. Zorzi controlled an extremely wide range of activities, from product design, graphic design and advertising through corporate identification systems to architecture, gift design, cultural activities, publishing, art exhibitions and design events. The structural centralization of these activities in combination with the strong personal involvement and presence of Renzo Zorzi is what made the cultural approach a driving force in the company.

Corporate Image has been shaping the outside image as well as the inside identity by consciously translating the Olivetti philosophy into visible signs in the company presentation. Com-

THE COMPANY UNDER DE BENEDETTI

78-80. Three examples of the Olivetti logotype in use, showing the variety possible within a clearly designed framework.

81. Ettore Sottsass.

pany activities are used as a conscious means of communicating a specific company attitude. In this way, Olivetti has created an image to communicate to the public which has more than just an economic perspective to it. In keeping with the Olivetti tradition, the company has striven for excellence and quality on every level: thus Olivetti's record in office and industrial architecture is justly well-known, while in graphic design and advertising Olivetti commissions from artists such as Pintori or Ballmer cannot be overlooked. In the wider world of contemporary cultural events the company has found an important role through its cultural activities and sponsorships. As to design, Olivetti products created by Sottsass and by Bellini are certainly among the most famous and most often cited examples of product design.

Corporate Image's central position and overall approach to its different fields of responsibility allows for considerable synergy effects. For example, advertising and graphic design can take advantage of the quality of product design. Famous examples of this are Nizzoli's posters of Nizzoli for the Lexikon 80 (1949) or Pintori's advertisements for the Lettera 22. Showroom material and exhibition design can be treated as a means of underlining product design. Investment in typography, colour research or keyboard research can be a way into a whole range of other activities

It has often been asked what could be the common basis for such different activities as product design, typeface design and architecture, especially as in the Olivetti corporate image the formal similarities that one might expect are not to be found. Co-ordination is not created through formal rules but by the central spirit of the company, embodied in and interpreted by those at the head of the Corporate Image department. Instead of a formal set of standards there is the concept of a pluralistic and personalistic company style – pluralistic because it is not one designer, nor one hand that has shaped the Olivetti image but a whole group of designers consisting of an 'inner circle' of those working permanently with Olivetti and an 'outer circle', who work infrequently, often only on specific projects. The Olivetti style is linked to a long list of names; in the field of graphic design and architecture almost all of the important architects, artists and graphic designers of the last fifty years have worked for Olivetti and have contributed to its overall style. Product design is the most striking example of this pluralistic attitude. Here two outstanding designers – both in the 'inner circle' – work within a common company style, despite their completely different approaches to design. This is in considerable contrast to the received view of how corporate identity functions. Olivetti's concept of design and corporate identity is highly personalistic, as the senior designers are given free space in which to develop their own styles. Designers such as Nizzoli, Sottsass and Bellini have not only worked with Olivetti for long periods of time, but have developed an individual design tradition within the company which has helped the company attain an outstanding and original presence in the commercial world.

In house design with independent designers

Olivetti has been building its design image using external freelance designers since the time of Adriano Olivetti. He introduced the strategy of creating a core of special individuals allied to the company. Outside the company, such individuals are able to interpret and develop the cultural values of society in the industrial world, through their independent work. By involving such people in the industrial process, the company found a direct means of participating in the general and developing cultural life of society, thereby avoiding the separation of the industrial world from society in favour of a common, live and continually progressing culture. With hindsight we can see that one of the main strengths of this original idea was its openness towards cultural change and its readiness to think of change as a major necessity of civilization. This original notion mainly has determined the personnel strategy in the field of Corporate Image activities. The basic meeting points of industry and society are to be found in the field of product design, advertising, graphic design and architecture, all of which fall within the brief of Corporate Image and which, planned or not, provide a visible and tangible vehicle for the company spirit.

The personnel strategy is twofold. Firstly, there the directors of the Olivetti design offices and their staff. The directing master designers such as Sottsass (fig 81) and Bellini (fig. 82) are personalities of international importance and reputation. They work with Olivetti on a long-term, freelance basis. It is these directors and a small group of designated 'senior' designers such as De Lucchi and Sowden (see below, on the Sottsass Design Office) who interpret and continue the Olivetti philosophy. Being themselves freelances they also work with a number of freelance assistant designers, who may come from all parts of the world and are often very young. This group of design staff usually stays with Olivetti for about five years before moving on to other work. A second group of collaborators consists of an outside circle of designers, architects and artists who work with Olivetti irregularly, and on specific projects. Most of the time, these people are important representatives of their professions or talented young people in whom Olivetti sees great potential. In this way a lot of architects, artists and designers, some already famous, some to be famous later, from Le Corbusier to Stirling, from Milton Glaser to Folon, and George Nelson to Castiglioni, joined the Olivetti company and contributed their names and image to the illustrious circle. This type of collaboration is frequently practised in architecture, advertising, graphic design and cultural activities whereas product design remains the exclusive domain of the inner circle. The designers of the inner circle are responsible for what is referred to as 'in-house design'. Olivetti provides these directors of the design offices with office space, equip-

82. Mario Bellini.

ment and administrative staff. They have a ready-made, permanent base inside the company and their long-term relationship with the company gives them experience of the whole structural organization of the company and its philosophy. Their contracts are on a yearly basis as consultancies rather than on a project by project basis. Therefore they are involved in all kinds of design matters with different departments and people. The number of in-house designers, counting only the inner circle of design masters and their assisting staff, is only about 50; an extremely small number for a company of Olivetti's size. Furthermore, these designers should not be compared to normal full time design staff, as all of them do other outside design work. This fact has made many wonder what are the reasons for the particular efficiency of this system. One main reason that is often overlooked lies in the continuity of approach, discussed above, which has led to design becoming a major resource within the infrastructure of the company. Without the established design commitment and experience of the engineers, the designers would never be able to realize their concepts. For the designers, the respect and positive attitude of the technicians are basic preconditions for effective work. To some extent, the design success of Olivetti is due to the fact that it has created what we might call a reserved area, one almost untouched by any other function within the company, to designers and technicians to work out new design concepts. For many years this area enjoyed a greater positive force than marketing and sales.

Another factor of great importance is Olivetti's design image, experience and relations in the international world of design and culture. This renown enables the company to attract the best designers to Olivetti. Similarly, Olivetti is well known for leaving designers free to work on their ideas and visions undisturbed. This idea had great appeal for once unknown designers such as Nizzoli, Sottsass and Bellini, as well as for designers who were already well known throughout the world. This heady mixture of very considerable responsibility with almost complete freedom of procedure provides a great challenge. The nature of this challenge, and the combination of factors in it, explain how it is that a small group of designers is prepared to take on such vital responsibilities, and work for Olivetti under financial conditions that are rather unattractive.

Another aspect which makes Olivetti's small group so effective is their independence and their outside design activities, through which designers receive wide-ranging experience in all kinds of design fields, including furniture, architecture, consumer goods or graphics, and come to understand their particularities with regard to materials, aesthetics, design trends, manufacturing requirements and markets. This leads to what the design management calls 'efficient cross-fertilization', whereby the fulltime employed Olivetti staff will always be confronted with new and different ideas with which to experiment and develop new concepts, while the external designers have the freedom to move independently within the company structure. They have 'vertical access' to all levels and can proceed in projects as they desire, as long as they use and respect the existing structure. How they bring a project through this structure is left to them. As shown in the next section, it is very much a self-organized process and the company takes advantage precisely of this self-organizing capacity in its external designers. By providing in advance the facilities of an office and the necessary administration, Olivetti intends to create conditions which will allow the designers to use their time to a maximum for creative work with. Designers with these offices of their own are in effect used to organize and manage projects. Olivetti supports the independence of their designers both inside and outside the company, in order to utilize the strength and creativity of independent minds that are prepared to take risks for their ideas. This concept is made possible by the specifically 'Italian' mentality and conception of the design profession in Italy, as we shall see shortly. It is hard to tell whether such a constellation of talents freewheeling through a company would be so successful in cultures with different design mentalities and design training, as for example in America or Germany. For Olivetti, apart from the qualitative advantages, this arrangement has considerable cost advan-

83. Paolo Viti.

tages, as the freelance designers are considerably less expensive than fully employed staff. Thanks to Olivetti's reputation and its active promotion of its designers, master designers of the highest international reputation are ready to work for lower fees for Olivetti.

This system of in-house independent designers is successful as long as the Olivetti image identity and choice of designers represent high cultural quality. So long as Olivetti can also offer an independent realization of ideas the company will attract the best designers and link them to the company on a long term basis. As Olivetti's history shows this is a matter of continual investment in the designers who have been growing with the company. It is largely this relationship, developed over many years, which gives the Olivetti its specific style. The basis and centre point of the Olivetti style within product design is in this sense different from the other image-building activities. These other activities act as satellites of the product design system, using outside designers to create an impressive surrounding to the centrepoint.

OLIVETTI

84. Antonio Macchi Cassia

Italian culture and drama as components of design management.

Before describing the design process in more detail in terms of the work of the design offices, we should turn our attention to Olivetti design management and its roots in Italian culture. The Italian understanding of man and society had been shaped over thousands of years by the frequent experience of occupation by foreigners. The family environment has become a stronghold of individuality and self-determination against an imposed system; family and friends are considered necessary for survival in a world of enemies. Consequently, the struggle for a democratic organization which would respect the rights of the individual is a driving force in Italian society. Personality is a key factor in Italian management. Management is not with a faceless workforce but with individuals who expect to be treated as such. Respect for the individual means the freedom to act develop, to find a human basis of interaction between the different levels in companies instead of a purely hierarchical one. Personal relations in the workplace are considered vital. Probably in no other country are there so many friends to be found within the workplace as in Italy; friendships bring contacts and information, on which all workers become dependent, as official rigid structures and procedures do not have the same importance in Italy as in more Protestant countries. The Italian tradition goes back to a positive model of man's life and fate in the Catholic Mediterranean tradition. Contrary to the Protestant ethic, work can be not so much a burden but a pleasurable and fulfilling experience. As such it is approached by the Italians with a positive attitude.

Bureaucratic rules can oppose basic cultural values. They limit personal freedom and the pleasure to experiment, and curtail openness to all new developments. Clear, tight orders are seen as showing disrespect to the individual, or even managerial incompetence, as such orders do not allow the individual to develop his or her own ideas. Another characteristic factor, and one particularly important for Italy's success in design, is the general enthusiasm of management for new ideas or projects. Architects in Italy are of particular importance in this context. With an education that encompasses all kinds of cultural expressions, and with the long and important cultural tradition of the profession, they are expected to provide new ideas, especially when working as designers for industry. Contrary to the specialist education of designers in the rest of Europe and America as, for example graphic, industrial or textile designers, Italian designer-architects are more autonomous. Their education as architects is rather the precondition for applying themselves to work in a wide field of activities instead of depending only on one industry. In combination with their high social standing in Italian society, this contributes to a great confidence and optimism, certainly more so than in other countries. So, for example, to give architects strict orders would surely be a reflection on their capacity and creativity.

These basic cultural attitudes and values largely determine and characterize the Olivetti approach to design management, and can clearly be seen on the operational level in specific methods of co-ordination, motivation and personal interaction. An important factor here is what can be called the 'Italian drama' – the consciously created and accepted chaos that is caused by the reinforcement of different approaches, overlapping competences and extreme time pressure, all of which results in apparent confusion and explosive personal interactions. Design managers and designers see such confrontations as a challenge, even as a necessary way towards achieving excellence. Unplannable, uncontrollable and always exciting, the best individual performances are given in a highly emotional atmosphere.

OLIVETTI

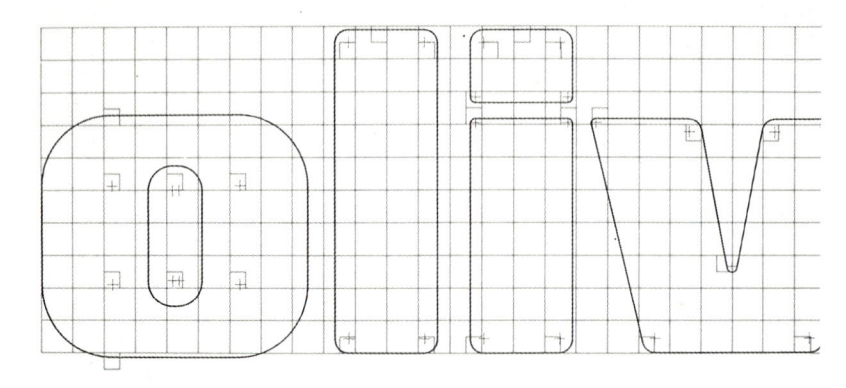

85. Study design for the Olivetti logotype by Walter Ballmer, 1970.

Self-organization and co-ordination in the design process.

Self-organization always has played an important role in Olivetti. It goes back to the management style of Adriano Olivetti and the Italian roots of the company. Adriano Olivetti saw Corporate Image and design as an area of self-organization. By choosing the right people, providing them with a company based workspace and giving them direct access to the company, he intended to create a society of visionary personalities who were able to interpret and organize company requirements, as we have seen. The common basis for action in this environment was the company philosophy and during the years of his reign it was mainly Adriano who personally transmitted this philosophy to the designers. This basic approach to organized design work still characterizes Olivetti. Freelance designers are given maximum independence as far as individual working methods and organization are concerned. They have vertical access to all company levels, are free to use the Olivetti office infrastructure, even the choice of the design assistants they work with is more or less in their hands. The only requirement is that they have to adapt and work within the existing company structure in order to achieve co-operation. How they proceed in working with the company staff during the design process is left to them. They have to learn how to bring their design concepts through the structure, to motivate and organize their staff and to convince the development engineers in order to realize their ideas.

Self-organization is possible because the conditions for practical co-ordination exist in Olivetti. Co-ordination within the design strategy is particularly strong due to its clear philosophical positioning by Adriano Olivetti and its continuity in strategy, structure and personnel, as described in above, on continuity and change. This has created a sense of identity within the design staff, which is handed on to anybody joining. It is a system of common values, attitudes, unwritten laws and procedures that nobody can explain in detail but that everybody respects and follows, protected and maintained by the directorate of Corporate Image. The director himself has always acted as the personal guardian and even embodiment of this code of values. Basic investment in co-ordination on this level is also seen in the choice of the right designer for a project, more so than any briefing especially when dealing with projects which require an innovative view: this became clear in the development of new keyboards, as we shall see in the next chapter. Personnel policy also plays an important coordinating role at the level of the single design offices. One small circle of design directors has been working for Olivetti for many years. Each of the younger directors has passed through the 'school' of Sottsass, whose role in the education of young designers is invaluable for Olivetti. Most of them have worked in several Olivetti design offices, and because of the company's emphasis on exposing creative staff to new situations, all of them have worked on projects belonging to other design offices. In this way, their broad educational background and their outside interests give Olivetti designers a high degree of sensibility to the context of their work with regard to the other design offices and their requirements.

Another aspect, vital for the co-ordination of

the design offices and between design and non-design areas of the company, especially engineering, is the fact that the main designers, although independent, are based in-house. In contrast to the classic external consultants, the in-house arrangement involves the designers in company activities. Their offices form a permanent part of the company structure and are available for consultation on all kinds of design problems by the company staff. Between designers and the other departments a network of relationships and experiences has been established with information channels enabling all parties to work on projects with greater efficiency, alongside the official structure for co-ordination, by which the director of Corporate Image department looks after strategic questions and the relevant design manager operational ones.

Long-term investment in design

The general long-term perspective of identity and image-building in Olivetti has been outlined above, but there are aspects which require more than a token discussion or defence in terms of the traditional conditions of continuity, aspects which demand real investment, a continual contribution in terms of finance and activities. One of these investments is in personnel. Designers like Sottsass and Bellini were not found in design consultancies. When Olivetti started to work with them they were young, unexperienced and unknown architects, as were many others who worked for the first time on important industrial projects under Adriano Olivetti. Following the idea that extraordinarily strong personalities are rare and take time to develop, Olivetti has given much time and energy to the search and subsequent development of young designers. They are given unusually high levels of responsibility, and are put into situations in which they can gain a broad understanding of design problems, particularly concerning Olivetti. Work and study visits to foreign countries, time for purely experimental studies and trips around the world to study the different conditions of culture and design, are given to promising young designers by way of investments for the future, paying off in cases like Sottsass, De Lucchi and others.

Part of the building up of designers as future investments includes the public promotion of their achievements. The work of Olivetti's designers has been presented with special care in commercial advertising and has been made a general cultural topic in exhibitions, at design conferences, and in catalogues and books. Olivetti's tradition of promoting and supporting the

86. View of Bellini's Museaum of Modern Art exhibition in 1989.

OLIVETTI

Design commitment at the top level

Top level design commitment in Olivetti means more than just the positioning of the design function in the company structure or its direct access to top management. It encompasses a personal dedication to design from top management and their identification with the humanitarian aspects of design as we have described in the section on continuity and change. Adriano Olivetti represented both top manager and design manager and personally looked after all kinds of design matters. Between 1960 and 1978 it was the close relationship between Renzo Zorzi and Bruno Visentini, who in most of these difficult years was President of Olivetti, which led to a further and particular top level design commitment. Both these men followed high ethical values in their work and understood the role of design in the culturally oriented approach of the company. They built up the institution of Corporate Image, which in those years of change was a major factor of continuity in the company philosophy. This commitment has been continued under De Benedetti with the guardian of design, Zorzi, and his staff and designers given the same central position to continue their work. The relationship between Zorzi, his successor Paolo Viti and De Benedetti is more difficult to comprehend. Perhaps only time will reveal the potential of top-level design comittment in the new era of Olivetti.

87. View of Bellini's Museum of Modern Art exhibition in 1989.

cultural values of industrial activities, not only of Olivetti but on a general basis, has made it a protagonist in the international world of design events; there is no other company of comparable influence and importance in design journalism, exhibitions and conferences. It now has a network of personal relations and influences and is involved in all the latest developments and discussions with the most interesting people in the design world. Access to this potential of people and information is an invaluable source of new ideas for design activities. At the same time it is just this position in the world of design which makes Olivetti a pinnacle; one of the most attractive and inspiring partners to work with for outstanding designers.

Design management functions on different levels of the company.

In turning to look in more detail at the present procedures of Olivetti's design management, it has to be drawn to the attention of the reader that the fundamental, personalized design structure as described above makes the detailed procedure a highly informal process. To ignore this foundation when considering present developments would be to risk a misunderstanding of design procedure in a successful company. The following discussions regarding present day questions are of necessity to a high degree subjective interpretations of an extremely complex network which nobody is able to trace and identify in great detail.

Due to the organizational structure of the company as a whole (fig. 76) and the structure of design (fig. 77), design management functions can be seen on four levels. These are the company board, the directory level of the Corporate Image, the operative level of the Corporate Image and the level of the design offices.

88-90. Three covers by Walter Ballmer for Olivetti annual reports, late 1970s.

OLIVETTI

91. Poster by Lucio del Pezzo for the 1981 Aspen Design Conference, which took Italian design as its theme.

The level of the company board.

The company board has direct responsibilities for design and some basic functions with regard to the management of design which cannot be delegated to other levels. The two primary or basic decisions that have to be made by the board are to define the role of design in the corporate strategy and to locate design in the hierarchy of corporate power and to equip the design department in terms of personnel, finance and structure. An equally vital and necessary further element in the general attitude towards design in the company is the board's informal commitment to and support for the design function.

The following is an attempt to analyze the position of the Olivetti board with regard to these functions and to present some of the questions and problems that arise in this context. It must be emphasized once again that this is largely a subjective interpretation by the author.

From an outsider's point of view the role of design in De Benedetti's strategy for the 1990's is a vital one. Technical standardization on the one hand requires design to act as a medium for distinction and differentiation of Olivetti products, and as a quality instrument to fight low price competition. On the other hand, technical developments and complexity demand user-conscious concepts which make products easy and pleasant to use. As information technology takes on a considerably bigger role in work and in everyday life, requirements for ergonomically planned, easy to use technology will increase in the future.

As in the past, the strategical orientation of design is towards design excellence. De Benedetti obviously builds on Olivetti's traditional design image, which offers a unique potential for knowledge, creativity and expansion. Thanks to the new economic and technological order of things in general and Olivetti's strategy for the 1990's in particular, the design department in the future will undergo some basic challenges and be posed new questions that will not be easy to overcome.

Within the strategic concept of offering integrated information networks using the latest technology, design will have to develop basic solutions regarding the adaptation of technology to human needs. Some solutions will concern hardware, where components have to be combined into systems adaptable to individual requirements of performance or assembled as individual work units with limited space both at home and in the office. These solutions increasingly also concern software design. The more complex technology becomes and the more possibilities it offers, the more an easy and friendly method of use and learning will be necessary. The problem is not simply one of pure software technology but a matter of software and the user's point of view, a matter of the relation between man and machine, the so called 'interface, which needs to be redefined. Ranging from the design of the keyboard as a central interacting field between man and machine (see chapter three), interface design has to deal with the general requirements of work from a human and cultural point of view. In the past Olivetti through designers such as Sottsass and directors such as Adriano Olivetti gone beyond a purely economic solution to a cultural interpretation of new technology. Companies producing information technology will now more than ever before shape contemporary culture: a fact which gives Olivetti's traditional approach to the design of technology an even greater importance.

The way in which Olivetti will respond to this situation cannot be foreseen. De Benedetti has explicitly declared himself to be aware of his cultural responsibilities and ready to meet them. He has reinforced basic research covering the field of man-machine interface and software. Remaining questions in this context include the ways in which designers can be involved in research, how the results should be made applicable to them and in what ways they will be able to develop such research. Moreover, the development of new design concepts for highly innovative technology has to be achieved under extreme time pressure and significantly reduced development times; a factor which opposes any new orientation for top

92. Cover for the 1980 Olivetti Annual Report by Franco Bassi.

OLIVETTI

93. The Cimabue Crucifix
exhibition designed by Allan
Irvine, 1981.

quality design.

A further new problem for design is caused by the interruption of the formerly integrated cycle of design, manufacture and marketing. Especially with Olivetti's new strategy of integrated information networks, a whole range of externally manufactured components and products are offered and have to be taken into consideration when developing personalized network solutions. Design has to be used to solve the new task of creating homogeneity between Olivetti and externally manufactured products as well as compatibility from an aesthetic point of view.

All the problems mentioned here finally point to the need for a basic new definition of the personnel, financial and, beyond the hierarchical, the living position of design in the company, and it will fall to the product companies to force this new definition of design. Their strategic aim is to use differentiated, specialized marketing instruments to meet the requirements of that segment of the market each serves. A company such as the Olivetti Office which in terms of turnover and staff is bigger than many of its competitors will naturally put more pressure on pursuing specialized design and image interests. Product design in Olivetti is a central part of the corporate image, and this presents an obstacle to the activities and specialized interests of the groups. Each of the three independent product units are confronted with extreme changes in the market and technology and cost pressures, all of which tend to oppose a central, long term approach to design and corporate image.

For this reason, the strength with which the holding management of De Benedetti and his managing director present design is vital. Without their support, Corporate Image runs the risk of loosing its influence as a central unit and its main importance in defending Olivetti's image and identity.

94,95. The Venetian Bronze Horses exhibition and the cover for the Milan catalogue, 1980.

Design management functions on the directorial level of the Corporate Image department.

The department of Corporate Image is the centre of design management as it has the function of planning design and corporate image activities, and has the set task of implementing these strategies in the various design offices. In the substructure of the Corporate Image department, a distinction can be made between the directorial level of design management and the operational level of design management.

Paolo Viti was Director of Corporate Image from 1987 to the end of 1989, and this text discusses the work of Corporate Image under his directorship. The directorial functions range from the strategic definition of design quality, through budgeting of design offices and projects, personnel policy to overall co-ordination and control. Viti took over the responsibility for Corporate Image during the new orientation and organization of the company which represents a new, maybe unknown form for Corporate Image within Olivetti in the future. In fulfilling Corporate Image's basic aim he was faced with a situation in which maintaining and continually interpreting the corporate philosophy is a question of primary importance. Due to the decentralisation and new market strategy of Olivetti the traditional approach of design and image building is confronted with new interests which demand a redefinition of its general role. Coping with the new challenge without diminishing the company's design and image does not only need classical management qualifications but in addition requires an understanding of and a strong commitment to the corporate culture. In this situation it is vital to have insights into specifics of long-term image building: here Corporate Image's infrastructure, developed over many years with the help of outside contacts, internal relationships and special knowledge, allows for results that other companies with a maximum of means are hardly able to attain from scratch.

As several times before in its history, Olivetti today has reached a point where personalities with understanding and idealism play a decisive role for the continuation of the Olivetti culture. Viti with twenty years experience in the direction of Corporate Image and his deep commitment to the Olivetti philosophy was such a personality.

To maintain the position of Corporate Image, Viti had to represent its interests and needs on different fronts within the company. One such front is the Board with Carlo De Benedetti as President and Managing Director and his partner Vittorio Cassoni, well known for his directness of approach. The other fronts are the company partners involved in the realization of design projects; the management and product management of the product companies, who are placing the orders for final products, development engineering as partners of design and production, and in a wider sense with marketing and sales.

The strategy Viti seems to have followed is to demonstrate the benefit of the existing central system of design and corporate image. For this reason major importance was given to proving the quality of design performance capacities under the different pressures of time, cost and specialized interests. Solutions might include shorter routes to gain access to information, better co-ordination of the interaction between product units and design offices, reduction of cost by better co-ordination of projects in design offices and rationalization in the use of techniques and elements in design and engineering. With the creation of the new position of operational design manager and the appointment of Antonio Macchi Cassia, Viti also invested in keeping forward the Olivetti spirit on an everyday basis.

Viti's management philosophy for design, as far as it can be identified, is built on the idea of a co-operative system of open-minded, independent personalities, in order to open new fields of experience beyond established systems and structures. In a co-operative system strong, independent personalities inspire one another and take advantage of free personal relationships in order to organize and realize their

96. The Masks of Mexuico exhibition designed by Hans von Klier, 1981.

ideas. It is this interpretation of Adriano Olivetti's approach which also determined Viti's management policies and his investment in personnel. His aim was to keep the system as open and flexible as possible and he worked to keep his collaborators under tension, to expose them to new situations and challenges whilst asking for the highest degree of self-organization from them. Inside the structure of Corporate Image there was always change and experiment.

Apart from the above functions Viti also represented design outside the company, playing an important role in the long-term interests of Olivetti, as we have seen. He did this through Cultural Activities, which he personally directed. The work of this department covers a wide field. The fine art exhibitions initiated and supported by Olivetti are one main category. These included presenting cultural 'monuments' from the past of Italy and other countries – examples are *The Treasures of San Marco*, *Masks of Mexico* and the *Studies for Leonardo's The Last Supper* (figs. 93 *et seq.*). In such cases Olivetti's patronage also involved a contribution to the restoration and maintenance of these masterpieces by important painters of the past.

A second category of cultural activites covered the field of design and architecture. This goes back to Adriano Olivetti, whose idea it was to make the achievements of those working with Olivetti into features of the company's communication to the public. This communication policy contributed on the one hand to the society's knowledge and awareness of industrial culture, while on the other hand this kind of specific public relations was an important means of motivating and encouraging Olivetti's chosen helpers. Publicity contributed a great

97. Cover for the recent Gauguin exhibition catalogue.

deal to the image of Olivetti as a protagonist of industrial culture and design. With exhibitions such as *Concept and Form*, *Dall'oggetto finito alla fine del oggetto* (an exhibition about Sottsass), *Italy – The New Domestic Landscape* at the Museum of Modern Art, New York, or *Hochschule für Gestaltung Ulm*, about the famous German design school, Olivetti has given a real push forward to the debate on design matters on an international level, while at the same time helping by their input to create a public forum for the representatives of its design culture.

The organization structure shows that, as Viti durected it himself, Cultural Activities was given especial importance. He worked with a small group of full time assistants. They were a highly self-organised and highly co-operative group of people with a major sense of responsibility and personal committment. Management here was mainly exercised by objectives and review. Apart from the core group, a wide range of freelance designers and architects, historians and public relation people, experts of diverse background in art or design, from all parts over the world, were involved on specific projects. A separate unit within Cultural Activities is the office of Renzo Zorzi, who today as a freelance consultant has a special responsibility for publications and catalogues within the department itself: almost all departments within Corporate Image work on an occasional basis on projects for Cultural Activities. One such official permanent function has the Corporate Identity staff responsible for the archive of corporate design materials, and also involved in the material outfitting of design exhibitions, just as the Graphic Design department also works on catalogue designs for Cultural Activities. Olivetti designers such as Sottsass and Bellini are asked for exhibition design ideas or to contribute to designing exhibitions about their own work. Sometimes they are also asked to the design catalogues (for example King and Mirandas work for the cover page of the *Design Process* catalogue) or to make contributions to conferences and exhibition openings. Other independent designers are also sometimes involved in exhibition design. To all of the regular

Olivetti collaborators this occasional work for Cultural Activities is welcome and stimulating. It helps to foster a growing feeling for cultural responsibility and acts a kind of common basis of understanding for the groups within Corporate Image.

Over the years there has been an increasing emphasis on art exhibitions. Investment in this field, because of its seeming remoteness from traditional business activities, has not always enjoyed the full agreement of all those in the commercial and sales departments. They tend to prefer activities that promote business much more directly. However, in retrospect the past ten years of violent technological change has caused considerable disorientation in the whole company (and this still lingers today), against which Olivetti's art activities started to build up an image of cultural commitment and cultural values that gave one clear point of orientation in a situation where nobody was able to locate the human and social consequences of the new technology. This image may come to serve as a marker, helping future markets differentiate between copmpeting products, and building up confidence in the name Olivetti, be it in the extremely competitive, but opaque personal consumer market, for office products or for the new integrated information networks such as the big sectors of education and public service now require.

98. Cover of Notizie Olivetti celebrating the Gauguin exhibition.

The operational level of Corporate Image

Corporate Image design management covers what is sometimes referred to as the 'up front' approach to design. This function is now of particular importance for the maintenance and continuation of the Olivetti philosophy and the efficiency of the design department. By appointing Antonio Macchi Cassia as design manager, Viti was investing in the continuation of the Olivetti design tradition.

Macchi Cassia has been a designer with Olivetti since 1969. He started in Bellini's office, which at that time was still based in Ivrea, and became familiar with technical development and production work. Educated as an engineer, he combined both a design and an engineering point of view. In 1979 he joined the Sottsass design office, just in time to participate in the development of Olivetti's first electronic computer, the M20. It was this particular experience with the two great design masters of Olivetti, a familiarity with the 'system' of employed staff in technical development and production in Ivrea as well as with the economic departments and their design requirements, which – from the point of view of experience – made him such a good candidate for the position of design manager. Macchi is one of those who believes in the Olivetti philosophy and ideals, being ready to maintain the Olivetti spirit on course through all the changes.

The on-going transition of Olivetti to a supplier of global information processing equipment has considerably affected conditions for the designers. Their work has become more complicated because of technical changes as well as because of other factors. Continual reorganization in the product units has contributed to a seeming divergences between the workers' roles and the interests of the company. Product development, in the past the preserve of the designers and now must take account of marketing and economic interests and the requirements of the new business units. In addition, the partnership with AT&T and the increasing need to use ready bought parts in the design of products and product systems means that designers have had to deal with people with a different understanding of design. The network of people, interests and requirements is now far more complex and yet design has to be developed with greater speed, under the pressures of production costs, and the increasing restrictions of technical standardization and technological change. All this causes unavoidable tensions as it cuts against the traditional understanding and procedures of the design process. Consequently, the designers have had to invest considerably more effort in informational and organizational activity, keeping them away from their real design work.

In an analysis of this situation, the aims of the operational design management have been defined as improving working conditions and efficiency in the design organization and supporting the traditional understanding of Olivetti design. Macchi's principal work is in the coordination of design offices and business departments during single design projects. His basic task is to gather and pool information from all the involved parties and to deliver it to the design departments when required. This kind of ready-made background information is especially important at the start of new projects when increasingly complex business and economic requirements have to be understood and interpreted in terms of design. Information about the strategic procedure of the business units is vital for the quality and efficiency of the designer's work; his success may depend on the quality of the information he receives. Procuring information is not only a matter of time and research but also of contacts within the company. Information from middle management is difficult to interpret because of different interests and ideas; it requires a knowledge of the background of the problem from an objective point of view. Macchi therefore has to liase closely with top level management within the business units. Through his continual work in various departments of the company, Macchi has learnt to identify developments and problems at each stage of a project's process. This allows him control from an early stage, so as to prevent developments in wrong directions and in so doing to contribute to a reduction in development time.

While a general and formal description of the course of the design process can be given, it is important to bear in mind that the informal side of the process is taken very seriously because of the personality-led management and the emphasis on self organization. Details will be given in the case studies in chapter three, although these concentrate on designs before Macchi's appointment, and therefore do not take his role into consideration.

In general the design process is initiated by the managers of product groups within the Independent Business units who decide on the introduction of new or reworked products. The next step is research on the commercial and technical requirements of the product by the product processes manager. He is someone with a technical background and is responsible for market analysis and managing product projects on behalf of the business units from the specification to production. His tasks are to collect information about market and technical aspects, to work out specifications and to organize the work with designers and development engineers and production. He also gives initial information about the project to Corporate Image, that is to Macchi. As design resources for product groups are fixed by the organizational structure of Corporate Image, Macchi will normally then inform the responsible designer of the product group. At this early stage it is possible for Macchi and the relevant designer to contact the project manager and others involved in the project in order to get background information and to discuss the product from a design point of view.

As soon as the technical functions and the costs of the product have been specified the development engineers are instructed to list the necessary technical elements within the basic concept. Once the commercial requirements have been outlined the designers begin work on the design concept, starting with the shape. Although the designers have to work with whatever the engineers give them as technical input in the form of the necessary technical parts, it is the designer who determines the technical 'architecture'. Interaction between designers and engineers is highly self organized, a result

99. External display for the Impressionists exhibition in Milan, 1988.

100. The Lexicon 82 typewriter, on which Macchi Cassia collaborated with Bellini, 1975.

of the Olivetti tradition characterized by the respect for designers and the openness of all to new design ideas. This specific relationship between designers and engineers has always been a driving force for creativity in product design, which while following a commercial point of view is not controlled solely by the market. With the new decentralized structure of the company, weight tends to shift in favour of the commercial departments, making it necessary for Macchi to be present in the various stages of the design process, particularly briefing and evaluation, to promote the value of design and educate non-design staff about design. Presentation of the design concept officially takes the form of showing a polystyrene model to the manager of the product group. At a final stage, depending on the importance of the product for the strategy, a prototype is also presented to the chief director of the whole business group and to the company board.

A second aspect of Macchi's work is the coordination of all projects within Corporate Image. Particular attention is paid to creating synergy in terms of the quality of contribution to a common line of activity and in achieving a cost-saving rationalization using some of the same basic design elements. This includes the standardization of minor elements such as cabling, ventilator slots and so forth, as well as checking whether solutions which have already been developed in areas like system products can be used for office products and vice versa.

Macchi has another function which involves the purely personal side of work and is a key factor in the personality-led design organization. He must be a person that individual designers can trust and with whom they can discuss their problems and worries concerning their work. His advice on how to bring a concept to realization through the system has become more and more important. Beyond his official tasks he is a kind of philosopher, always representing the Olivetti attitude to work and quality of design, continually nourishing and defending the Olivetti spirit. The fact that he has worked in collaboration with both Sottsass and Bellini in the past, acting as assistant on a number of projects, is of value here, as is his own work as an independent designer. Examples of his work are in the Design Collection of the Museum of Modern Art, New York, and he is a *Compasso d'Oro* winner.

His philosophy regarding his design management function is that important solutions are not the result of rules on how to work but of putting together the right individuals and supporting their ideas. The design department is not a

101. The TE 500 teleprinter, on which Macchi Cassia collaborated with Sottsass, 1980.

The level of the design offices

mechanism but a group of individuals, and he says that as 'Italians don't like regulations' he does not give out orders but just talks about design problems, bringing people together and trying to convince them that 'they may not have to work but they do have to be happy'. This statement, although ironic, reveals his basic attitude.

The Corporate Image department of today is subdivided into nine offices of design and the office for cultural activities. All of these, apart from cultural activities, are directed by external designers, who work with Olivetti on a freelance yet continual and long term basis. Olivetti in general provides housing and support for the departmental infrastructure thus making the offices in effect company design offices. Compare with this the two research departments, which are also always headed by external consultants but who work within their private offices.

In accordance with the personality-led management approach the directors of the design offices within Corporate Image are given a basic freedom to organize themselves, as long as this fits with and respects the existing organizational structure and the philosophy of Olivetti. How the directors of design fill this free space is best explained in outline, through the example of the most important offices within Corporate Image: the two offices of Sottsass and Bellini for product design and the office for Corporate Identity under Hans von Klier.

OLIVETTI

The design office for product systems and office furniture directed by Ettore Sottsass

The Olivetti office for product design which houses both the Sottsass and the Bellini office is in the center of Milan. The Sottsass design office is designed to serve Olivetti Network & Systems and Olivetti Synthesis, in other words a product range on the one hand of minicomputers, high level personal computers, bank machines, printers, and telephone and telefax machines, and on the other office furniture systems. It is a product field which encompasses some of the central elements of highly advanced technology necessary to realize De Benedetti's strategy of global systems and networks. In comparison to the more simple technology of the 'office products' created by the Bellini office the Sottsass product range is sold mainly by direct sale teams or agencies to industrial, commercial and government institutions. For this reason the designs here, in contrast to those of the Bellini office, are more minimalist and dedicated to functionality and user feasibility.

Sottsass has given operational responsibility – in agreement with the director of Corporate Image – to two senior designers, Michele De Lucchi and George Sowden. Both of them have worked with him on his other professional activities, both of them were part of that circle of friends who in 1981 were to found the legendary Memphis group. They spent a lot of their time together working for Olivetti, developing new design concepts for Alchimia and later Memphis, discussing food, love and everything of importance in life. De Lucchi, as we will see with the Delphos case study, is an example of how Sottsass employs young designers, to start with as assistants, mainly doing information collection for problem analysis, or making detailed drawings, or handling follow up with technicians and organizational work on Sottsass's own concepts and designs. By and by Sottsass gives them conceptual work on parts of the ob-

102. Sketch design by Sottsass for the M40 project.

THE COMPANY UNDER DE BENEDETTI

103. The Sottsass office: left to right (back) Antonio Macchi Cassia, Michele de Lucchi, Ettore Sottsass, Adolfo Dallatea, Theo Gonser, Erich Gottein, (front) James Irvine, Simon Morgan, George Sowden, Marco Susami.

ject being designed, and finally control of whole projects.

Today the senior designers, after more than ten years with Olivetti, are not only responsible for single projects but have responsibility for whole product ranges year in, year out. De Lucchi, who is also appointed as Sottsass's representative in the Olivetti office, oversees mini computers, high level personal computers, bank machines and furniture systems. Sowden is responsible for printers and telecommunication machines. Their task is to organize and realize project work with the assistant des-

104. Model of keyboards developed for the M40.

OLIVETTI

105. Detail of the DM 309 Printer designed by George Sowden and Simon Morgan.

106. Telephone set designed by George Sowden and Simon Morgan, 1988.

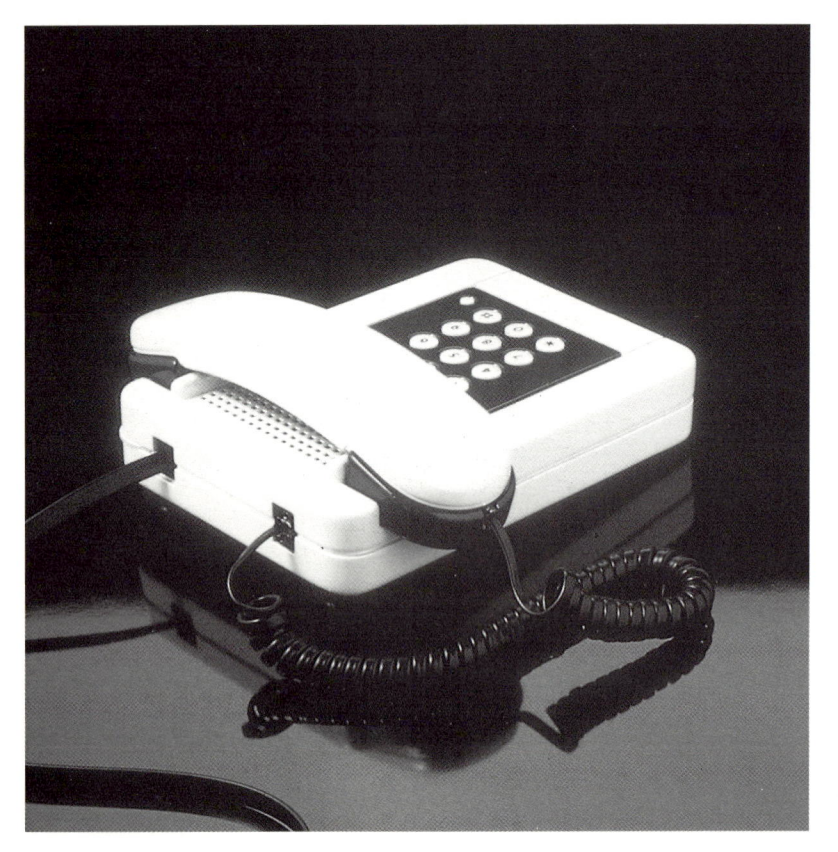

igners, as always in closest connection with the engineers of Olivetti and the operational design manager Macchi.

Sottsass's 'management' (though he would hate to be called a manager) of the design office is based on giving responsibility to people who have his personal confidence, people who in ethics and temperament are close to him, strong individuals of high personal autonomy and with a natural capacity for working independently. One of his collaborators from the 1960's said that one of Sottsass's most striking qualities is his knack for finding and recognizing talented strong personalities, always in extremely young people, who may not have a long record of proven experience and knowledge to present. This is to be seen best in the foundation of Memphis and also when he established his own design company with four very young partners. However this is only part of the phenomenon as it is mainly his charisma that attracts the most interesting people and it is his charisma which inspires them to follow the highest standards

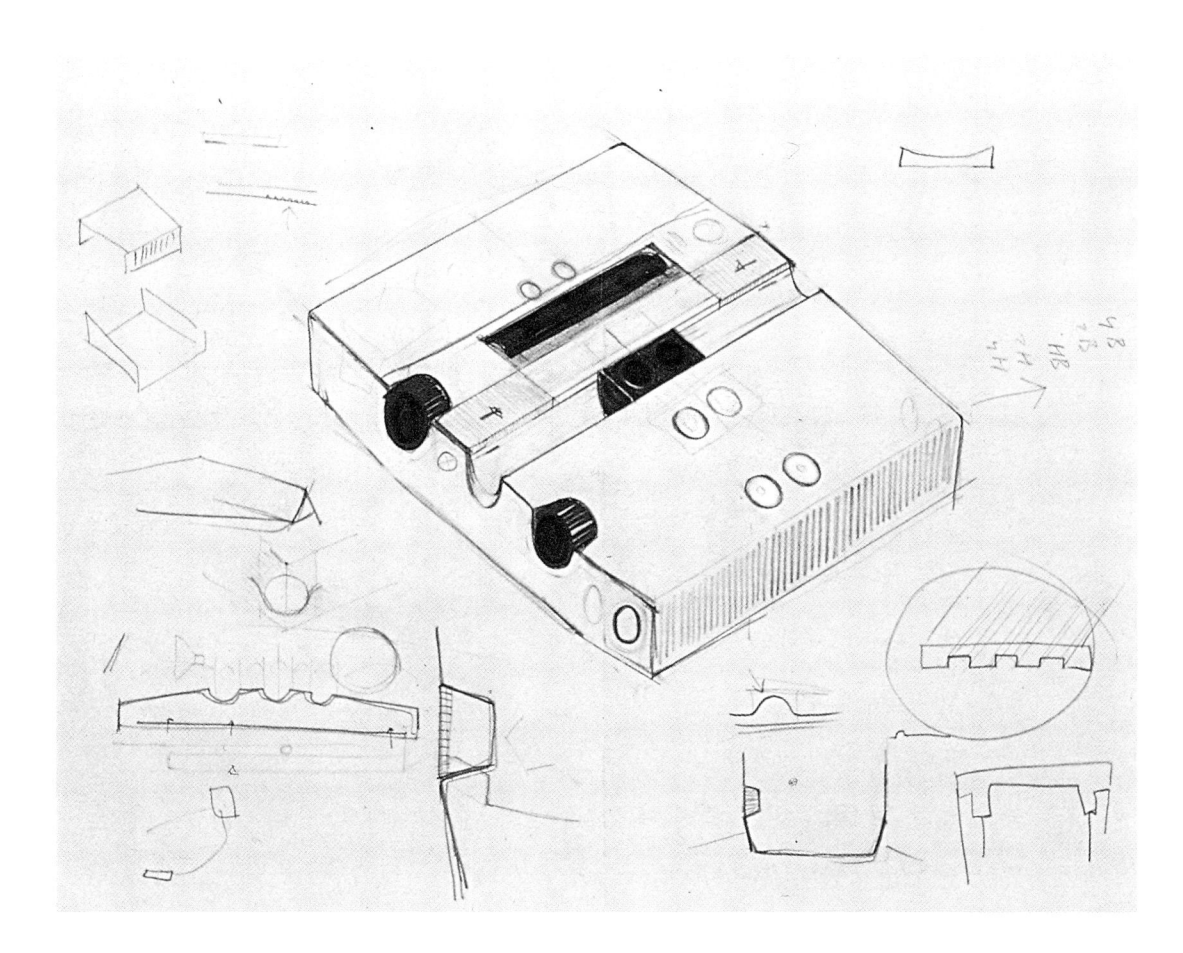

107, 108. Two sketch designs by Sottsass.

and aims. In this sense he is very much an inspiration: a teacher who by questions and discussion of the world, the design and so on, rather than by rules, can develop specific ways of understanding and working. Working on design to him is part of life and as such it has to be lived with friends with whom you talk, eat, share and search for new ideas be it for a specific problem or for the world in general. With this kind of relation to the people of his choice and in his confidence over the years Sotsass has always kept himself informed about everything in the Olivetti office and has been able to be involved in and direct design at its roots, that is in the minds, as it were, of the designers. The one decisive rule his collaborators had to follow without being asked was to keep him informed, continually and in detail. His direct involvement in the years of 1978 to 1987 had usually been at the beginning of each project, when the basic lines of the design concept were established, and through his later control of the different steps of realizing the design.

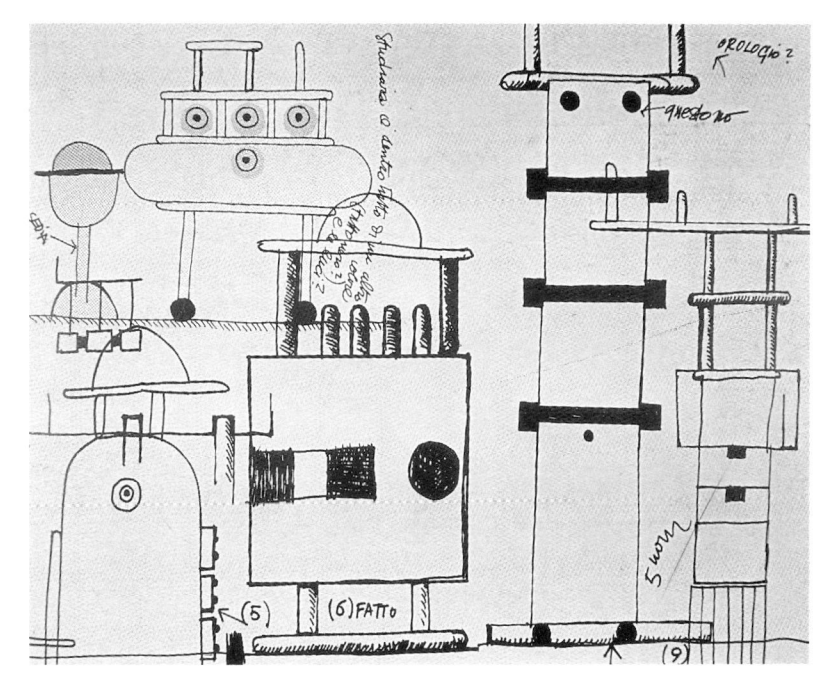

OLIVETTI

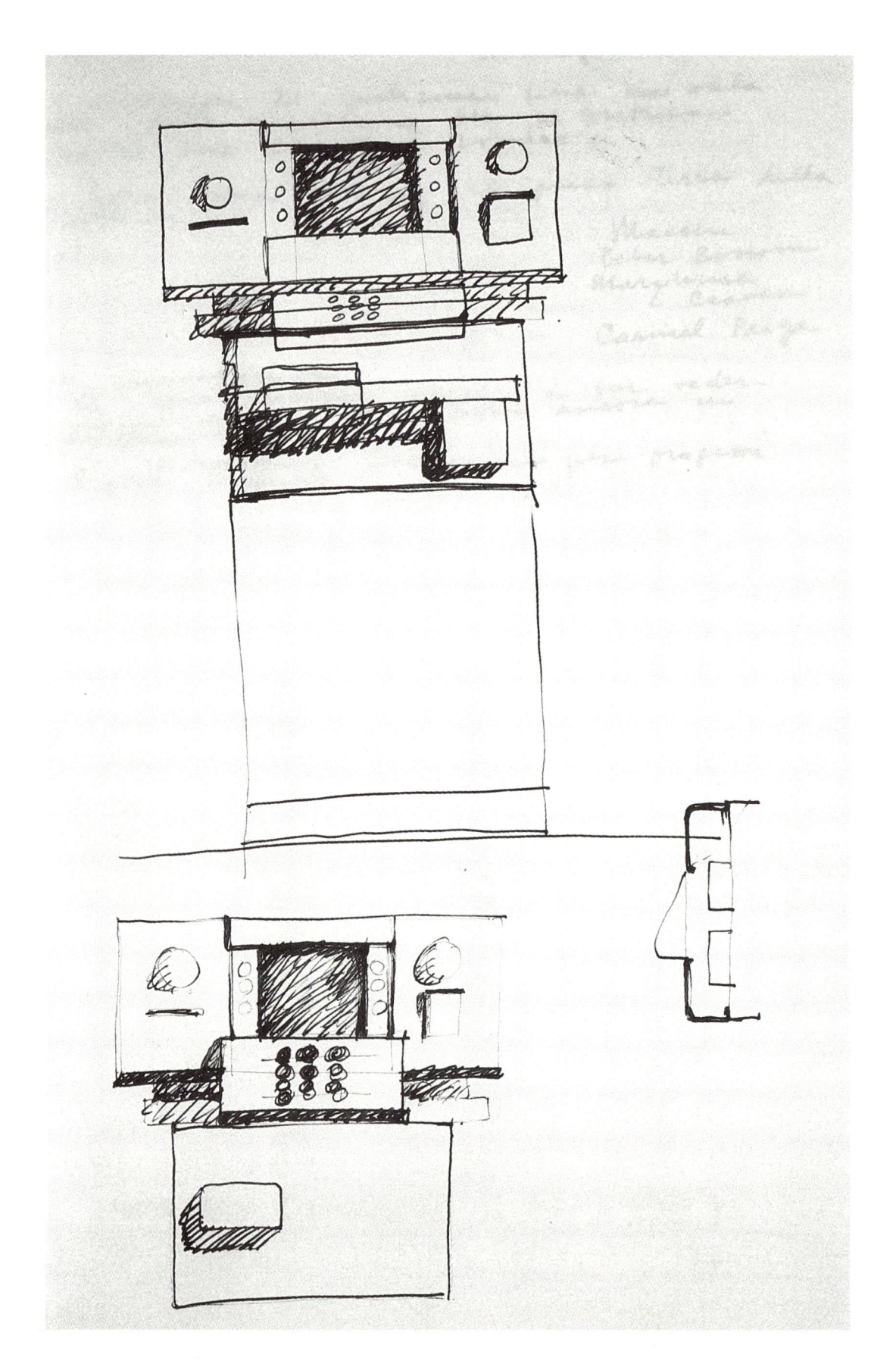

109. Sketch design for a banking machine from the Sottsass office, 1989.

Since the reorganization in end of 1987 Sottsass has taken a step back in favour of the two newly created senior designers. He still has responsibility for the office as a whole which he fulfills today via general supervision. Each project at the end of the creative phase, on the basis of a model, is overssen by him before being presented to anybody else. He is always the partner for any kind of discussions with his senior designers. In the cultural activities of Olivetti Sottsass is today one of the company's strongest assets. His designers follow very much the same attitudes towards their work and for this reason attach considerable importance to having close personal relationships with their assistant designers and to giving responsibility to those in whom they have confidence. Project planning and organizing is done by the senior designers with the departments involved and the design manager Macchi. Conceptual work starts with outline drawings and concept ideas by the senior designers followed up and discussed with the assistant designers who take over a lot of organizing and technical detail work. The senior designers keep always in close contact with the engineers in Ivrea.

In the Sottsass office a vital part of the design process consists of making sketches, drawings and roughs (see figs 107-111). This deliberatley creative, almost anti-rational approach to problem solving begins with Sottsass and his group of designers exploring their individual attitudes to and understanding of a problem through drawing. This artistic approach allows subconscious ideas about a project to surface before the detailed needs and requirements of the project are fitted in, putting free expression before constraint. In the Bellini office the same initial creative input is, as we shall see in the next chapter, more likely to be in the form of models in wood, foam or plaster (see figs 112-114), a difference of approach in some ways, between two and three dimensions, which should not however be exaggerated in comparing the two offices, as the Bellini office also uses drawings (figs 115-117, for example) and *vice versa*. In using drawings in this way Sottsass and his group stand within the Olivatti tradition started by Nizzoli: one consequence of this is that the Olivetti archives contain some of the finest modern product design drawings and models.

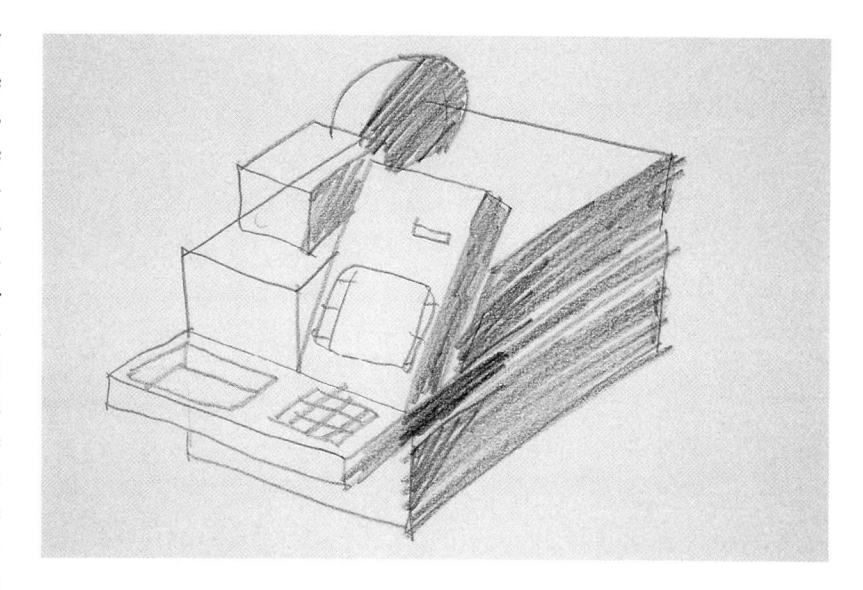

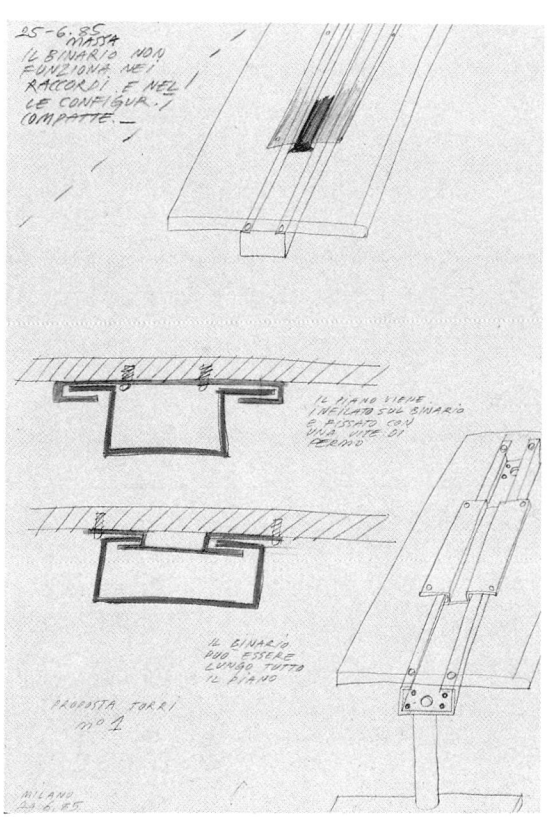

110. Sketch design for a cash register by Michele De Lucchi, 1989.

111. Development sketch for keyboards by King and Miranda.

OLIVETTI

112-114. Block models for evaluating the Logos Class 50 calculator, Bellini office, early 1970s.

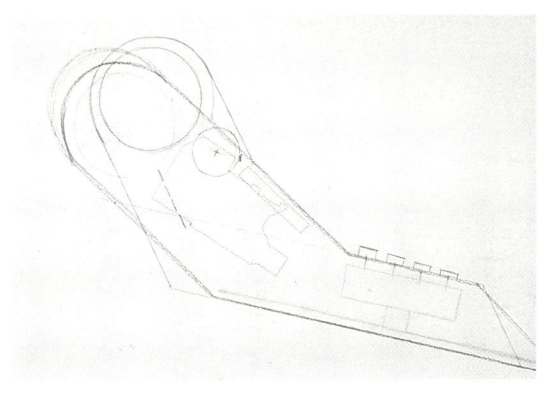

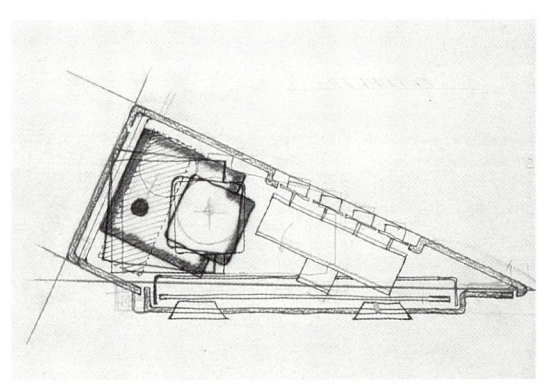

115-117. Drawings developing themes in the models.

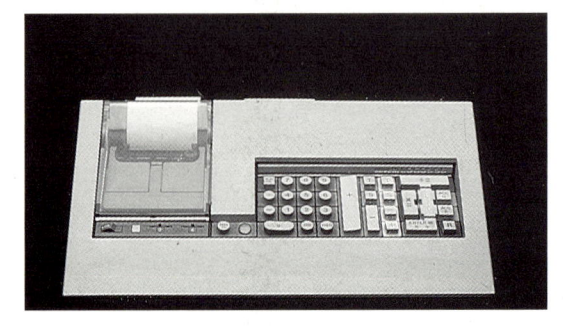

118. The Logos 50 calculator designed by Bellini with De Vries, Macchi Cassia, Pasini and Pasqui, 1973.

I. A detail of the Praxis 48 typewriter designed by Sottsass.

100

101

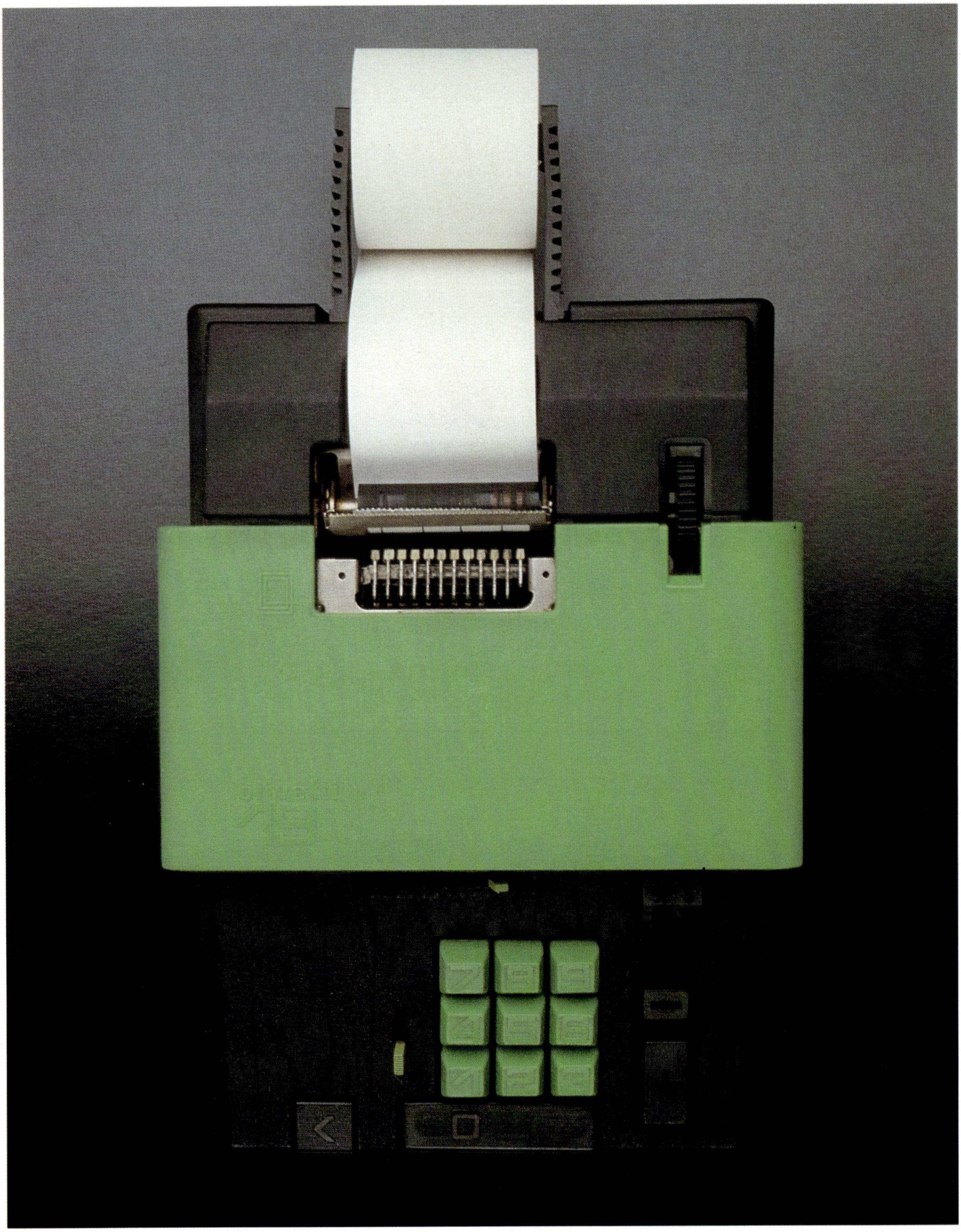

II. The Summa 19 calculator, designed by Sottsass.

III. A recent project drawing by Ettore Sottsass.

103

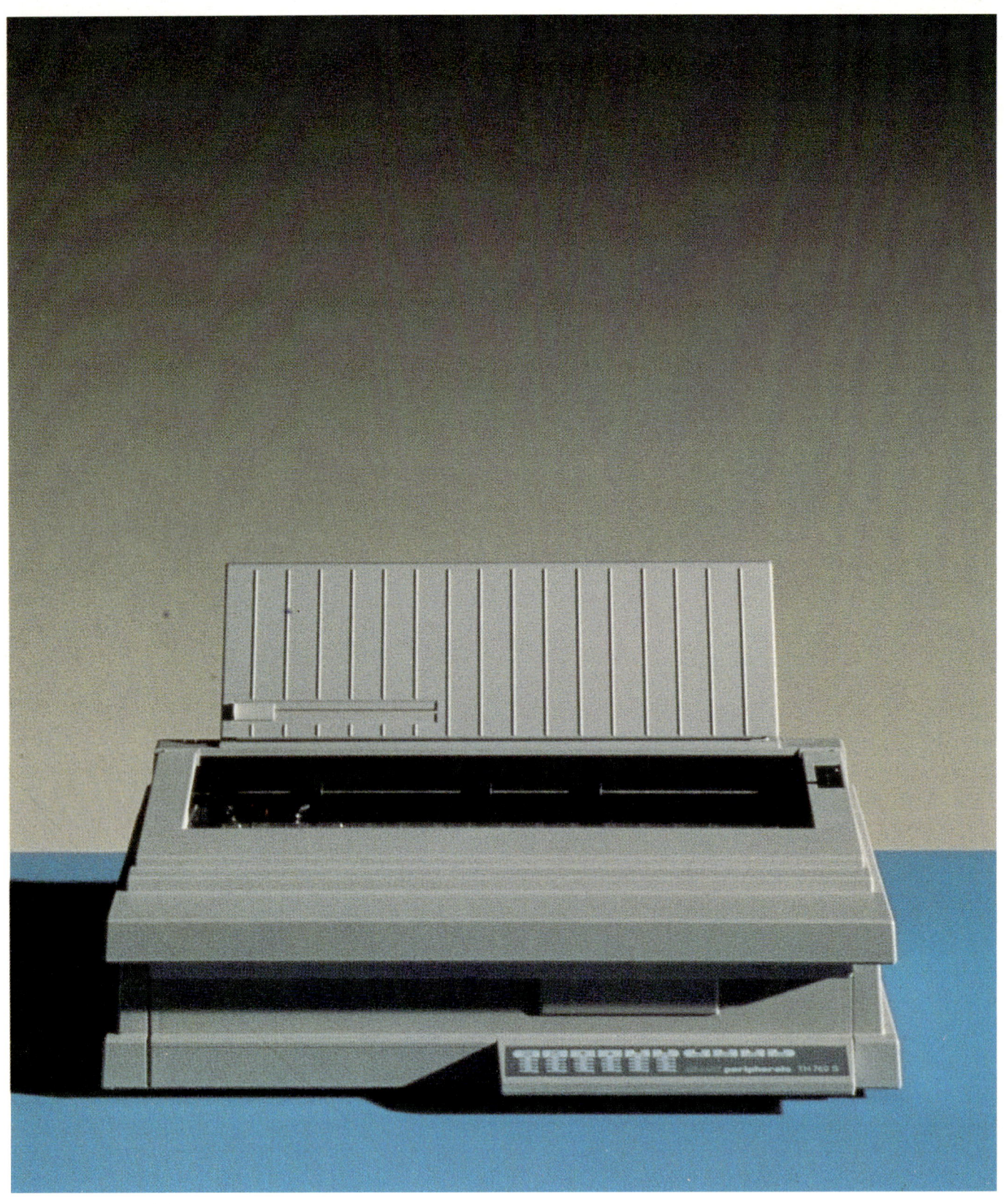

IV, V. New products include
the TH7605 printer and the
ET65 typewriter, designed
by M. Bellini and A.
Chiarato.

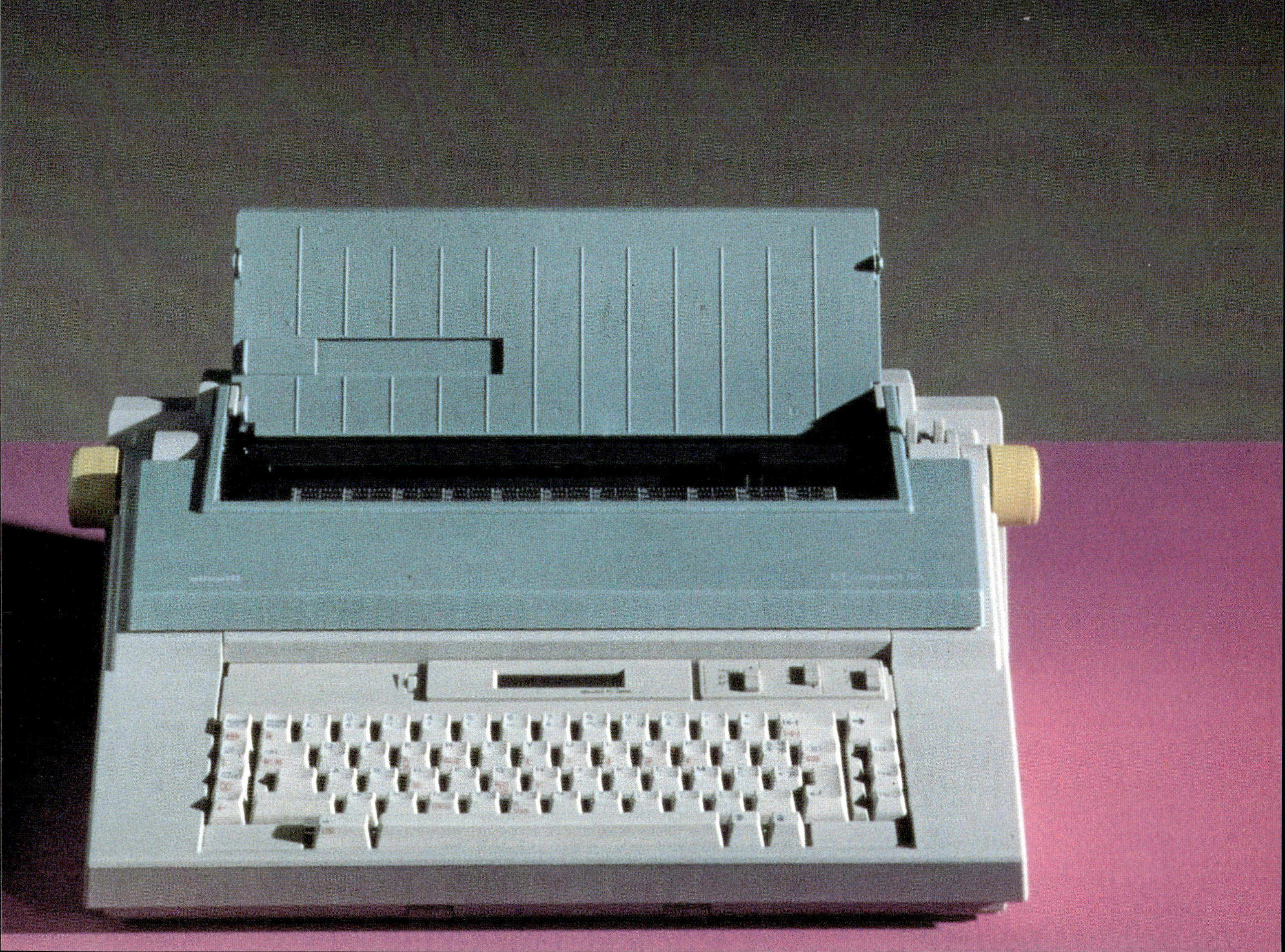

VI, VII. A design and a model for a cash dispensing machine, by Michele De Lucchi, 1989.

107

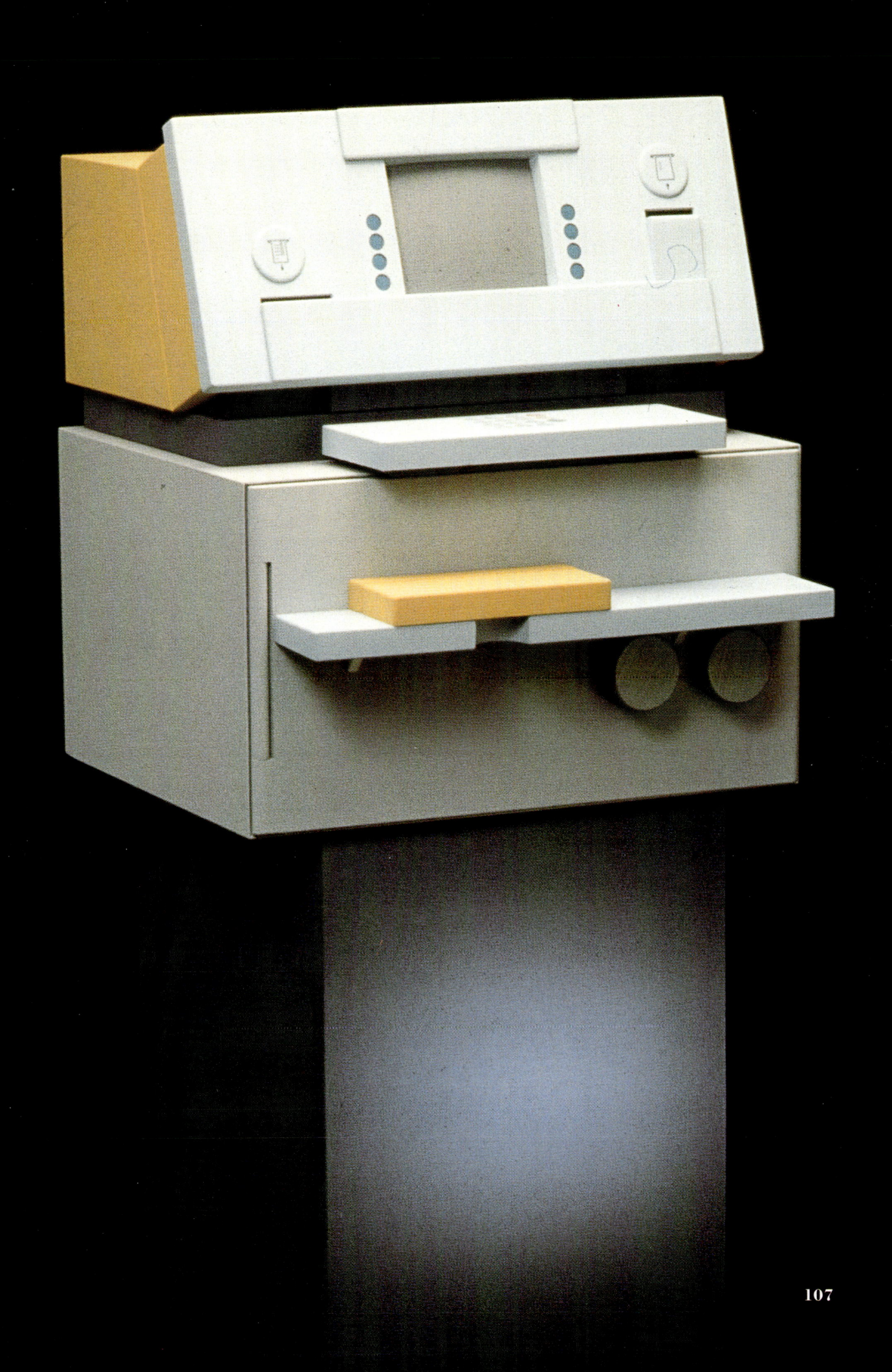

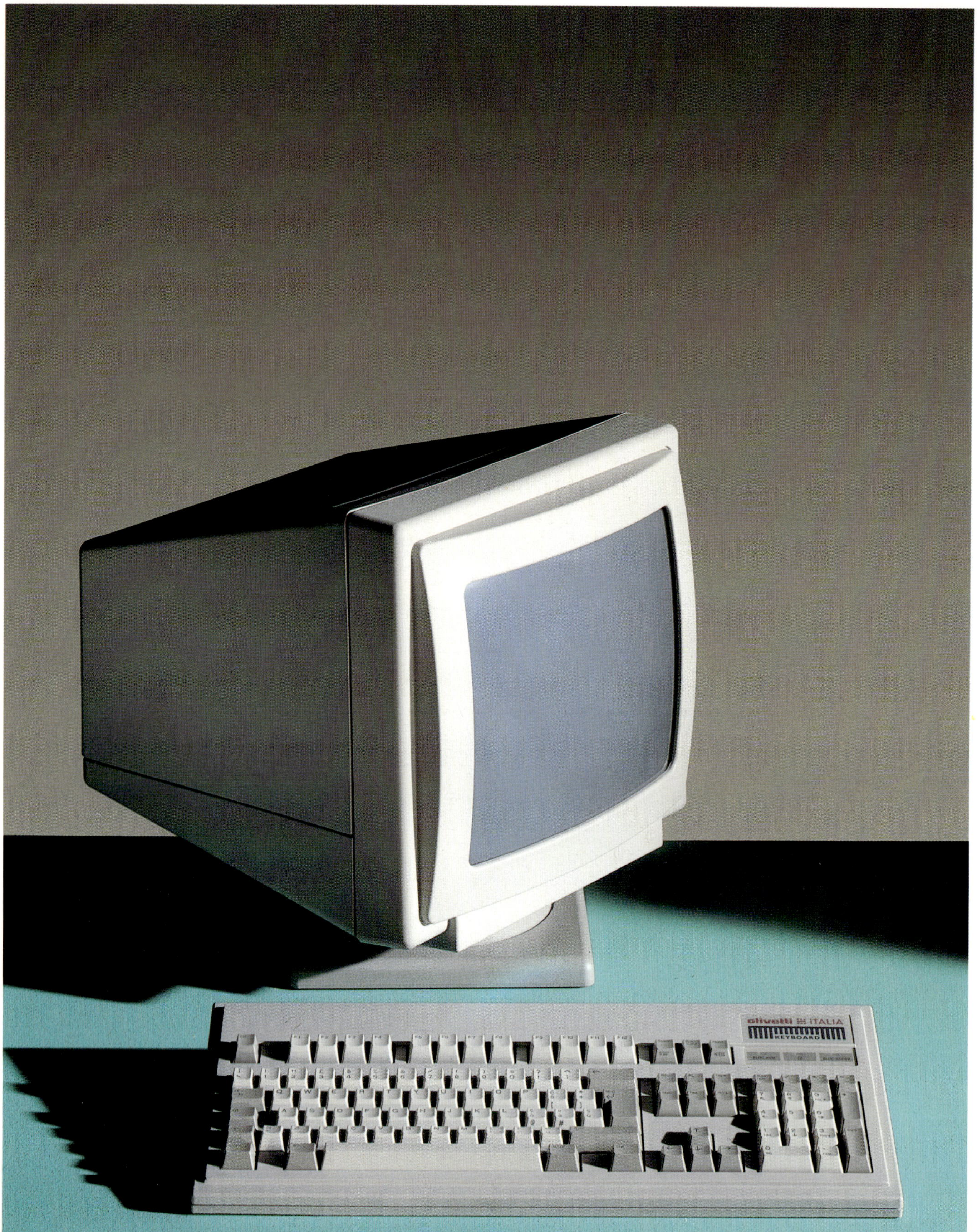
olivetti ITALIA
KEYBOARD

The Bellini design office

Bellini, with his assistant designers and technical draughtsmen, looks after all design matters for the independent product company, Olivetti Office: that is typewriters, calculators, cash registers, word processing systems and, since the end of 1987, personal computers. It is a field of products in which there is an increasing market among private consumers, for the home office of the future. The shift from purely professional use in an office environment and with specialist professional customers towards the private customer and more individual type of offices led to distribution via mass channels such as HiFi, radio and television shops and shopping centers. While the products remained technically refined, they as a consequence required a more consumer-oriented design stance.

Bellini's approach in his machine design is a symbolic and iconographic one. His machines very often seem to have a kind of animal-like character in their overall shape or the shape of some elements which Bellini likes to describe ironically his 'zoo of strange animals' ready to be domesticated by the user. Other ideas he uses in a symbolical way are, for example, the old concept of the inclined writing desk he saw in a painting by Piero della Francesca – this so-called wedge shape was to become a new standard in the design of electronic desk machines taken over by almost all the range, or the idea of a racing car with spoiler which inspired his design for ETP 55 (see the case study in Ch. 3). This general attitude to machine design as an object of personal relation, an object of a kind of hidden fantasy and emotional stimulus makes Bellini the ideal designer for the new kind of consumer product of information processing.

In managing, Bellini follows a more autocratic or patriarchal style with responsibility for the office and for representing it resting clearly and solely with him. He has his assistant designers follow tightly the conceptual line he works out for each project in the beginning. They are – each of them for a different product field – responsible mainly for the working out of details and the organization of technical realization together with the technical draughtsmen, developing detailed drawings and the first models in polystyrene and later in wood if necessary, apart from fulfilling the more routine work of realizing smaller tasks of minor updating of products. As Sottsass, Bellini uses his design assistants as information media keeping him in closest contact and up to date on what is happening on the 'front line', in particular the engineering and production departments as well as the commercial. His method aims to get maximum information and follow-up organization in

119. Portable typewriter designed by Bellini, 1985.

VIII. The new M 380 keyboard and screen.

OLIVETTI

120. The Bellini Office: left to right, Pier Giorgio Perotti, Alessandro Chiarato, Chiora Novella, Luciono Lumelli, Erminio Rizzotti, Mario Bellini, Bruce Fifield.

order to concentrate on the purely creative part. For this reason, one of the three technical draughtsmen, who has been working with Bellini for twenty years, has also administrative responsibility for the office, deciding how to organize out of house work, how to organize the work space and controlling the administrative staff. All of the technical draughtsmen for the different product fields work in the design office in Milan. Each of the assistant designers is expected to organize his work in terms of time and relations with other people and departments totally independently. The only key area is what is presented to Bellini during the different stages of a project, for in this Bellini controls every step

The full time technical draughtsmen and the freelance design assistants in the Bellini office work together very closely, all of them following the same approach from different starting points. Through knowing Bellini for such a long

THE COMPANY UNDER DE BENEDETTI

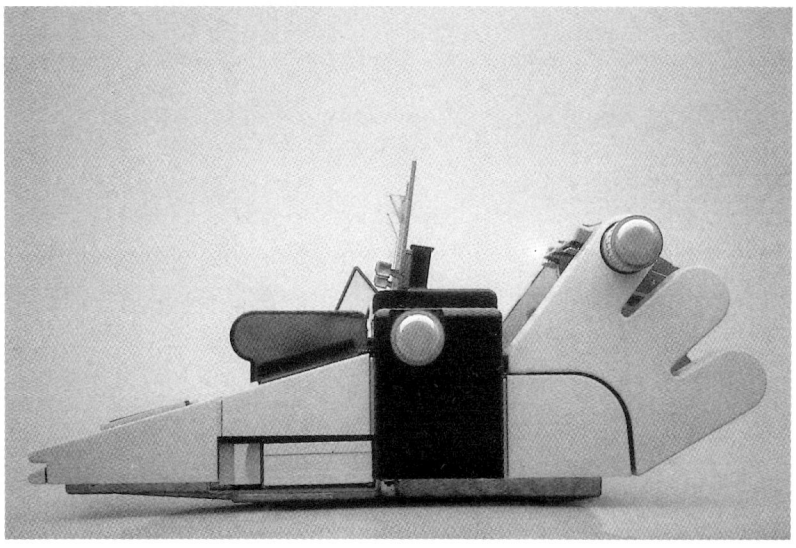

122. Detail from a Renaissance painting showing an angled writing desk.

123. The A4 accounting machine by Bellini, with De Vries, Macchi Cassia, Pasqui and Pasini, 1978.

124. The ET 201 electronic typewriter, 1978, by Bellini: both this and the A4 show the use of a sloped work-surface.

OLIVETTI

125. The Copia 2000 by Bellini, 1978.

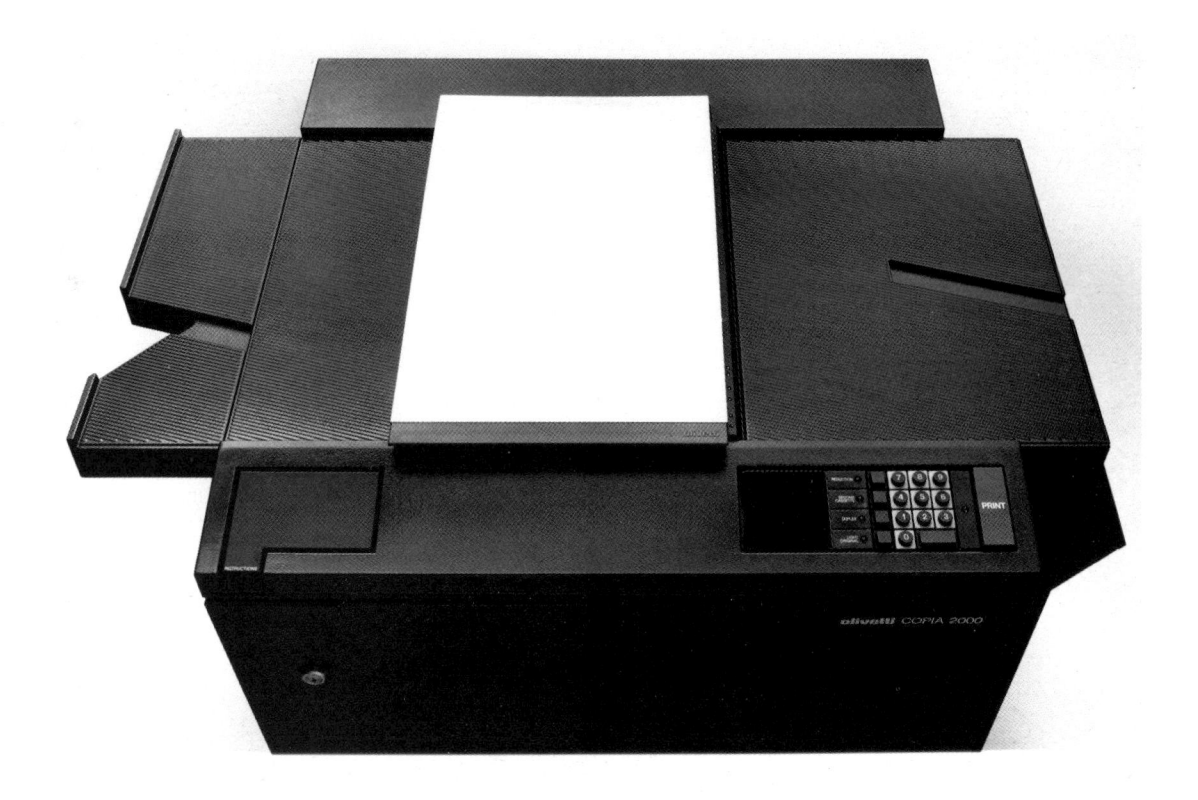

126. The Logos 80 calculator designed by Bellini with Macchi Cassia, Pasini and Pasqui, 1980.

time the technical draughtsmen are already able to experiment and to seek out possible problems in the earliest phase of projects. The shared location contributes to discussions about both design and technical ideas and the two groups inspire and drive each other in a common line. In comparison to this Sottsass keeps almost all of his technical draughtsmen at the production site in order to keep them in close touch with the engineering side.

Besides this Bellini is also a cultural ambassador for Olivetti. This is not only based on his work for Olivetti but also on his numerous outside activities as an architect and designer and as editor of the famous magazine *Domus* for the last three years.

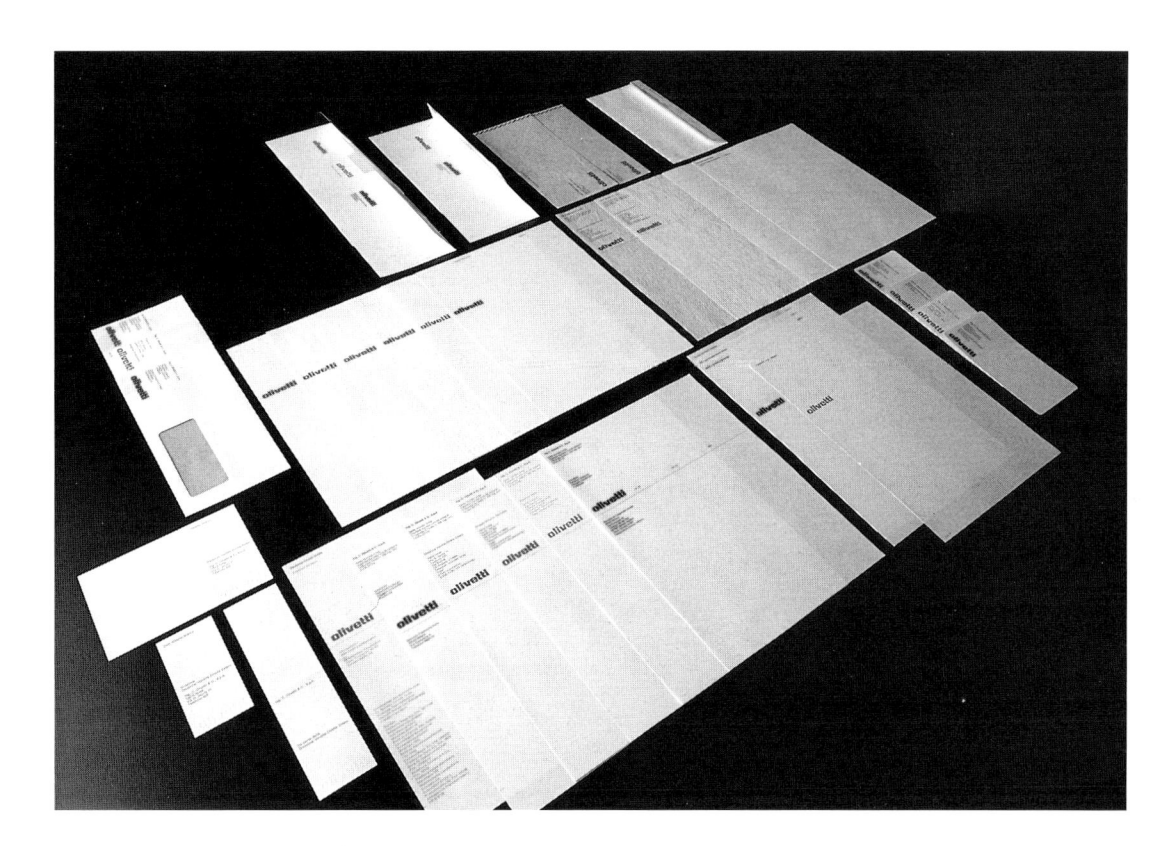

127. Letterheadings and corporate stationery, from the Olivetti 'Red Book', designed by von Klier's department, 1982.

The department of Corporate Identity directed by Hans von Klier

The department of Corporate Identity today is serving mainly three different 'clients' in the Olivetti empire. The first is the direction of Corporate Image, which oversees central tasks regarding the corporate design of the parent company Ing. C. Olivetti & S.p.A. as a whole. Such tasks are the development, follow-up and supervision of the 'corporate identification systems', covering the company logo and colours and their application in letterheads, external and internal signs, on company buildings and company vehicles. The identification system of Olivetti is laid down in the famous 'red books'. Furthermore, this work for Corporate Image as a whole encompasses the design of interiors and renovation of company offices, the design of the corporate system for Olivetti dealers and exhibition design for cultural activities.

A second category of work is for the indepen-

128. Hans von Klier.

OLIVETTI

129. Dealer identification systems designed by von Klier's department, 1982.

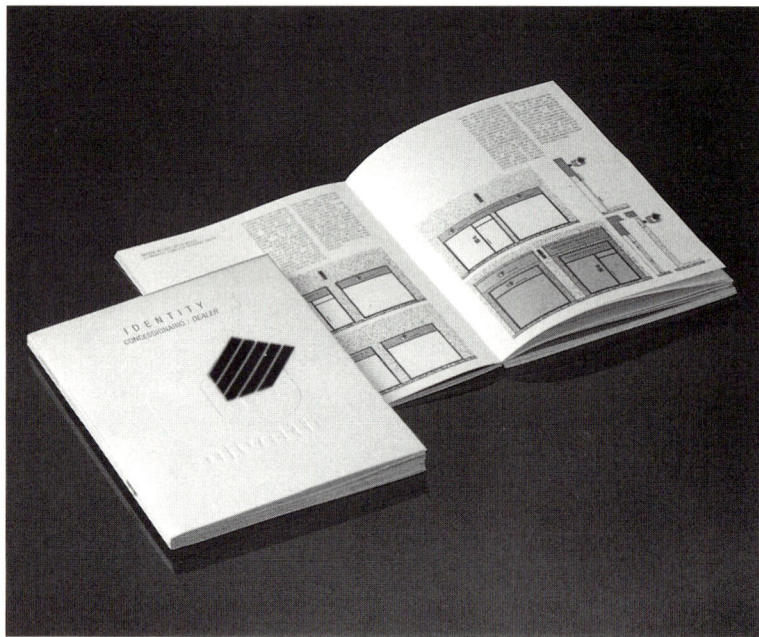

130. Packaging for office supplies designed by von Klier's department, 1982.

dent business units, that is Olivetti Office, Olivetti Systems & Network, Olivetti Information service (see diagram p. 67). This work includes design concepts for product identity, such as product logos, product presentation, display and media and press material on product launches for the three independent business units. Packaging design and graphic design for product communication is in a separate integrated office for graphic design under direction of Roberto Pieracini. He is also responsible for other graphic tasks such as the graphic design for exhibition catalogues or other projects of the Cultural Activies office. Exhibition design for commercial events is done by a special sub-department of Corporate Identity headed by Alfred Leclerc.

A third category of clients are the Olivetti controlled companies using the Olivetti name, whose number since De Benedetti's taking over has increased considerably.

Von Klier's department consists of about twenty people. His managing style is a centralist and rather patriarchic one, though it does explicitly ask a conceptual contribution and self organization from the staff. Control is exercised

114

131. Example of Olivetti identification on a vehicle, 1986.

in each of the project phases by individuals and in collective meetings, in which the actual development is presented and further procedures decided: here continual contact with the central departments and the product units or controlled companies on a operational basis is vital, as is reporting to von Klier. Von Klier had direct contact to Viti, though such information exchange, even in important strategic matters, was mainly informal.

Corporate Identity brings together many threads, from the traditional spirit of the company as well as the driving forces of the independent groups. Due to internationalization, diversification and decentralization Olivetti is increasingly becoming a system of autonomous groups, each of these, with own interests in its own profile and identity, which by their nature tend to scatter the corporate identity of the whole.

The identification system of von Klier which had been introduced in 1970 already at that time took into consideration the strong need for individuality which is typical in Italy. For that reason a kind of minimum solution was worked out which only determined the typography of the

OLIVETTI

Olivetti logo and its colours and their application (size, position, support material) for all kinds of applications such as letterheads, documents, catalogues, entrances, buildings, carparks. His system of six colours was to give freedom without putting into danger a holistic image. The aim was to have a simple striking identification system concentrating on the name of Olivetti and using it as a graphic sign thus leaving a maximum free space for individual interpretation.

However in the highly competitive markets of today and tomorrow managers tend to require stronger identification systems. This means in most cases having more striking and more individual signs, whereas the concept of visual corporate identity of the whole emphasizes the necessity of rather few, constant elements to use on all fronts of the company body in the same way, as focal points and constant, material bearers of the corporate connotation, ever changing and imaginary as that might be. Here two attitudes meet head on, where in the future Olivetti, along with many other multinational decentralised companies, will need to seek a new kind of reconciliation.

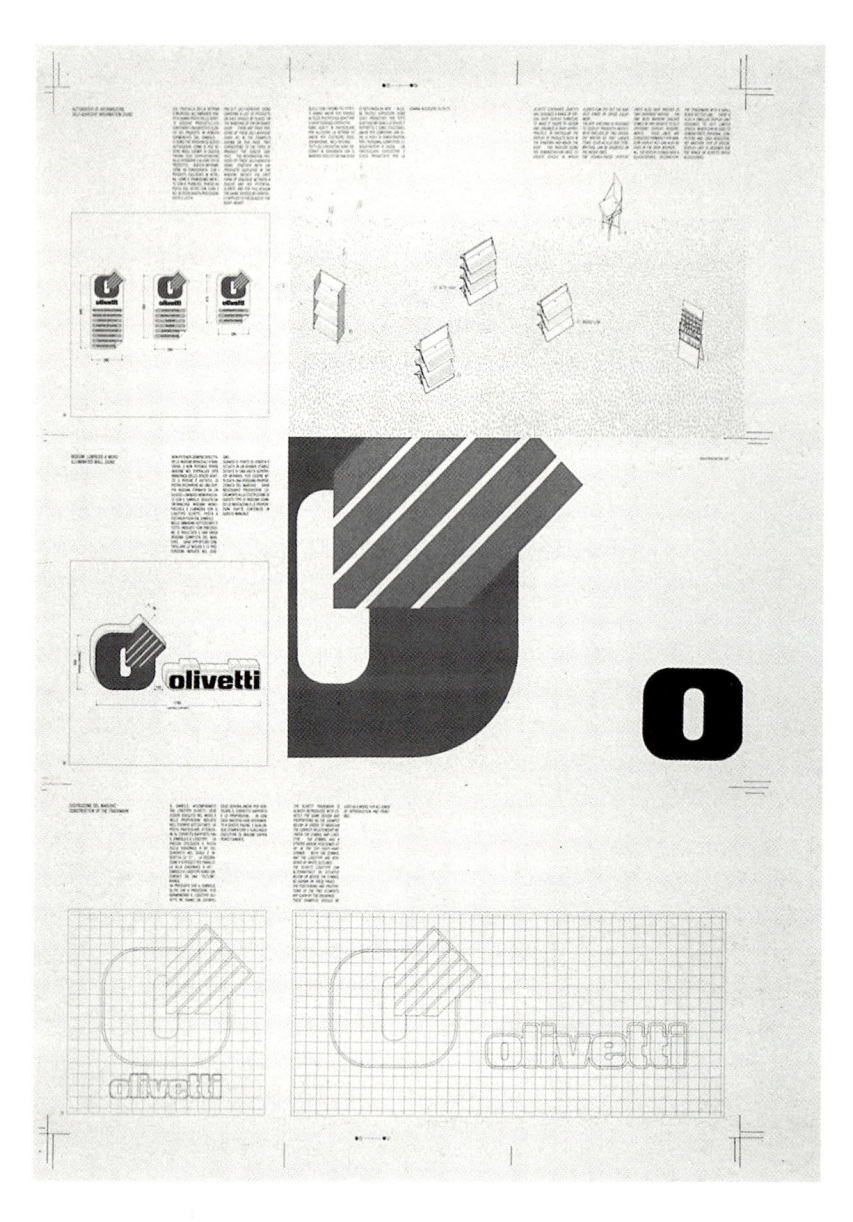

132. Example of Olivetti logo on a sign, from the Olivetti Red Book, 1986.

IX. Olivetti's showroom in
Venice, designed by Carlo
Scarpa, 1958.

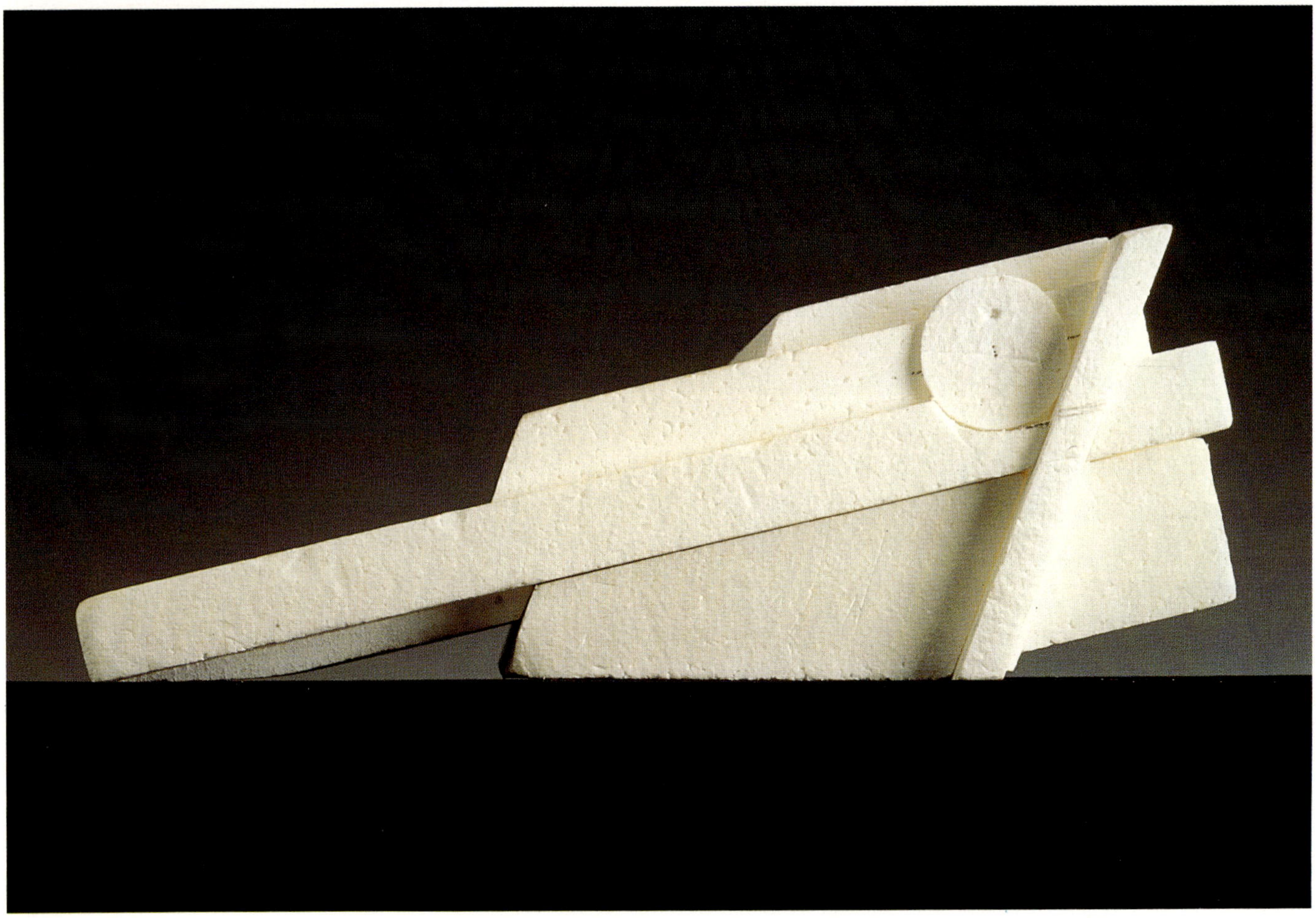

X, XI. The finished ETP 55 typewriter and one of the block models used to develop the design.

XII, XIII. A drawing for the Delphos layouts, and the completed system in use.

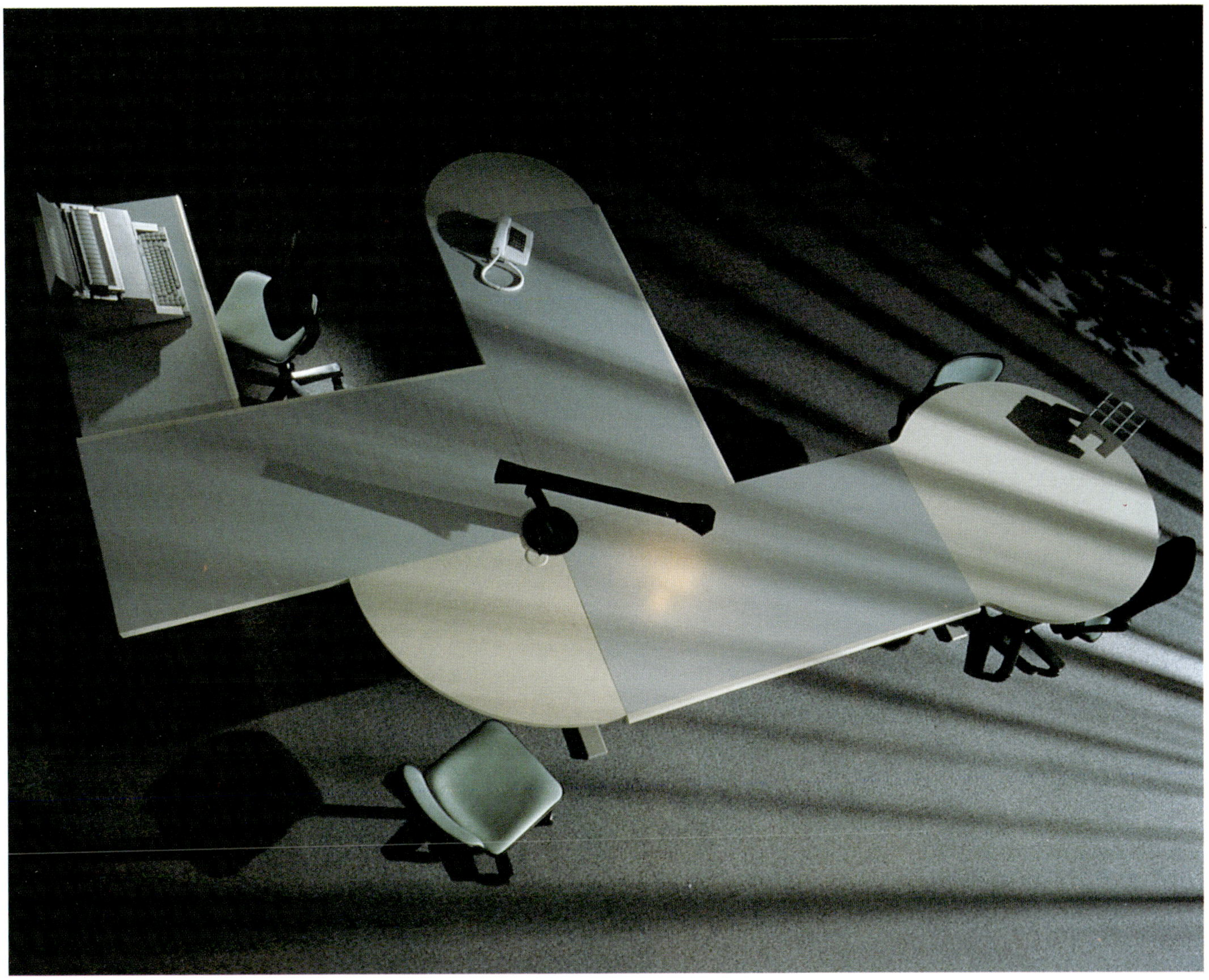

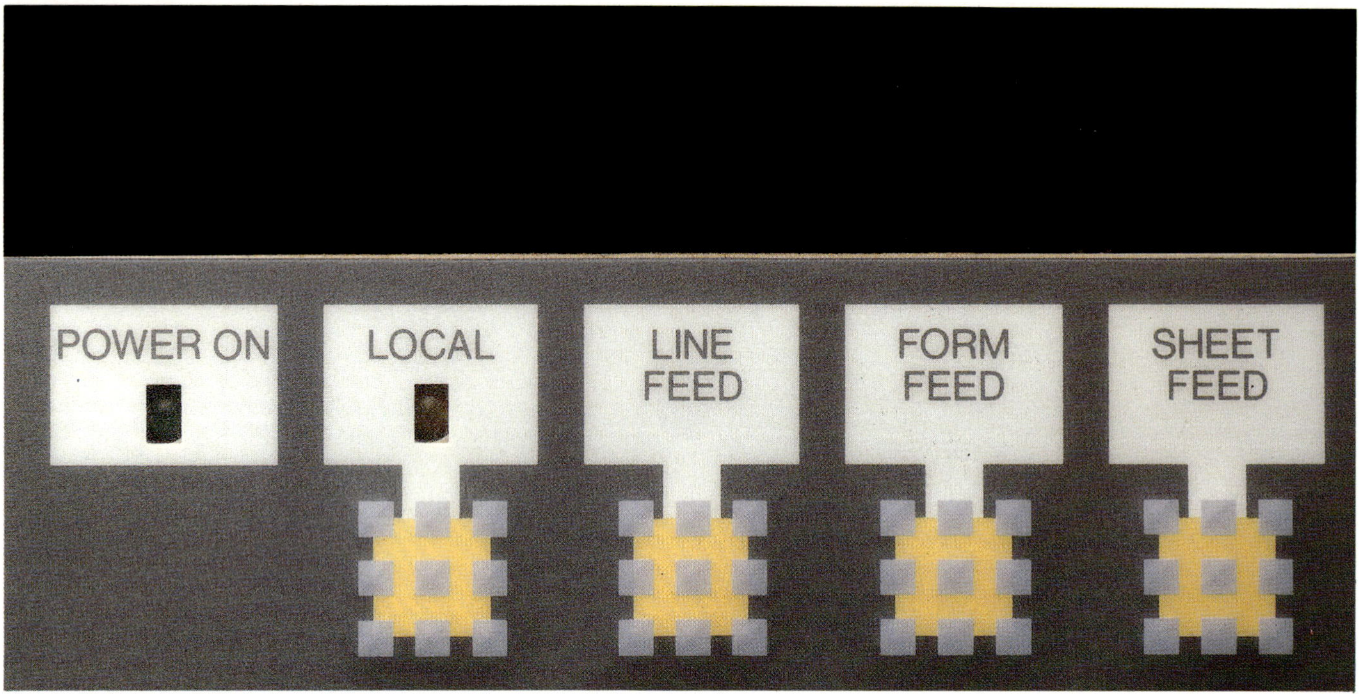
POWER ON
LOCAL
LINE FEED
FORM FEED
SHEET FEED

XIV, XV. One of the study drawings for keyboard finishes, by King and Miranda, and a detail of a finished system.

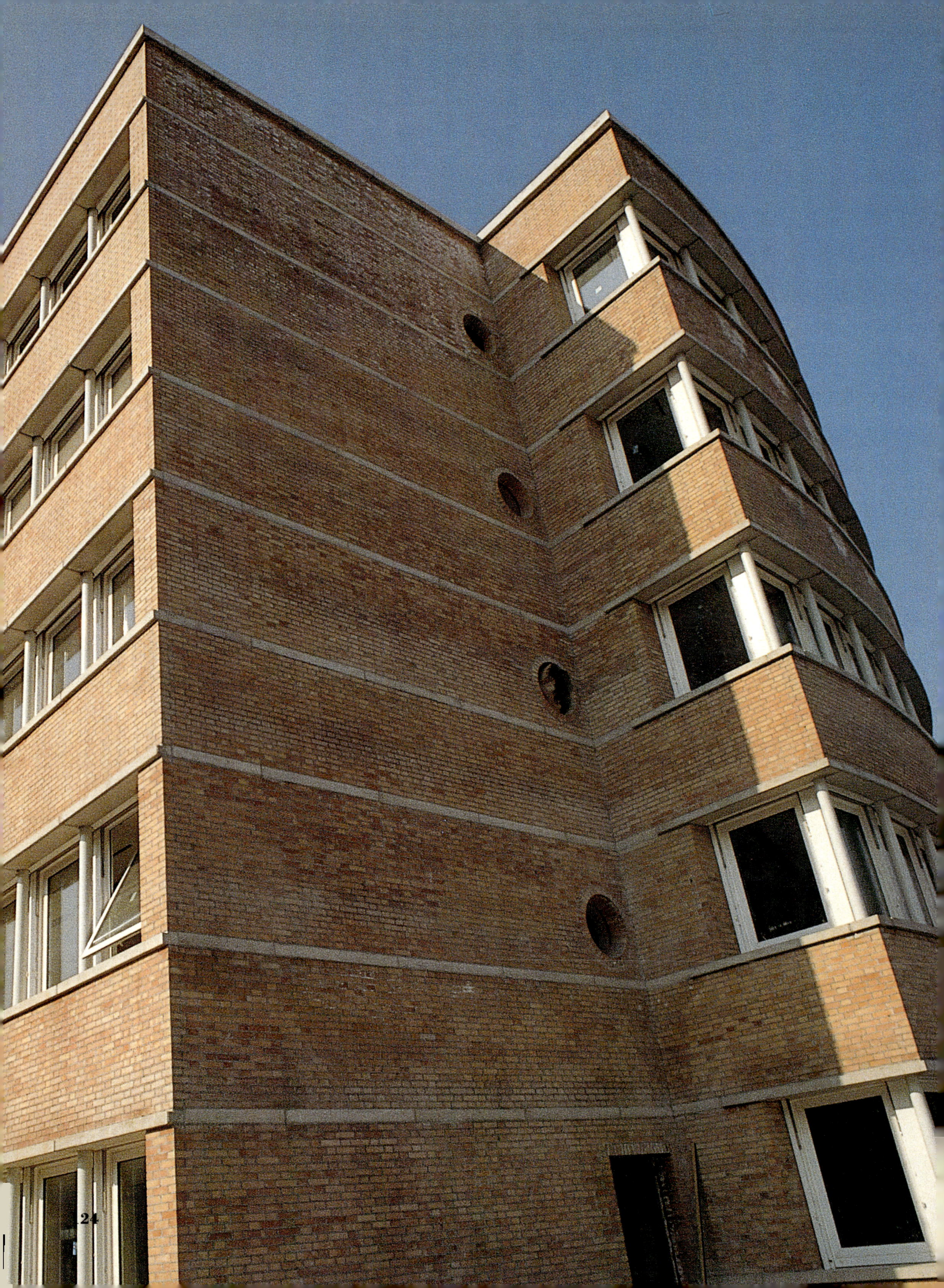

PART 3
PRODUCT CASE STUDIES

XVI. The new Olivetti central building in Ivrea, by Valle, 1989.

The design process from idea to finished prototype

This chapter presents three case studies of design projects in close detail, as mentioned above. Points of particular interest include the way in which a design project proceeds from an idea to the finished prototype, which personnel are involved and which criteria stimulate decisionmaking and achieve results.

It has to be drawn to the attention of the reader that the following text cannot be more than a incomplete and necessarily subjective interpretation of a most complex and evasive phenomenon. While there is one reality of officially approved facts and structures, there is also a second reality of contacts and events that lie behind the visible, seemingly logical pattern. The attitudes, personal beliefs and personal interactions of the protagonists, which are highly informal processes, provide the driving force behind the design process to a considerable degree. These things are not catered for in classical analysis models, which see the design process as a purely logical and structured one.

In Olivetti what happens 'in between the lines' – the informal process – seems to be more fundamental and decisive than any 'official' organisation. For this reason our understanding of the Olivetti design process may have to start with identifying the structurally organized frame with its hierarchy of departments, staff responsibilities and so on, but it has to go beyond into the field of the living informal processes which are the basic forces at work. These processes in Olivetti stem directly from company tradition and culture, as we have seen in the last chapter, and they are understandable only with this background.

The following case studies try to shed light both on the organisational and cultural frameworks as well as on the living processes. Each case study covers a different design unit with its own background inside the company. And each of them emphasises different aspects of the living culture driving the design process in Olivetti.

Case study: Portable Typewriter ETP 55

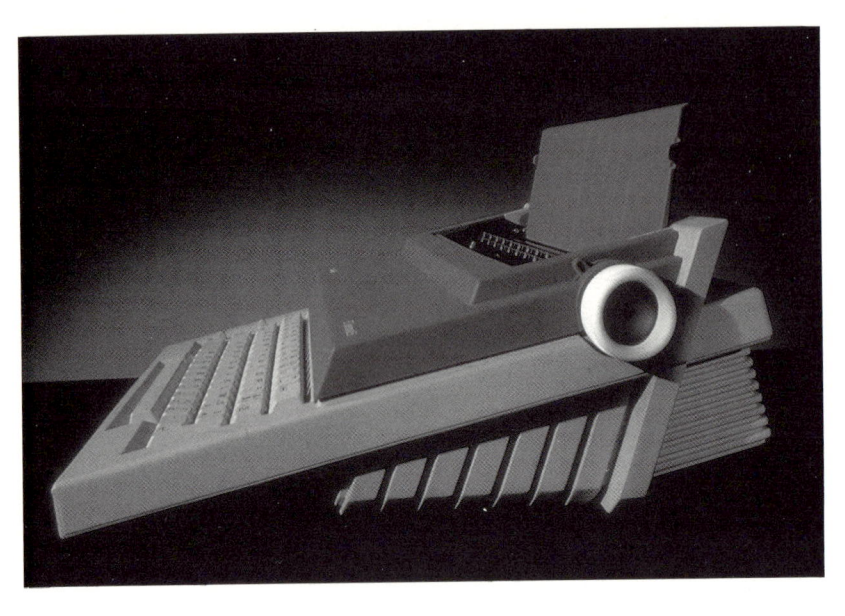

134. The ETP55 typewriter designed by Bellini and Chiarato.

Historical and business background.

The design process of the ETP 55 began in 1985. The machine was intended to replace the Praxis 20 (figs. 134,135), which had been on the market for three years, with a more up-to-date technology and design. The international market for this type of machine is extremely competitive, as there are numerous other producers, many from the Far East, and with low cost production and price strategies. From a technological point of view, the portable typewriter is a simple but mature product that has followed the general pattern of development from mechanical to electrical to electronic. The only innovations for today's typewriters are in the printer systems. The Japanese were the first to introduce the laser printer, in the same year that Olivetti changed its sales organization from one consisting mainly of concessionaires or Olivetti approved dealers to a wider distribution chain through independent dealers and electronic marketers.

The strategic background, which also led to a new organization with independent business units (see Ch. 2) involved both a broader and a more specialized covering of the mass market, with the aim of increasing sales and market share. The situation with the ETP 55 was the typical one of a company dealing with a saturated mass market and using a quality and design approach to counter excessive price competition. The ETP 55 was to symbolize Olivetti's claim for quality through design leadership, in a market where goods of low quality and passable appearance play an important role.

Organizational structure of the project

The ETP project was started by the two managers responsible for the portable typewriters product group within the Office Products Independent Business Unit. Others involved were the marketing group responsible for the market research and who calculated the product requirements of electronic typewriters from a commercial point of view, in terms of price, performance and fittings. A central part within the product development process was taken by the planning product manager who works on the technical market research and co-ordinates the project for the business unit. As such he plays the part of a project manager, responsible for the process from the initial briefing through to the prototype. He is a meditator between the commercial and technical sides of the IBU. Due to the design organization of Olivetti the design function lies outside the business unit with the central department of design (or Corporate Image, see Ch. 2). Bellini's office is responsible for the design of portable typewriters for the business unit, with Bellini himself as director and Alessandro Chiarato as operational designer. There also two technical draughtsmen brought by Bellini from the design center in Ivrea to produce the technically detailed work in direct relation to and parallel to the development of the design concept involved on behalf of Corporate Image were the Pieracini's graphic design office, responsible as always for the packaging, and more indirectly the consultants King and Miranda for research and design of keyboards and product graphics. King and Miranda had already developed the new standard keyboard which was also to be used on the ETP 55. Indirectly involved was the consultant for colour research and design, Clino Castelli, who had just completed a comprehensive central colour programme to be used in all product fields. In 1985, the director of Corporate Image was still Zorzi and the director of Design was Viti. Both fulfilled their usual functions with regard to design projects from consultants, providing information and control of the finished product. Finally development and production engineers were also involved on behalf of the business unit.

135. The Praxis 20, which the ETP 55 was to replace.

The course of the design process

When the marketing and project managers had finished their market and technological analysis, a rough briefing was worked out and approved by the responsible managers, the main points of which were to use already existing parts in creating the technical concept. In order to save cost, production was to be by Olivetti Singapore. The new product had to be an inexpensive and lightweight machine with a strong image to distinguish Olivetti from its main competitors Nagashima, Brother, Olympia, Sharp and Canon. The design was to be a clear symbol of the Olivetti claim to leadership in quality and design and would attract interest from a broad field of potential customers, mainly from the home market.

Official orders to start work on the ETP 55 project were given to the Bellini office in August 1985. The designers had to work on the basis of a given technical concept with a 50% reduction in the number of mechanical parts, for a cheaper, lighter and smaller product. As usual they received the 'box' with the technical input from the development engineers. In this case it contained a memory, a transformer and a metal frame to carry the printing system and cartridge as the main components with which to work. The metal frame showed that the Olivetti engineers were still following the old philosophy of producing solid, long lasting machines.

In contrast to Olivetti, Japanese companies produced plastic typewriter bodies. Sharp and Canon offered portable typewriters with thermo printers which allowed a very flat shape, whereas Olivetti had always planned to use its tried and tested 'Margherita' printing system which in the opinion of the Olivetti engineers represented the best quality of printing apart from extremely expensive laser printers. It had already been decided that King and Miranda's recently developed electronic keyboard would be part of the input of the machine. The specification gave as point of reference the Praxis 20, in comparison to which the ETP 55 had to be quieter, lighter, to have smaller dimensions es-

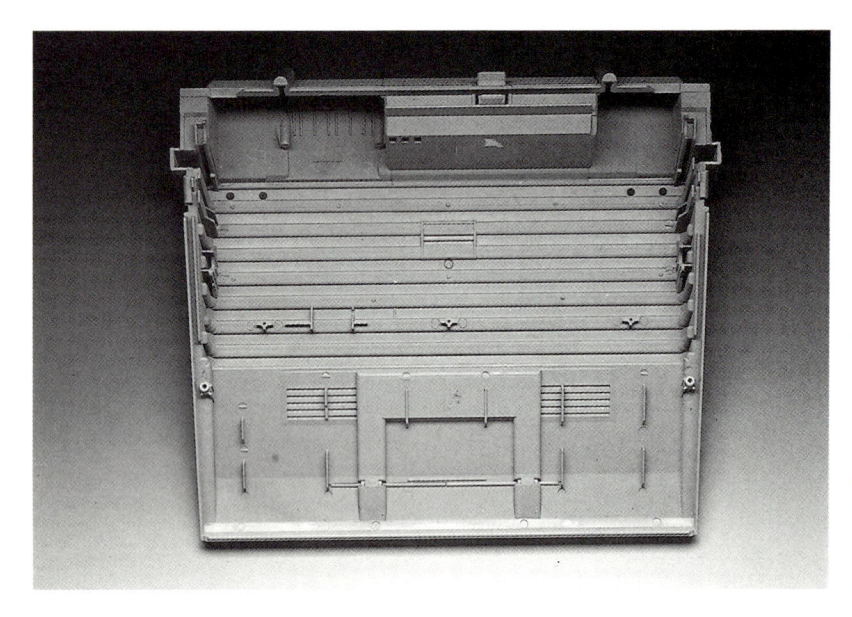

136, 137. The technical models, showing the position of the printer unit (top) and transformer (below).

pecially in length, and to be cheaper to produce.

The technical elements to be used were determined by the steel frame for the housing which had to carry the printing system and cartridge, with the transformer in the rear (see figs 136,137). The architecture of the technical components once this basic shape was decided was left to the designers, in co-operation with the development engineers.

Creative work in the Bellini office has as central 'spiritual' input from Bellini's interpretation of the Olivetti philosophy and his products for Olivetti as a guideline on which to continue (see Ch. 2., above). In this case Bellini gave his interpretation of the project in the form of a basic idea for the structural shape and the image to Chiarato who worked on the details of a structure within the given guidelines. As usual he presented all the detailed proposals to Bellini who decided how to continue from the alternatives developed by Chiarato.

The main idea was to stay with Bellini's invention of the wedge form, which has provided a strong image for Olivetti typewriters since its first introduction in 1978. Its influence on the whole typewriter market is quite obvious, although the many imitations might not please Olivetti from an economic point of view. The wedge shape meets all ergonomic requirements. Instead of the optimal 5% inclination of the keyboard on standing machines used on special lower typewriter desks, the portable machine is used in the home on non-specialized desks. With the table at this height, the position of the hand automatically becomes steeper when typing. For this reason the designer planned a 10% inclination of the keyboard instead of the average 5% for standing machines, and the wedge shape of the typewriter body exactly follows this inclination (fig. 138).

Another idea Bellini wanted to achieve from the beginning was to create a visual realization of an advanced, high quality electronic product. The symbol for Bellini was a flat, short and light-looking exterior. Instead of producing a single volume as with the Praxis 20, the designers created an architecture of different elements: an inclined slab with the keyboard crossing a vertical slab in a lateral x shape to build the frame of the architecture. Three additional volumes were added, one in the rear carrying the transformer, one below containing the electronic components, and one covering the cartridge and the paper roller. These volumes interact with the architecture of the wedge and are sculptured with differing decorations, to evoke starting grids or racing cars and other technically sophisticated vehicles. Using this technical imagery in an artificial way achieves the friendly impression of a robotic toy.

The symbolic aspect has always been a vital

element in Bellini's design approach. He once described his office products for Olivetti as a zoo of strange animals ready to stimulate the user's fantasy and the desire to domesticate them. In the case of the ETP 55 the image of the strange animal is quite obvious. Bellini's second image of a racing car has been incorporated by the vertical cut of the housing.

Bellini uses iconography in his designs; he hides the volumes by cutting them into slices, by dividing each volume into smaller elements. In this way it is possible to save space and to cut out empty parts of the machine. In consequence, the composition as a whole appears much lighter, shorter, more dynamic and less static, even though it had to fulfill the requirements of a minimum radial distance of 3mm from every machine surface, as a safety zone.

While the ETP 55 was being developed, another design group for colour research directed by Clino Castelli was about to finish a new range of Olivetti identity colours for product design. The research included colours for every component of products for every company producing Olivetti parts, and the group faced the huge task of changing the coding of every coloured component in the whole Olivetti catalogue. From this point on, all decisions concerning colour for product design were to be centralized and controlled by the design management. Inspired by the possibilities available, Bellini decided to use not only one basic colour of grey but additional blue and yellow to differentiate the ETP 55 from the monochromatic approach common in many similar professional products. A polychromatic product also makes the object more appealing and captures attention faster in the consumer market. Throughout the whole design structure, colour is seen as symbolizing emotional effect.

The design concept was a result of the rational reflections of the designers and of a process of negotiation with the technical designers and the engineers. Yet a great deal, probably

138. Preliminasry sketch for the ETP55, showing angle of keyboard to user's hand.

OLIVETTI

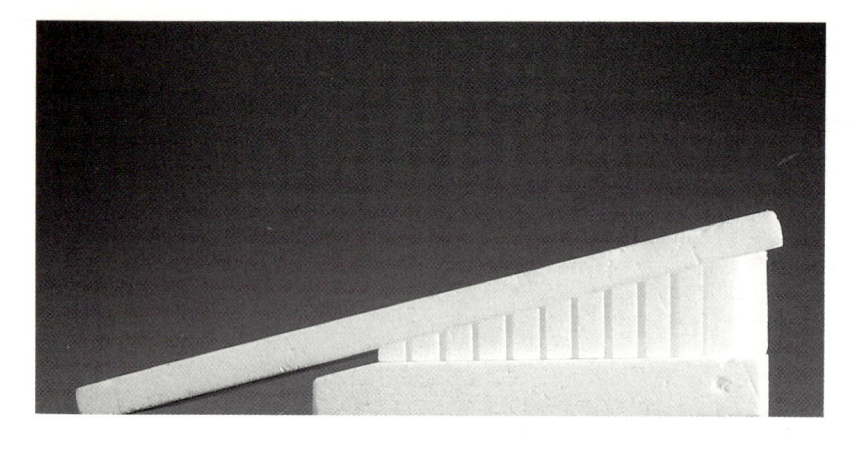

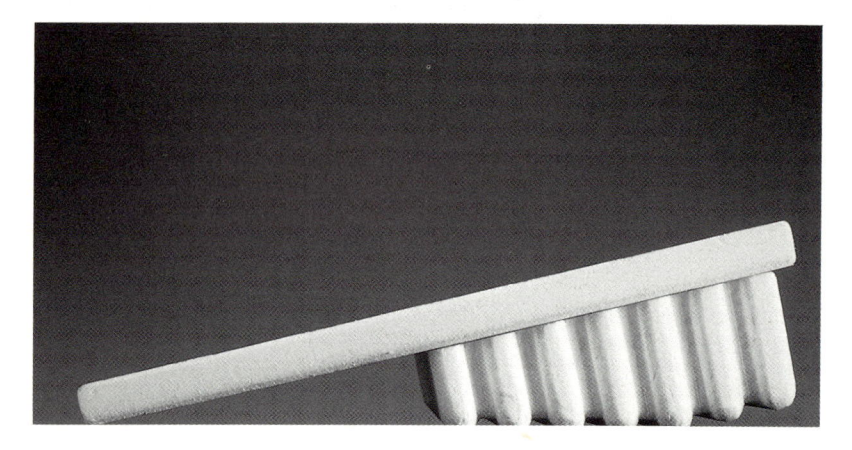

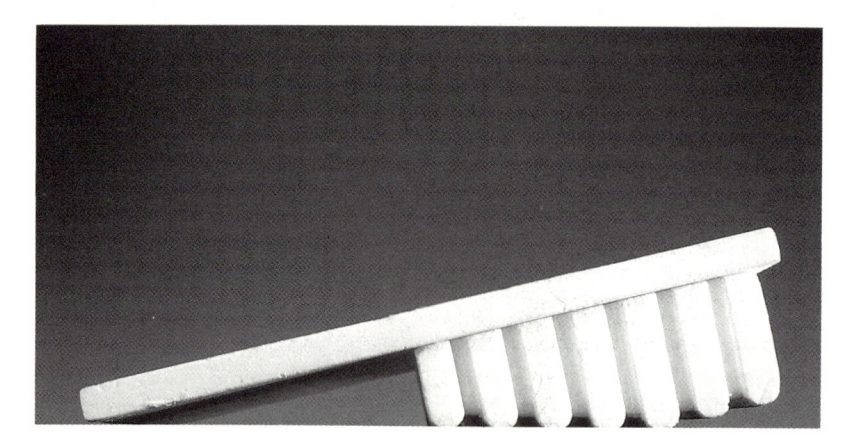

the main part, is the result of intuitive, personal attitudes and abilities of the designers, realized here with great freedom. What Bellini clearly rejects as creative input is a specific analysis of his competitors' products. Such knowledge should be part of the general expertise of the designers in any case.

The first presentation of the design concept in rough sketches and drawings was to the project manager Mr. Giglio. He in turn presented and discussed the basic ideas to the relevant planning and production representatives. As far as evaluation in this phase was possible, the project met with approval and was followed up in more detail. Chiarato worked out detailed solutions on a polystyrene model. Each step had been presented to Bellini who decided about future developments (see figs. 139-148). A difficult problem to solve was how to reduce the dimensions of the technical input elements in such a way that intended overall expression could still be achieved by the design. The whole co-operation with the engineers was left to Chiarato who continually informed Bellini about possibilities and problems. Any problems were mainly a matter of saving centimeters and millimeters here and there, but these kept the designer and engineers working for some time until a solution could be found.

Wood is the prefered medium for the final presentation model as it is more durable and conveys sculptural values more closely.

After the final model in wood (see fig. 149) had been presented by the project manager to the responsible product staff and later to the director of the division and to members of the top management in December 1986, preparation for production started. Problems were incurred in finding a type of moulding that could contain the unusual sculptural volumes of the central shape within the given tight budget and the particular production conditions in Singapore. Solving this involved Chiarato in going to Ivrea every week.

A realizeable solution was found with the designer and engineers compromising to find new, detailed solutions which met the requirements of the design concept (figs. 150,151). It took six months, almost three times as long as usual,

CASE STUDIES

139-140. Part of the series of foam models used to explore different profiles and relationships between volumes, using the theme of a single plane keybard.

141-144. Other foam models with a further layer over the keyboard and a more traditional base layer.

133

OLIVETTI

145, 146. Increasing complexity and sophistication of forms in further foam models.

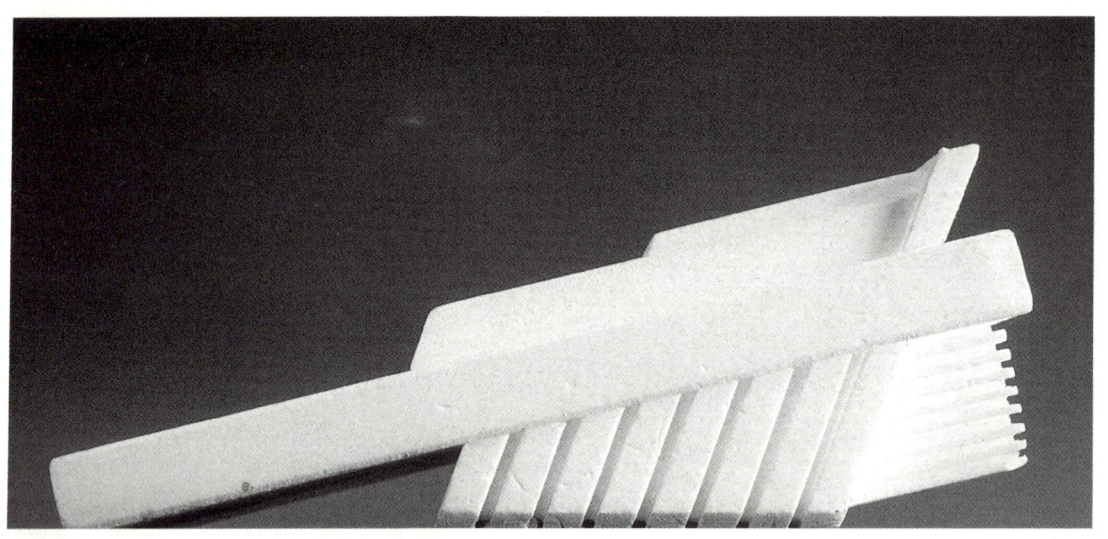

147. A front-on view of the foam model.

until the typewriter was ready for production, partly because of the need to adapt to the production technology available in Singapore and partly to the long and complicated methods of communication between the engineers in Singapore and in Ivrea and the designers. The packaging design, meanwhile, was conceived by Pieracini in the department for graphic design. The product designers had no influence on the advertising and promotional material, at that time dealt directly by the central advertising department.

ETP 55 was first introduced to the market after an agreement with the dealers in Brussels in November 1987 and introduced to the world market in mid-1988. Its image has been remarkably successful, not only as a result of the exhibition in the Museum of Modern Art in New

CASE STUDIES

148. Further development of the foam model to include the carriage control.

149. The woooden model presented for final acceptance: wood is selected for its greater durability and better volume to weight ratio.

York of Bellini's design work which attracted enthusiastic attention to the design of this typewriter. The design clearly realized the aim of distinguishing the ETP55 from its competitors. It communicates the company's cultural identity in an unmistakable way and is a medium for the technically advanced imagination of the company, even although in this case the technical concept itself is not an avant garde one. The product has been made lighter, shorter and flatter than the technological structure itselfwould seem to dictate, and in its category of consumer office products the design justifies the higher price of the product.

135

OLIVETTI

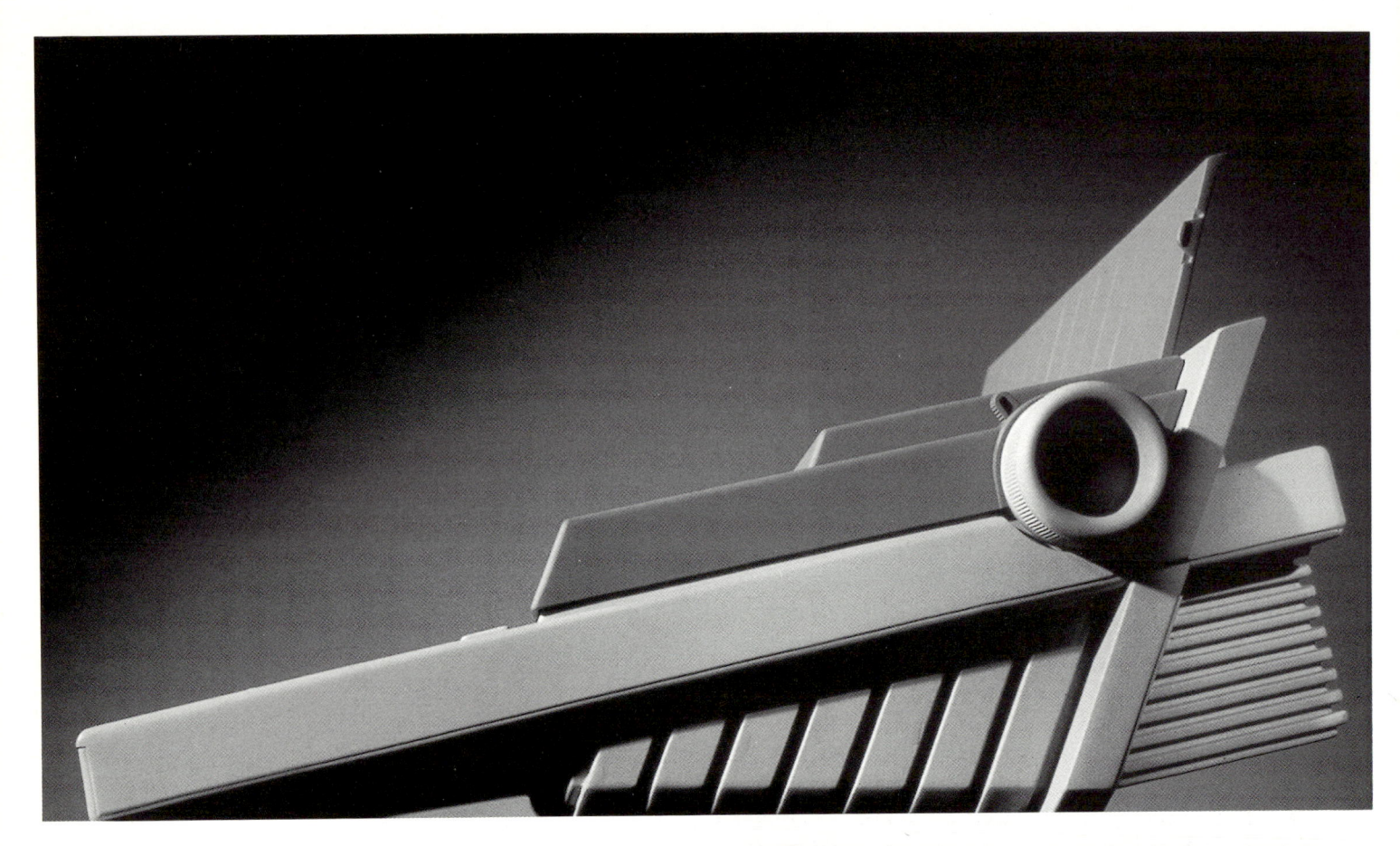

150. The finished product,
ETP 55, launched in 1987.

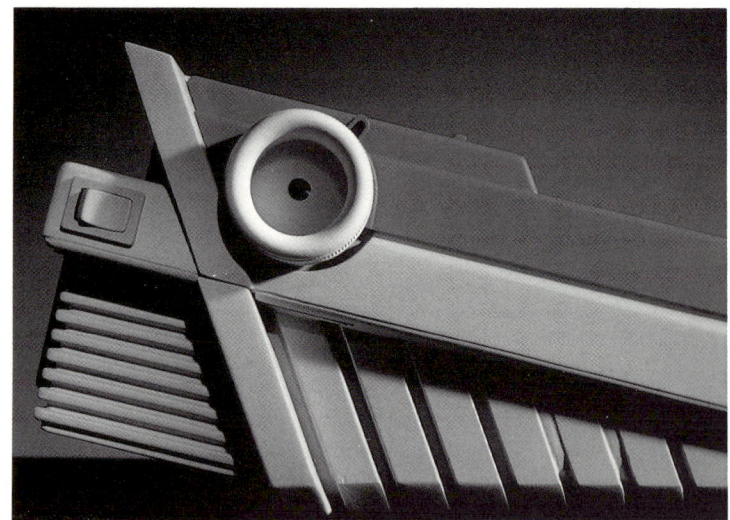

151. Detail of the finished
product.

Case study: the 'Delphos' office furniture system

The historical background of office furniture in Olivetti.

The Delphos furniture system was introduced to the market in 1986 (fig. 152). It is produced by 'Olivetti Synthesis S.P.A.', an independent company within in the Olivetti group which is located in Massa with 600 employees. Synthesis began as a division of office equipment in 1930 and became autonomous in 1978. Its creation can be linked to Camillo Olivetti's ideas: he maintained that the primary aim of production should not be lost during industrial activity, although the whole range of possibilities from these activities should always be kept in mind. In this sense Olivetti has always enlarged on what it has to offer, not by specializing in one product or technique but in looking to the field of office work as a whole. Having started with mechanical machines for writing and calculating, it made sense to add filing cabinets, which were available from 1930, later followed by matching metal cupboards and supports. This was a consequence of a vocational understanding of office work in its broadest sense; Olivetti considered the organizational and qualitative aspects of working conditions necessary to gain a specific awareness of design as a medium to meet the requirements of the office worker. In 1969 the first line of office furniture 'Spazio' (designed by Belgioso, Peressutti and Rogers, see figs. 153, 154) was created. The first Italian office furniture system named '45' was produced in 1973. These systems consisted of a group of components such as legs, tops for desks and shelves which allowed for individual and flexible arrangements in an office environment, instead of a range of single unit products on traditional lines. Whereas the 45 (fig. 153) was an inexpensive and simple desk system, the second Synthesis system, Icarus (fig. 156), is still one of the most sophisticated and expensive office systems on the world market, offering both maximum quality and highly sophisticated technology.

152. The finished Delphos system.

OLIVETTI

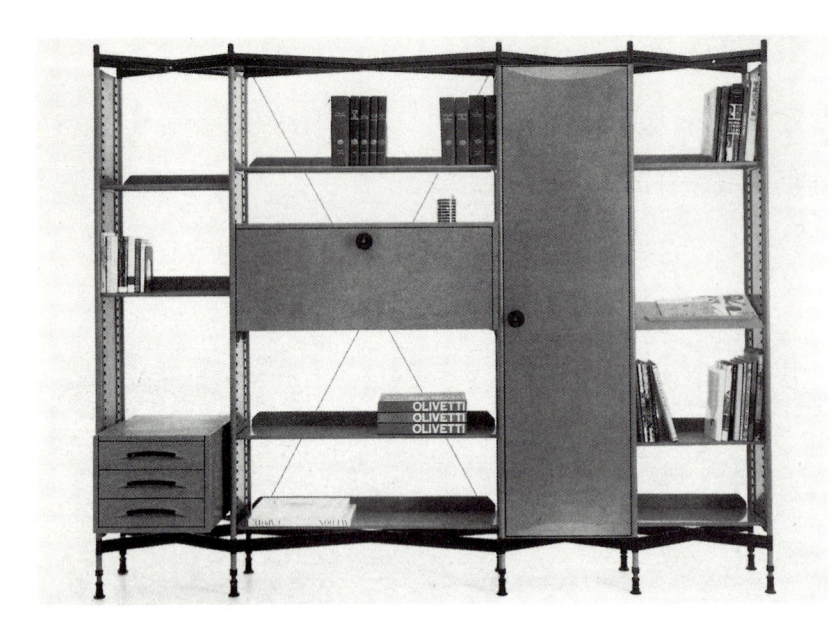

153. The Spazio system in an office setting.

154. A desk from the Spazio range.

serie SPAZIO   Scrivania S 1613

The Business Strategy of Olivetti Synthesis.

Olivetti Synthesis mainly serves the home market and its export rate is less than 10%. In 1983, it led the home market with an 11% share of the sales for office furniture, ahead of the most experienced manufacturer in the market, Castelli (5.6%), FARAM (4.8%) and Tecno (4.6%). The market for office furniture can be divided into three categories: small offices with a staff of one to three buying mainly single units such as desks, chairs, cupboards at a time; professional engineering and architectural studios, usually requiring higher quality products, and, thirdly, large scale customers such as banks, large companies and public institutions. Olivetti Synthesis concentrated on banks and large scale customers with an initial small group of potential customers, most of whom were already clients of one of the 800 Olivetti concessionaires.

A basic problem for Synthesis was that of identity – it clearly belonged to the parent company and could take advantage of the Olivetti image and knowledge of office technology, but at the same time Synthesis had to ensure its independence in order to be more flexible and open to new possibilities, ones not perhaps covered by the parent company. With the production of office furniture systems, Synthesis took a first step away from being a producer of office machines, complementing elements of single furniture that were known for their quality and technology regarding metalwork, towards offering a comprehensive set of solutions for office furnishing. It was not until 1981 that Synthesis became a company from an organizational point of view and established its own sales service: up to then sales had been handled directly by Olivetti.

A clear strategic concept for the company as a whole was developed in 1985, after Emilio Torri had taken over the general management in August 1984. His analysis of Synthesis showed that despite the 45 and Icarus product ranges, the company was still perceived as only a producer of functional mechanical filing and storage systems for the office. Synthesis did not have a public image as an office furnisher and was not regarded as having the aesthetic and architectural approach of a furnishing company. Torri saw the main reason for this in the obvious lack of furniture systems for the middle ground between the two extremes represented by 45 and Icarus in terms of market and price; one was a simple, inexpensive concept of a desk system for a traditional market and the other was a high price, high standard panel system. The market analysis did not cover the important area of the middle ground, and so the potential of that market did not come in to the calculations. Similarly, the sales organization followed Olivetti channels through concessionaires and direct selling by representatives serving large scale

CASE STUDIES

155. The 45 system.

customers. From the beginning, Torri worked to develop a new strategy which was to make Synthesis an office furnishing company offering high quality, comprehensive solutions, and together with the unique aspect of Olivetti as the only producer of both office technology and furniture, so that Synthesis could take advantage of Olivetti's experience in office machinery and the high standard in design and architecture of the parent company. The new strategy is for high quantity and high quality, serving all three segments of the market with a new priority for the middle range customer, including the offices of architects who were to become leading customers for the new Synthesis image.

The first step towards this strategy, which required major changes in sales, distribution and communication was the creation of Delphos. Instead of continuing the work of his predecessor who had asked the designers to produce a new desk system to replace 45, Torri decided to produce a system to fill the middle ground between 45 and Icarus which was also to bring an increase in turnover of at least a third. This decision was not only based on strategic analysis but on his personal discussions with the Synthesis staff. Indeed, the first meeting between Torri and the designers saw Torri inquiring about the designers' point of view with regards to the strengths and weaknesses of the Synthesis programme.

139

The infrastructure of Synthesis

Torri introduced new marketing and commercial directors who were responsible for sales and distribution, but otherwise he had to work within the existing infrastructure of Synthesis. Of central importance for the new product strategy was the fact that in terms of design, Synthesis was directly connected to the central department of Corporate Image in Olivetti (see Ch. 2). It used this central service of the parent company in more or less in the same way as the business units within Olivetti, by working with the various offices designated for specific design tasks such as graphics, exhibitions and specific product areas, by completing the planning and evaluation of the design projects in agreement and consultation with the directors of Corporate Image and by getting the approval of Corporate Image for the design concept. Because so many of their projects are planned on a considerably smaller time scale, the directors of Corporate Image and the top management of the Olivetti group have agreed to budget Synthesis design on a yearly basis.

Responsibility for the design of Synthesis furniture systems is under the direction of Ettore Sottsass, Michele De Lucchi and assistant designer James Irvine (see Ch. 2). One peculiarity of Synthesis is that apart from this group, Olivetti designers and design offices are sometimes used for specific projects such as office chairs, for example by Bellini, or furniture systems for executive offices, such as the Executive Line by Hans von Klier. This use of external designers for one-off projects is standard Olivetti practice, as we have seen.

Apart from the organizational bond between Olivetti and Synthesis, there is a personal bond which ensures that the Olivetti philosophy of design is continued, not only through the personalities and beliefs of Corporate Image management or the personal capacity and attitudes of the designers but also through the fundamental and personal attitude of the business management of Synthesis. Emilio Torri lives and breathes the basic Olivetti values. It is not a coincidence that a man with twenty year's experience and a deep conviction about the quality approach of Olivetti has been named as manager but rather an application of the typical Olivetti management principle of the personalized continuation of the company tradition. For Torri, design is an intrinsic factor in a product and has to be considered at an early stage, long before the engineers present a technical solution. Discussions with the designers are vital for an understanding of the quality that a product can contribute to office life and so solutions are not developed just to fulfill market and sales requirements but as a representation of the company vision of quality. According to Torri, design quality requires close and continual interaction between the designers, and to realize a continually advancing company concept the designers have to share and interpret basic beliefs, instead of developing their own solutions outside the company context.

Course of the Design Process

The following groups of people were involved in the Delphos design process as a result of the structural frame of Synthesis: the general manager Torri, the marketing director who acted as a project manager and was responsible for the co-ordination of staff and work, the marketing planner responsible for commercial research and strategic planning, the commercial director responsible for technical development and the production engineer. In addition the management of Corporate Image, Viti and Zorzi, were on hand to give advice, to control progress and to ensure the continuity of the design and image approach of Olivetti. The product designers were Sottsass, De Lucchi, Irvine and Pieracini from the graphic design office, and Clino Castelli, the Olivetti consultant for colours and materials also played his part.

After the decision to produce a new system in August 1984, Torri asked the technical development engineers to analyze the costs. Product meetings started with the representatives of sales, marketing, technical development, design and production to clarify the product concept. These discussions, the result of technical analysis, a further analysis of the market by the marketing department and of cultural trends in the office by the designer, led to the design briefing. Its aims were to develop a design concept for a new desk system with panels to fill the middle position between 45 and Icarus; it should be in the middle price range, more flexible than the earlier, simple 45 system, and it should meet the needs of middle-sized offices. The new product was of particular importance to Synthesis as it was to cover a major part of the company turnover and in terms of corporate image Delphos was to substantiate Synthesis's claim to be a specialist comprehensive office furnishing company of high design quality: this was to be achieved through demonstrating also the versatiliity of the existing range of products. In addition, Delphos had to incorporate an existing set of storage elements, and use the specific Synthesis knowledge of metal folding and the same tools. A further technical proposal concerning cost savings suggested the necessity of using a wooden top (the top represents almost 80% of the production cost) and using wooden panels instead of the costly metal frame as in Icarus. The time allowed for the development of the design concept, including the prototype of all the system elements, was eight months; extremely short in comparison to the two years each allowed for in the design concepts of 45 and Icarus. The designer's briefing, which contained mainly only rough points, came directly from Torri.

Behind these facts regarding the passage from product idea to the design briefing lies another story, a network of specific relations and experiences of the designer and the Synthesis staff. The officially nominated design group for Synthesis furniture systems was within the Sottsass office. Ettore Sottsass chose Michele De Lucchi as assistant for this project. They started to work together with the renewal of the 45 in 1979, in 1981 they developed the design for a new line of supporting elements and in 1982 they worked on Icarus. For the latter, De Lucchi was appointed by Corporate Image to produce an international analysis of office cul-

The work on Delphos started with Torri's arrival in August 1984 and progress can be schematized as follows:

August 84: market analysis, first informal discussion with De Lucchi, technical study on how to save cost.

September 84: first product meetings, research on cultural trends in office design by the designer, design briefing.

September/October: creative work on design concepts, first checks of the idea with technical development, first styrofoam models.

November 84: first presentations of design concept to Torri, decision on one of the three alternatives.

November/December: work on design details and technical concept of the chosen solution.

January 85: presentation to the management, commercial, marketing, technical development and production staff of Synthesis.

January/February 85: detailed work on design and technical concepts, development of the final styrofoam model.

March 85: presentation to Corporate Image Management and Franco De Benedetti by Synthesis staff and designer.

April to August: work on technical details and prototype, the development of an exhibition, communication design for Delphos' first public presentation.

September 85: first public presentation in the Salone del Mobile in Milan.

October to February 86: tooling up begins, with production engineering consulted, safety aspects tested and international safety and copyrights registered.

March 86: production begins.

ture and the position of Olivetti's competitors, which involved a six-month trip around the world to visit relevant companies, shops and offices. De Lucchi gained a profound knowledge of the market and its particularities and reported his findings to the commercial, marketing, technical and production departments of the Synthesis group whenever they needed information or support as, for example, in presentations to large clients or for detailed market information regarding technical solutions. De Lucchi, the in-house designer was always present in the follow-up of Synthesis products and he was always available for consultation on design problems in the various departments. As the designated design office offers a continual service with a yearly budget to the business unit, it was possible to establish a close link with the Synthesis staff who appreciated and took advantage of the work and services of De Lucchi. When he began the conceptual work for Icarus he became even more involved in the company. The main people in management, marketing, production and technical development became real friends, mutual help and information were taken for granted. Most of them were not permanently based in Massa but came from Milan: the extended dinners in a fish restaurant on the beach became something of a ritual for discussing the events in and plans for the office. It was here that many of the new ideas were born and everybody understood what they had to do. This is why nobody remembers when exactly a designer had been officially informed and put in charge of a project; official briefings were seen as minor information by designers. By this time De Lucchi already had an extensive understanding of the problem and of what information was still missing and he would carry out his own research into office cultural trends.

The results of his analysis and his interpretation were as follows.

The typical European office - and particularly the Italian one - is located in an old building with office space limited to small rooms. Apart from large industries and service institutions such as banks, there are a vast number of middle-sized offices, housing from five to twenty people in which work spaces have to have multi-functional and even multi-personal uses. Individual work spaces, the traditional system of work organization, have to be combined with collective spaces, the new open plan approach. There is now a growing desire for individually designed work spaces, probably in opposition to the multi-personal use of working places. As a counterpoint to the increasing use of technical information processing machines there is also a demand for a 'softer' environment. In clear distinction to the American 'vertical' design of work places with the worker's head looking towards the wall where storage systems are attached, there is what the designer calls the 'Mediterranean' ideal of working with the head overlooking the worker's surroundings to give the feeling of space. For this reason, office planning in America starts with the creation of walls with the panel as a fundamental element for the rest of the work space, whereas in Europe the starting point is a free standing desk to be followed later by the walls. As a desk system with panels, Delphos clearly followed the European model.

Influenced by this type of European office ideal, partly through his own research and also through the many discussions with his friends in Synthesis, De Lucchi developed the idea of Delphos as a 'compact configuration'. This meant a new system, in which a metal beam integrated into the structure acts as a support, connecting element and cable tube. De Lucchi took this principle of structural integration from Icarus, saving costs and allowing a combination of furniture without additional elements. The innovation came in the form of a beam with points for cross connections over half its length, which allowed much tighter combination and connection between desks, storage elements and panels (see fig. 158). Whereas a cable beam – a necessary feature – would normally allow only a couple of configurations, the compact configuration offers an almost infinite variety. To add aesthetic possibilities to the range of functional methods of combination, De Lucchi developed a set of different forms for the working surface, three different legs as supporting elements for single desks, multiple desks, desk panels and desk storage elements (see figs. 159-161)

CASE STUDIES

Other ideas originally developed and used for Icarus included a vertical unit enabling service and storage elements to be attached to the wall (see figs), and in order to save costs the wooden inlay of the Icarus panels with its simple aluminium beam was used instead of a metal support and a plastic cable channel. De Lucchi took these important developments for Icarus and added new elements to make a new desk system with panels that were less expensive, and also more compact, flexible and light and therefore easier to install.

The first step towards the presentation was to show drawings (see figs. 162-164) to the technical experts to check that the design could be produced within the given frame of cost and equipment. As there were no basic difficulties, the designer and technical development engineer worked together on three styrofoam models (seen in fig. 171) in the laboratories in Massa. When he had the full agreement of the technicians, De Lucchi presented the drawings of the three alternatives to Sottsass who approved the general approach and only advised him to emphasize some parts more than others and to evaluate the costs further. The decisive presentation of the final solution and the go-ahead for the development of the prototype took place informally one afternoon with Torri and the designer in the Massa laboratories. The designer explained which alternative he had chosen for Synthesis and why, as the general approach in all three alternatives was the same principle of the integrated beam system. Two of the concepts used the so-called compact configuration. The main difference between them was a different set of desk tops, legs and connecting parts, giving each prototype a different appearance and making the systems more or less complex and solid from a functional point of view and more or less expensive. The first decisive criterion for the choice of the compact concept was its outstanding flexibility which allowed a maximum number of easily installed combinations. The second was that it was the least extravagant and the least expensive as every element could be used in a multi-functional way. In two of the alternatives, the drawer had already been used in the Icarus

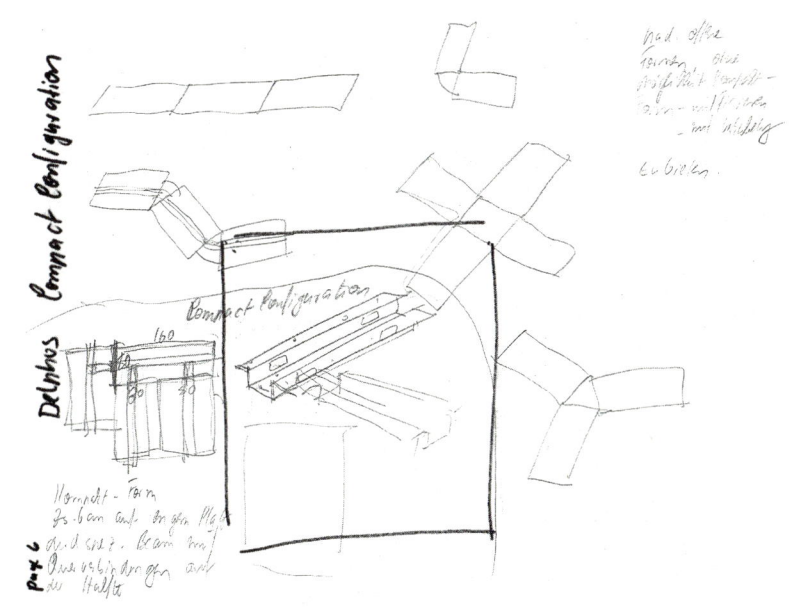

156. The Icarus system.

157. A drawing for the crossbeam in Delphos, annotated by the author.

143

OLIVETTI

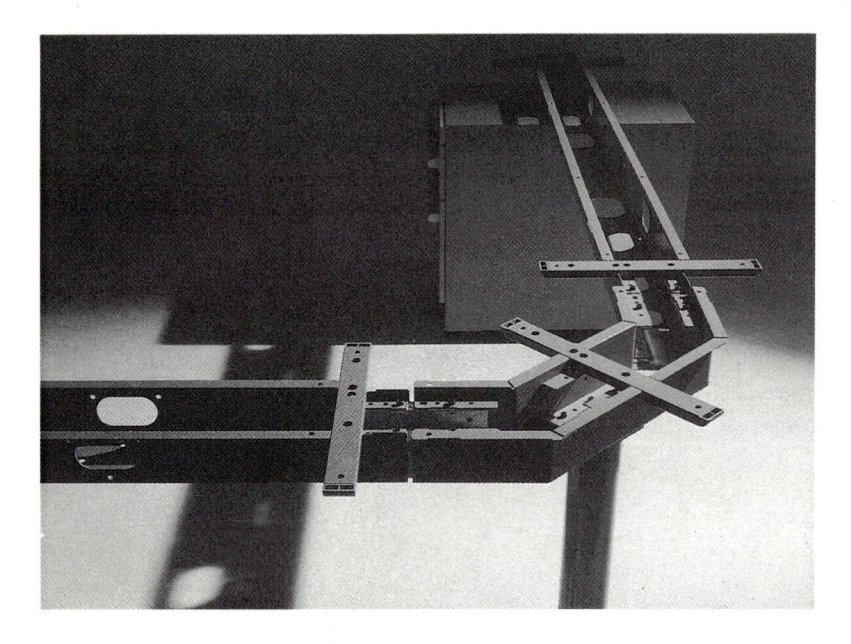

158. The Delphos crossbeam.

159-161. Drawings for incorporating Delphos into structures.

desk, whereas Delphos used the drawer as support element for desks to save elements, cost and space. The multitude of compositions using the same components enabled Delphos to stress its particular potential for personalized work space layouts: the architectural possibilities were particularly important (see fig. 159).

In January 1985 another, this time official, presentation was given to all the departments involved in Synthesis – the management, marketing, commercial, technical development and production departments. It was a critical review of the refined design concept based on drawings and the styrofoam model, and concerned the requirements of the market as well as a cultural

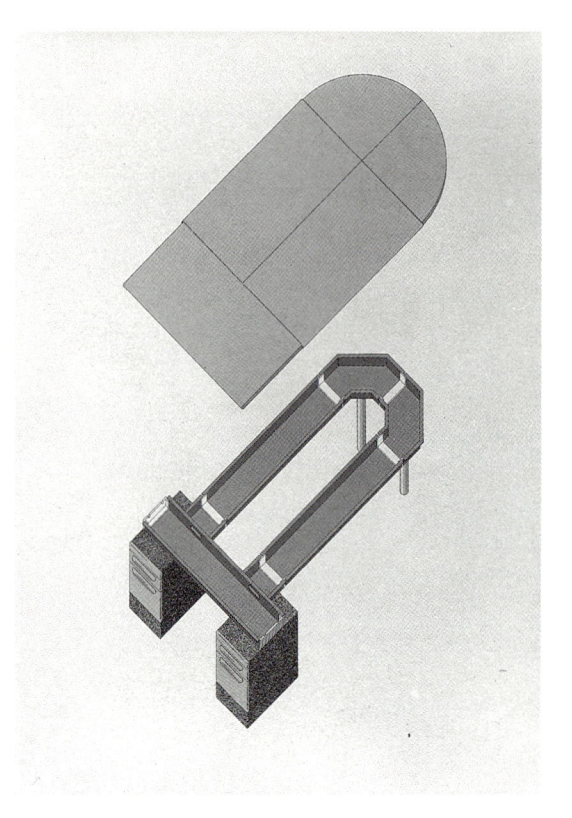

CASE STUDIES

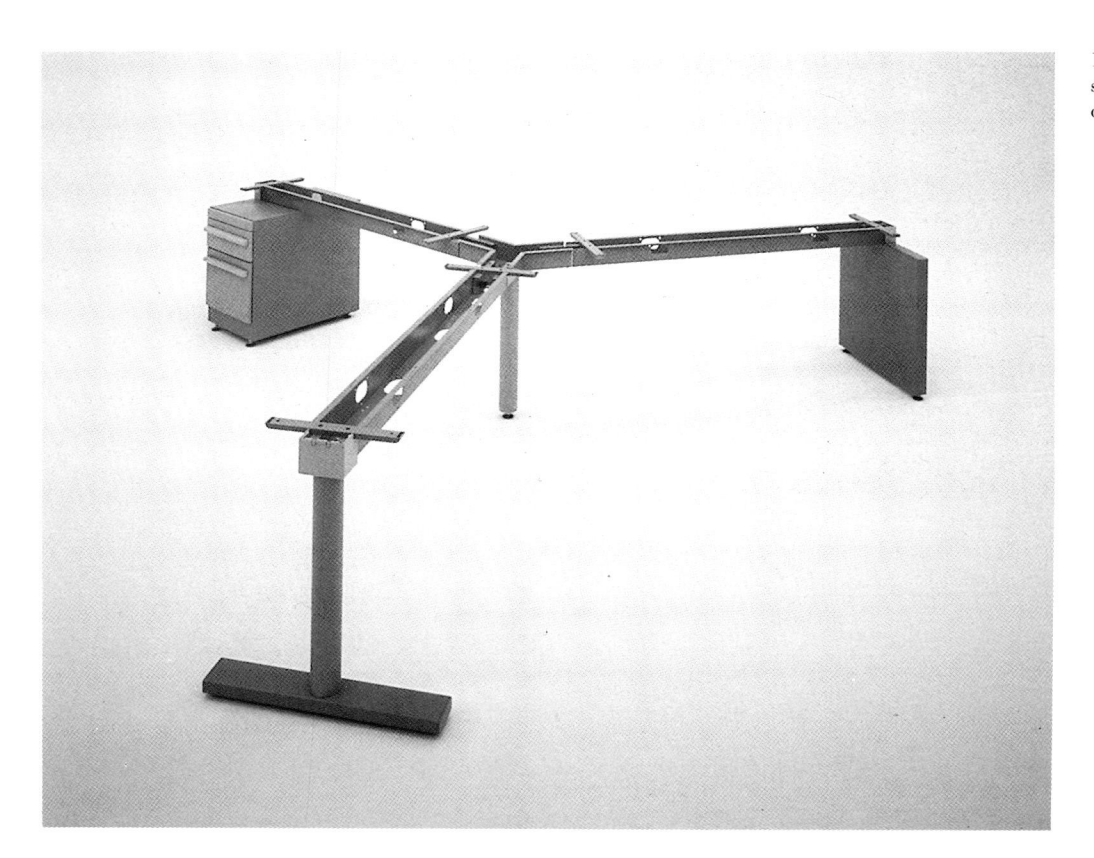

162. The Delphos support structure showing the cablebeam.

163. The support structure with table top in place.

164. Detail of fit of separate units.

145

OLIVETTI

165. The finished unit, showing its architectural possibilities.

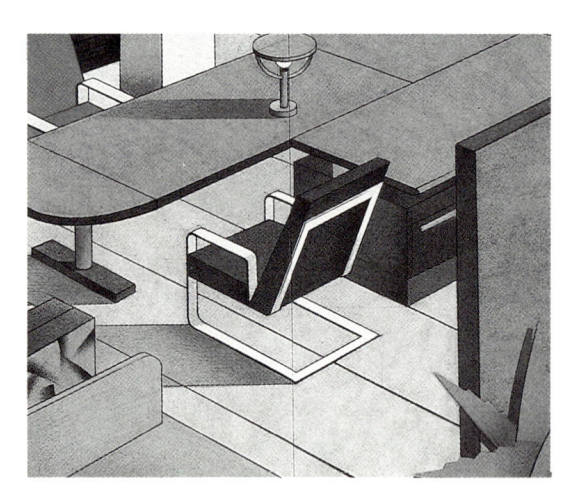

166, 167. Premilinary sketches exploring different combinations of the proposed units.

146

analysis. The second official presentation was to Carlo De Benedetti and the directors of Corporate Image in March 1985. The Synthesis management and the designer presented the new design concept and product strategy. Torri's introductory comments referred to the importance of the project for the company, the marketing director presented the results of research on the Italian and European market and the designer demonstrated cultural trends and particularities in office development before explaining details of the solution. The function of this last presentation was mainly to give information to the parent company for their general approval and to ensure that the Olivetti approach had been followed. Torri drew attention to the fact that the solution also needed an adequate adaption of sales, distribution and communication. The whole concept was greeted with applause.

Work on the prototype was in closely observed by the two designers, Sottsass and De Lucchi, and the technical development engineers who discussed every detail: this work between the two groups went on without any interference or supervision from the management. However, the introduction of the finished product to the market was controlled by the marketing director. As is usual in Italy, the launch was arranged for the Salone Del Mobile in Milan – the Milan Furniture Fair – in September. Torri had given design responsibility for the launch to De Lucchi during the introductory presentation and in May 1985 De Lucchi started working on the architectural setting, the display, the lighting concept and, together with the Olivetti office for graphic design and its director Pieracini, on a catalogue. The latter consisted of a small book giving the background and details of Delphos, demonstrating a scientific and sophisticated approach rather than aggressive marketing. Clino Castelli, the designer responsible for colour in Olivetti, was also involved in the preparatory work for the market launch. Castelli had started work on a new colour system and on a programme of colour finishes for Synthesis, but as this programme was not yet complete, he developed in collaboration with De Lucchi a 'phantom' colour set consisting entirely of sha-

168-170. Axonometric presentations of different Delphos elements, showing alternative legs, tabletops and fittings.

OLIVETTI

171. Styrofoam model for Delphos.

des of grey. The final presentation before the launch at the Fair was made to Torri, who as always consulted De Lucchi.

Designers were involved with problem analysis, the development of the design concept and its technical aspects, with production and even with the development of the communication approach of Delphos. Involvement was informal: so designers had easy access to all the different departments and vice versa. Design was not a linear, step by step process but a network of different processes in different departments which interacted in a spontaneous way. The product meetings mentioned above were the only kind of regular, organized exchanges of information between all the relevant parties. They served mainly as a starting base for new individual interactions and as a system of mutual assistance and information, always available. Only with this background was it possible to realize the project in just eight months, compared to the usual two years. Apart from the Synthesis 'family of friends', De Lucchi had another solid point of reference in Sottsass who would always give advice and comments in

mutual confidence, so that although De Lucchi worked completely alone, he felt he had support. All the design offices and their staff within Corporate Image were also at hand to give advice and support.

Delphos was a great success in both economic and image terms. In 1988 it was responsible for almost 50% of the Synthesis turnover of furniture systems and as such has fulfilled its economic aims. The look of the Delphos system contributed to the new strategy of presenting Synthesis as specialists in furnishing of all types and of the highest design quality. Delphos was launched by a new distribution concept – out of 800 Olivetti concessionaires, only the 500 most exclusive were chosen – as representative of the new strategy – to stock the range, and a series of new showrooms was also established. This new way of communicating with the market was reinforced in all kinds of advertising and in the graphic design of catalogue illustrations. In particular, the argument presented emphasized the architectural aspect of office furnishing.

According to Torri, the close interaction with

the Synthesis designers was vital for clarifying and verifying the strategic concept. He uses this example to point out the importance of the Olivetti design organization represented by Corporate Image. It was the ever-available service of this institution with its design offices which provided him with a solid basis of knowledge and capability in both office design and image building, especially as he had no special experience in office furniture design when he entered Synthesis. He took advantage of the long experience and tradition of Olivetti and the way it had shaped the attitude and ability of its designers, technical staff and production engineers. Delphos was the result of a long term investment in design and in a young designer – De Lucchi was 28 when he joined Olivetti. His experience of work on the 45 and Icarus systems, the unusual chance for cultural research for the office in a trip around the world directly led to his ideas for Delphos.

Promoting this kind of long term design investment may look vague and unplanned, may not seem a clear plan for ensuring success. In fact it was arrived at by the operational design manager, Macchi, describes as the 'Italian belief in possibilities', an attitude of fundamental importance for the creation of the exceptional, even though it may contain an element of risk. For Torri, managing design in Synthesis requires, of necessity, understanding and respecting the existing corporate culture of Olivetti and using it in an open, flexible way, so that it becomes a lively and enriching experience.

172, 173. The finished Delphos system in use.

OLIVETTI

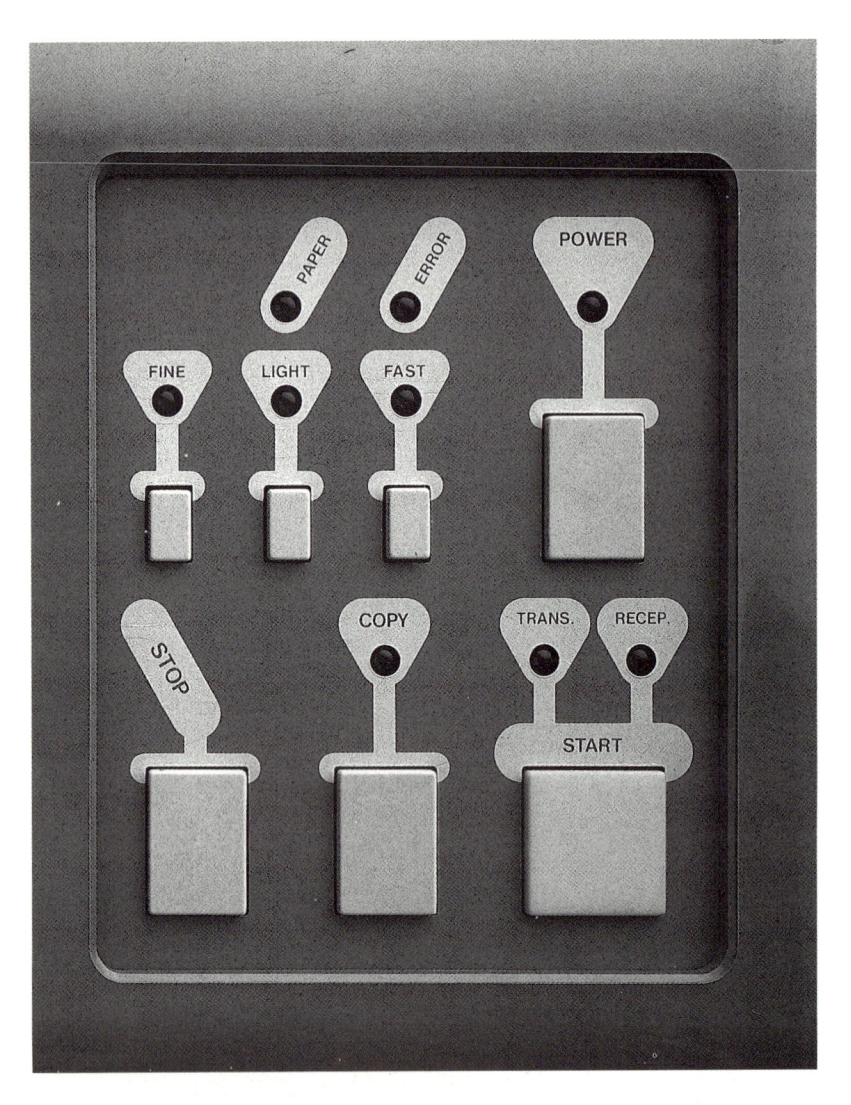

174. An early pressure
keyboard from the TLM 300
series telefax machine.

Keyboard design for the Olivetti Printer DM 309 by Perry King and Santiago Miranda

This case study demonstrates some of the basic principles of Olivetti design management as described in chapter two. To understand the design process for the latest keyboard, only recently introduced to the market, it is necessary to consider Olivetti's central principles concerning the history and continuity of keyboard design.

Starting keyboard research

Perry King points out that pure design research in Olivetti has always been undertaken with a specific project in mind, and it is in this context that his research from 1982 to 1988 has to be seen. In 1982 electronic and micro electronic technology had reached a level which confronted designers and those responsible for design with new opportunities in terms of the power and functions of the machines themselves and in ways of operating them. Technical achievement concentrating on small control surfaces and on the smallest possible elements had made mechanical operating devices such as levers, pushbuttons and moving switches quite obsolete. The energy needed previously – in the form of pressure to turn switches, move levers in operating the machine – was no longer even appropriate for the new technology, as the new technical mechanisms were highly sensitive, miniaturized elements, and the user had to adapt to this new interface between user and machine. Technology driven by what Zorzi describes as a new kind of 'sensory' keyboard developed with 'keys which were to be equipped with operating and monitoring signals and activated by simple finger contact, with no need for pressure, on a smooth and even surface'.

This keyboard demanded a totally new method of handling the machine, using touch instead of pressure. But pressure had given a clear feeling and control of action and reaction, and so in planning for the new technology special attention was given to the visual aspects of design and to a thorough study of the potential of the technology. Zorzi and Viti, at that time directors of Corporate Image and Design respectively, decided to break with the usual procedure of giving product design work solely to product designers.

The way in which this project was entrusted to the staff and the type of brief that was given was typical of the Olivetti management style. To choose Perry King and Santiago Miranda may at first have seemed rather strange as neither had any previous experience with keyboard design. However, this appointment can be seen as following Adriano Olivetti's original principle, which was to bring in young artists and architects with no specialization in industrial design in order to achieve new, culturally inspired concepts of design.

King had been working with Olivetti for twenty years in different offices and with both of the great masters Sottsass and Bellini. During this time he became deeply involved in Olivetti's history of design. From 1965 to 1970 he could be found in the Sottsass office working on the famous Valentine typewriter and the furniture system 45 for Olivetti Synthesis, among other projects. From 1972 to 1979 he was co-ordinator of the department of Corporate Identity which produced graphics for posters and catalogues as well as typeface design, especially dot matrix characters for printing and for electronic screens. King's dot matrix for OCR (optical character readable) applications was later adopted by the European Computer Manufacturers Association (ECMA) for optical character reader fonts. In 1982 King and Miranda worked on the graphics for *Design Process Olivetti*, a catalogue commemorating Olivetti's 75 year history, focusing on all those activities which gave the corporation such a high profile.

King and Miranda were both deeply convinced by the Italian approach to industrial design, and their work in compiling and designing *Design Process Olivetti* gave them a historical perspective on Italian design, as neither is Italian-born: Perry King was born in London in 1938, and Santiago Miranda in Seville in 1947. Compared to the educational and professional possibilities they had in their home countries, Italy offered such prolific designers as Sottsass and design-aware companies like Olivetti. There the possibility existed of becoming involved in living design as part of a modern society and a contemporary culture, from an intellectual, moral and political viewpoint. To both of them this implied a richer, more inspirational and challenging perspective on work and life. When they met in the early 1970's they soon realized that despite their very different backgrounds, they had in common a strong belief in Italian design, despite the arguments then in progress, for example in the Italian 'Radical Architecture' movement, about design and its relation to purely commercial interests and over the failure of utopian experiments to affect social realities. King and Miranda worked together on a self-defined project named 'Unlimited Horizon' through which they explored and developed elements constituting and separating public and private space, so defining public and private environments. It was the start of their work on the user-object relationship and a design approach which they now call 'interactive design'[1]. This background shows that King and Miranda are designers with the vision and drive to develop their own ideas. It was probably their independent research rather than their experience at Olivetti that convinced Zorzi and Viti to give them the keyboard project as it required an input of new values and insights. Zorzi later wrote that it required the 'greatest intellectual freedom, a wide ranging analytical ability and a considerable set of cultural and aesthetic references'[2]. There was no formal briefing for the designers who were left free to undertake their own research and proposals. 'They never specified what we had to do. We knew that they wanted something innovative and exciting......'. explained King and Miranda. The only defined task was to design the visuals of the new sensory keyboard paying special attention to the new technology and operating systems by the choice of symbols and highlighting.

Methods of study

It was completely left to the designers how to proceed on the project. King and Miranda decided that they 'wanted a wide ranging research project to examine the zone of the machine that allows the operator to establish a dialogue'. Nobody forced them to follow this linear course, they were completely free to start and continue as they pleased. One of the first findings in their research was that the symbolic communication between man and object has always had both rational and evocative connotations. They became more and more fascinated by such keys – devices that open up the secret passage to the machine, the well-defined sensitive zones that represent the mysterious centre of the emotional relationship between man and machine as well as being logical and functional devices.

A particular part of their research was the study of symbolic communication in ancient cultures. They discovered a fantastic treasure of communication signs that reached beyond the logical message alone. One source of information was the Italian archaeologist Enrica Fiandra's work on record keeping by ancient Mediterranean societies[3]. She drew their attention to clay seals, tablets and cylinders from the fourth millennium B.C. found between the Eastern Mediterranean and the Indus. They were used as a means of witnessing and administrating operations and represent one of the first communicative filters between man and his activities. Inspired by these discoveries, King and Miranda went on to search out signs with the same rich, evocative quality through other cultures. This included written and drawn descriptions of goods by the Aztecs, body painting both by American Indians and Africans communicating war and dance, Egyptian hieroglyphics and paintings and ancient heraldic symbols. As well as analyzing signs used for messages, King and Miranda went on to consider signs that amplify their own meaning by examining everyday forms of communication such as graffiti.

King and Miranda concluded from this analysis that there have always been two sides of communication between man and object, through formalization in algorithms and the hermeneutic richness of meaning. In today's age of computer rationalities we have reached an extreme point of formalization: binary language knows only either 'yes' or 'no', and so lacks any evocative content. The aim of enriching this language of communication became central to King and Miranda's work.

Their research by necessity also required from the first a logical and rationalist analysis of the requirements of today's man-machine communication. King and Miranda carefully studied all the standard systems for type sizes and letterforms, such as the Italian Uni, the American ANSI, the German DIN and the International ISO. They studied the ergonomic criteria of the man-machine interface which in Olivetti office products consists of an alphanumeric keyboard, control console and video screen. Each of these elements had its own ergonomic requirements such as the degree of inclination of the keyboard for the optimal position for the hand, the colours, size and clarity of the typography used on screens, and the treatment of the screen with non-reflecting layers for maximum legibility. Through their ergonomic studies, King and Miranda came to understand the need for a new, soft interpretation of ergonomics to meet the problem of the latest sensitive keyboards and operation areas. Ergonomics would now have to deal with specific physical aspects, the logical and the functional as well as with emotional and symbolic levels of communication.

Special attention was also given to an analysis of the user of the new keyboards and their established methods of man-machine interaction. The machines on which the new sensory keyboard could be used covered a wide range of printers, copiers and banking machines, all with different types of users. One thing they all had in common was a multitude of users in what could be referred to as the public corners of office buildings, as well as a large group of non-specialized users, in comparison with the former specialized operators for electronic office machines. Users were eager to use technology in an immediate way, simply to operate home machinery, such as what are called 'brown' electronic entertainment systems such as HiFi, video, television and 'white' kitchen appliances such as washing machines and microwave cookers. A study of the common codes for operating these machines gave an important insight into the average user's know-how and habits in interacting with machines. Another field of research concentrated on gaining an overview of future technical trends for the man-machine interaction, involving the use of the mouse, magnetic tablets, touch screens and experiments with voice synthesizers and analyzers.

Olivetti's long experience provided King and Miranda with a very full history of keyboard production. Early typewriter keyboards were not elements of detail but formed the central function of the machine, giving direct and visible access to the mechanical structure, even representing the mechanical structure itself. In a machine like the M1 from 1911, the mechanism lies open and is seen to be directly connected to the inside structure, revealing one side of the mechanism. Technology and design has resulted in a stronger separation between the inner and outer structure as the operational scope develops and the keyboard becomes smaller in relation to the overall size of the machine. Changes in the design of machine casings from 1911 to the present reflects changing attitudes towards the keyboard. Nizzoli's sculptural approach involved working on a holistic concept of shape and integrating the keyboard in the whole without treating it as a separate element. The most striking example of this is the Lexicon 80. A contrast can be seen in his later work, where he starts to divide the body of the machine into separate volumes and planes, a design concept that has not been fully appreciated by his admirers even though, in historical terms, it was the first step in a new direction. It was Ettore Sottsass who continued and perfected this architectural approach to office design, dividing the whole structure into different aesthetic and functional levels. He emphasized the keyboard of the Praxis 48 as a clear console directed to the user with the technical, functional structure for-

175. Drawing for pressure keys with separate target and information zones.

176. Pressure keys in use.

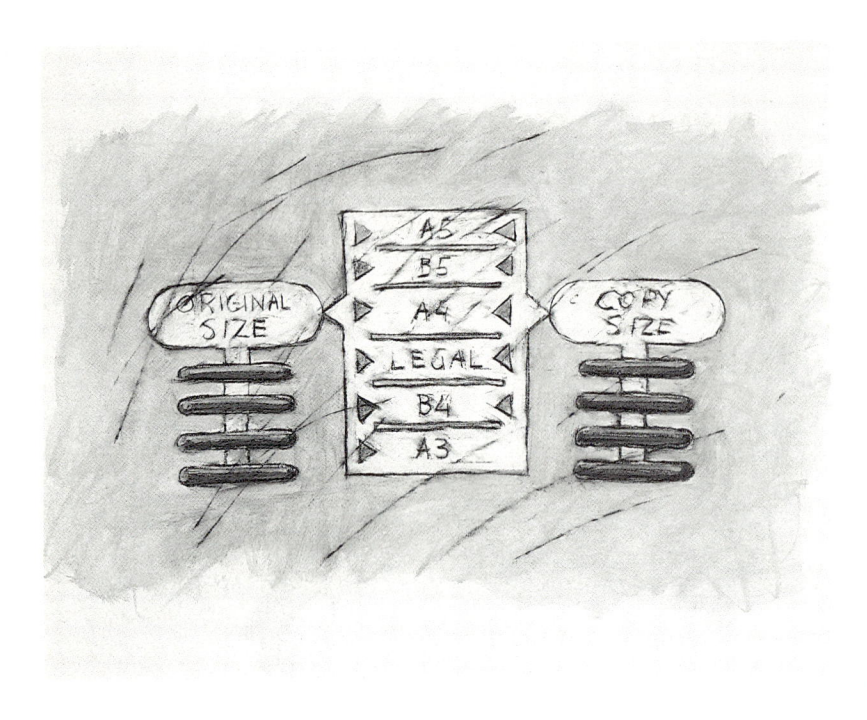

177. Drawing for a patterned relief key system.

ming the architectural backbone. Bellini's design for the world's first desk top computer, the Programma 101, also included a clear separation between the keyboard and the information display. In a sandwich structure the operational area was a console forming the bottom part whereas the information was displayed on an area separated in the upper part by being set back from the rest. With his wedge shape for typewriters and calculators, Bellini represents a more sculptural, holistic approach to design. However, there is still a clear aesthetic distinction between the operation and information and the functional side of the machine (see for example the Logos 240. The ETP 55 represents a sculptural shape as a whole and also emphasizes the different operational and functional areas for paper and printing as different organic elements of the one body. By 1973, Bellini's Divisumma 18 and Divisumma 28 calculators already recognised an operational zone that was not a separate element but part of the body itself. The surface of the Divisumma 18 in the operational zone was a like a soft rubber skin. It allowed sensually smooth operation through touching the surface of the body instead of pressing the keys in the usual, more mechanical way. This kind of interaction with the machine in a more emotional, less rational and functional way forms a common bond between work by all Olivetti's design masters who have been continually experimenting on the perfection of this ideal. The history of Olivetti design was King and Miranda's starting point on which they built and continued their design philosophy. It was not a logical, conscious use of Olivetti's history but an almost natural and automatic process.

The results of research

Through their studies, King and Miranda saw that they were not only confronted with the design for Olivetti soft keyboards but with the question of the interface between man and machine in general. They wanted to contribute to an emotional and symbolic enrichment of the interaction between man and machine – the interface, as it is widely called. The man and machine relationship in the twentieth century seems to have been represented either as one of man exposed to a overwhelmingly mysterious technology, for example in such films as *Modern Times* by Charles Chaplin or *Metropolis* by Fritz Lang, or as one of man wielding ever greater power with the use of the machine. King and Miranda do not follow either of these basic attitudes. Their aim has been to contribute to a playful interaction that involves and stimulates the human senses; the machine as an enjoyable everyday counterpart for an immediate and easily achieved activity, a role which in the future will fill more and more of mankind's time.

King and Miranda began with one of the most basic steps in design, by separating the two zones which are not differentiated in traditional keyboards. The active element which tells the user by a visual stimulus that the machine is ready and what it can perform is called the information zone, and the passive element by which the user puts the machine to work is the target zone. The traditional keys contain both elements: when a key is pressed the information zone is covered and so suppressed. With new technology being operated purely by touch, pressure would no longer instigate the automatic control process. This made it particularly important to give the user an means of to checking which operations he was using. In some ways the user of the new technology was forced to develop a totally new feeling for the machine which no longer provided a traditional response of reacting to pressure by giving in until the lowest point of extension was reached. From 1982 to 1988, design concepts for the keyboard as interactive operational zones continued and developed that idea, allowing the user to adapt to new technology step by step.

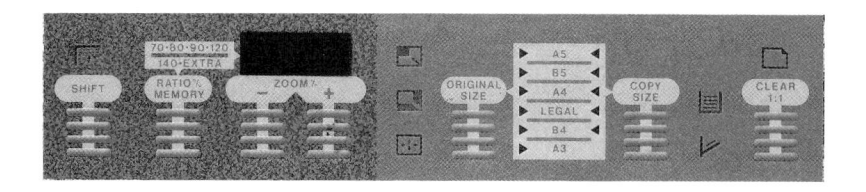

The first results came between 1982 and 1983 with consoles with divided information and target zones with three dimensional keys (see figs. 175, 176). The graphic elaboration of the information zone emphasizes the semantic content and underlines the hierarchical importance of the keys. Control lamps in the information zone work as a direct visible response to the user's action. The empty spaces are used in the same way as letterspacing is used in typography, to achieve a harmonious composition. This type of keyboard was first realized in 1982 on the TLM 320 and TLM 332 telefax machines.

The next step in 1983 to 1984 was the development of sensitive operational zones with braille effect to facilitate the identification of the target area whilst still maintaining the division between information and target areas. The braille effect consisted of a patterned relief system which created a reader text relation through tactile stimulation (see fig. 177). This type of keyboard first appeared in the printer PR 45 (see figs. 178, 179) and the Copia 900 and 1150 photocopying machines. A second kind of relief was made up of thirty six pyramid shapes

178. Patterned relief keys on the PR47 printer.

179. Patterned relief keys on the Copia copier.

put together in a six by six matrix target field (see fig. 180).

The change to sensitive zones without relief effects had been completed between 1983 and 1987. Keys in the target zone were highlighted by graphics, with coloured patches corresponding to the traditional three dimensional keys in size and shape (see figs. 181,182) The target fields were also separated from the information zone. Another type of sensitive flat keyboard was produced between 1985 and 1987. Using a postage stamp shape for the keys in the target zone, it moved away from the symbol of the traditional, three dimensional key towards and alternative graphic model (see figs. 183,184).

Olivetti keyboard research in 1988

Organizational background of the project

Since 1982 King and Miranda have worked continuously as design consultants for Corporate Image department, with responsibility for keyboard research and increasingly for product graphics. The latter became more important with the growing number of products manufactured outside the company and entering the Olivetti range. The only possibility left for design in such cases was in the colour range and product graphics. Apart from the application of the Olivetti logo and the product name, product graphics encompassed the keyboard design. Together with the economic background this further convinced King and Miranda that the keyboard of the future will become a central means of differentiation in terms of aesthetics and offer a potential of differentiation in the general quality of man-machine interaction.

Several stages must be followed with each new Olivetti product and the example chosen here is the production of the DM 309 printer series. The independent product unit for product systems would take responsibility for marketing all products within the business group, including printers. There must also be marketing direction and assistance for the specific product group on behalf of product planning within the business groups responsible for standard re-

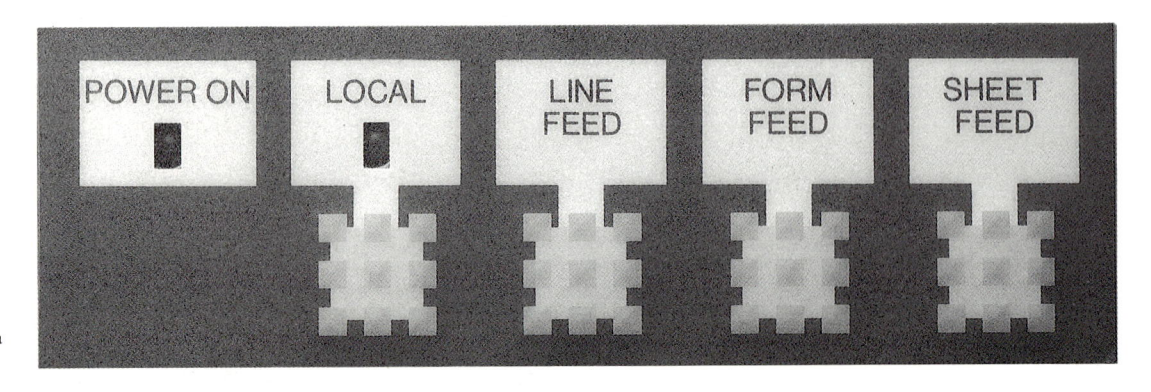

180. Alternative design for a patterned relief keyboard.

CASE STUDIES

quirements and the director and manager of product planning for each specific product. The project manager must establish marketing requirements and give a rough briefing with both commercial and technical requirements and standards for the product so that the development engineers for the relevant product groups can start to work on a basic technical concept that fits to the established requirements. The designers of the shell of the keyboard unit, in the case of the DM 309 George Sowden with Simon Morgan of the Sottsass design office, started to work with the development engineers on the design concept. King and Miranda also were involved in this phase of the process. Sowden and Morgan's own work on the double shell keyboard was a very important factor in the success of the overall design process.

181. Drawing for a touch-sensitive key that imitates the shape of a traditional key.

182. Model of a banking machine using such keys.

157

OLIVETTI

183. Drawing for an alternative graphic model for a touch-sensitive key – the 'postage stamp' approach.

The course of the design process

Whereas designers are nowadays informed about new projects by the operational design manager Macchi at an early stage, King and Miranda in fact first heard about the project in March 1988 through their close and continual relations with the development engineers. At that time Macchi was still working on the basic conception of operational design management and was not involved as much as he is today in everyday design work. Despite this, as we will see later, he played a vital role in the later stages of the project.

The briefing by the project manager was to develop a new series of professional printers to replace the preceding semi-professional line of DM 282 printers. As a professional product, the DM 309 was to offer higher technical performance and functional differentiation with higher design standards and finish, to correspond to the requirements of professional operators. Speed capacity was to be increased from 240 to 300 characters per second, the paper tractor was to be transformed from a pull system to an integrated push system and the number of printing points was to be considerably increased to improve printing quality. A main requirement was to reduce noise, to meet the new standard of 55 decibels maximum.

The product designers started by concentrating on how to reduce noise and to improve finish for professional use. Their aim was to achieve a softer, friendlier machine that offered special facilities for the professional environment. From the beginning of the project they worked with the engineers on a double layered housing for the machine, aiming thereby for a considerable decrease in noise: furthermore, all 'open' parts of the machine were to be covered with special noise-dampening devices.

King and Miranda saw an opportunity to realize something new and to develop their established ideal of creating a more emotional and interactive relation between man and machine, by allowing the user to use touch to cause some kind of emotional response. The braille effect with reliefs that they had developed in 1983 was the most important step in that direction, although for financial reasons it was not adapted for succeeding products. Higher costs are accepted for first, innovative models, but are not tolerated for later models on the home market. With this in mind, King and Miranda wanted to use this opportunity of working on the DM 309 and agreed with the project manager, marketing and product designers to develop a new approach to the keyboard.

Analyzing the competitors, Miranda understood that the flat keyboard had by that time had become the image of cheap and low quality; all of the low quality, low cost products on offer were characterized by flat low keyboards. The expensive, three dimensional and touchable solutions of the competitors had the keys set in the shell of the keyboard unit and covered with a rubber skin. Telling the engineers about their idea of a three dimensional, touchable keyboard King and Miranda created what they called an 'economic scandal' in the engineering group, as everybody knew about the expense of such keyboards on the market. They asked for more time to calculate the costs for this concept and although they experienced no hostility from the technicians, it became difficult for them to continue as the technicians are only allocated a limited amount of time for each project.

184. Model of keys developed from the drawing in 183.

OLIVETTI

185. A drawing developing the double layered solution to the body shell.

The design concept from the defined keyboard to the interactive keyboard unit

At the same time that King and Miranda worked to develop a three dimensional keyboard, product designers and engineers were working on a two layer concept of the machine body, which for a long time seemed to be impossible to achieve. King and Miranda believed in the possibility of the new concept and decided to work on an alternative to the previous traditional rubber keys that would be less costly to produce. It was mainly this concept of the machine design that inspired King to develop not only a new version for the keys but a totally new concept for the whole of the keyboard unit. The basic idea was to eliminate the existing separation between body and keyboard, with the keyboard seen as an outside element attached to the machine, by using the body itself as operational element. The designers saw no need to place the keyboard in any specific section of the machine and saw no sense in rigidly separating its hard and soft constituents. The idea of an organically designed 'leopard skin' with harmonious but unusual placements of graphic highlights around the body complimented the idea of using all of the machine body as a potential area of interaction for the user, instead of putting all the information into a small, compressed area. Stemming from King and Miranda's ideal, the traditional operational fields were to be replaced by interactive surfaces with tactile reliefs and graphics. As King and Miranda put it, the whole of the body of the machine becomes communicative; the ears, arms, breasts, shoulders, legs and hair as well as the head or face. The established product graphics were able to give a vital contribution to the design of the machine body; by freeing the graphics from a defined role and allowing them to be adapted in a completely free manner, the body itself becomes livelier. The overall design meant that the machine did not have just one point of communication, but that all of its parts and elements could be used for a more fulfilling communication with the user.

At this point in the design procedure, the engineers had completed their calculations on the rubber version of the shell of the keyboard unit. The marketing staff responsible had originally shown no interest in a solution for the keyboard during the first presentation of the drawings and ideas. When King and Miranda informed Macchi about the lack of interest, he came to see the form studies, discussed the design concept in detail with the designers and having been convinced of its qualities, made a personal presentation to the top level of the business unit, in this case the director of the product society for systems Panatone.

Panatone appreciated innovation and differentiation in a product field where mature technology tends not to offer striking developments, and this applied to keyboard design which was forced by market pressure to follow a conventional direction. With Panatone's approval and support, the discussions between the marketing and engineering departments were restarted. It was agreed that a concept representing an innovation in the market could involve higher costs and retail prices as long as the competitors were not able to produce the same innovation at a lower price. King and Miranda were given the go-ahead for their concept by the engineers concerned with the technical realization of the project. With more time, with inspiration from Miranda and with top-level support the engineers were able to realize the two layer concept of the shell of the printer and were able to co-operate efficiently and successfully with the designers. Before long, the technical concept was finished, with costs always in mind: King and Miranda had achieved what they called a 'perfect compromise with the technical'. (fig. 187)

The final solution involved taking the shell of the machine, designed by Sowden, and using it as a body with a double layered structure. The traditional solution had used a three dimensional keyboard with the keys placed into holes in the shell and covered with an outside rubber skin. The new concept was to have the technical structure of the keys inside the first level of the shell of the housing structure. This was to be completely covered by a second level, with the possibility for opening it. A rubber mat was introduced between the two levels to hold the outside sculptural structure of the keys. By touching the relief key from the outside, the internal part will come into contact with the technical structure, transmitting a clear feeling of this action to the user. This concept allowed the keys to be used decoratively, with their shape, material and colour independent of the body of the machine.

The higher cost of the keyboard in this way became absorbed in the overall cost of the machine, which was easier to justify and administer internally. By solving the problem of how to control the budget, King points out, they had already won half the battle.

As the photographs of the last model of the new keyboard show (see figs. 185,186), King and Miranda preferred to develop their designs and research continuously, rather than to make a series of radical changes. The potential that the new approach offered in using the whole body of the machine as an interactive surface started slowly, as it still referred to preceding concepts of the interaction between man and machine and gave the user the possibility to adapt to it at the speed he desired. This was also a result of costs, as the price of the electronic board for the sensitive technical structure was

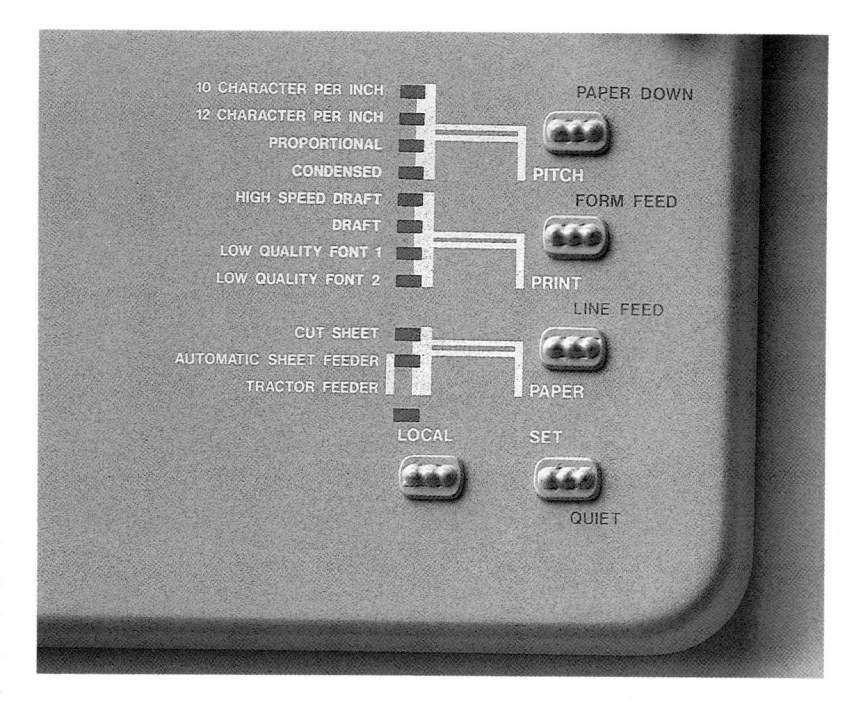

186. Model for the DM 309 Keyboard solution.

OLIVETTI

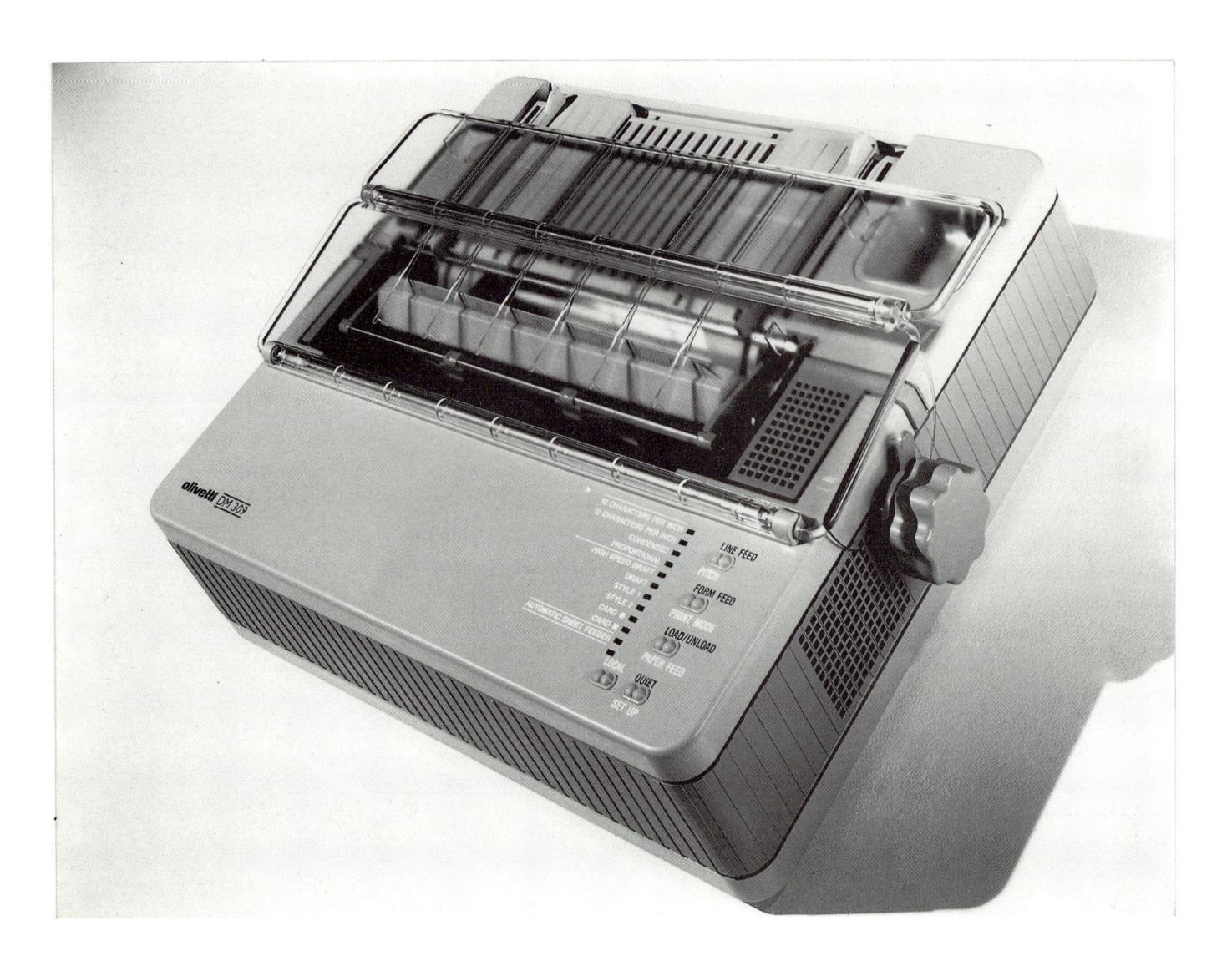

187. The DM 309 Printer,
designed by George Sowden,
with the keyboard designed
by King and Miranda.

measured in square millimeters. The closer the keys are put together in a small, defined area the more cost effective the solution. For this reason, King and Miranda chose to compromise and to concentrate on the graphic aspects of the keyboard. Introduction to the market was planned for June 1989.

Some final thoughts

The relief keys integrated into the shell of the machine represent the latest result of King and Miranda's research into keyboards from 1982. They are an extremely reduced formal interpretation of King and Miranda's concept which succeeds in meeting Olivetti's important principle of continuity in design (see chapter two). A retrospective look at Olivetti's design history shows that the basic idea was used by Bellini in 1973 in the Divisumma 18 and 28, although on a different basis. By 1989 it is possible to continue this newly developed conceptual line so as to open up a totally new approach to the design of both the keyboard and the unit.

King and Miranda's project is a most interesting and wide ranging example of Olivetti's living design philosophy for many reasons. It shows that briefing for innovative projects and their solutions is in Olivetti very much a matter of using the right designers for a project and giving them maximum freedom to develop their research and ideas. This principle, so difficult for traditional management, wedded to detailed planning at every step, to accept, can be seen throughout Olivetti's main design achievements.

We set out in chapter two the general principles of Olivetti management design. In this chapter each project has been chosen to show what is required for this special method of working to be successful. First of all it needs designers with independent ideas and mature views about the cultural aspects of design as well as the capacity to apply these ideas to concrete industrial projects. It also demands the experience and ability to carry such ideas and projects through the company structure, taking into consideration both human and economic factors and using all the advantages and possibilities of the vertical access given to designers by the company. Finally it demands a strong belief in Olivetti's philosophy and tradition.

Note on Sources

The early history of Olivetti is well-documented – the main titles used here are given in the bibliography below. However, much of the material on the contemporary activities of Olivetti and the company's development since Carlo de Benedetti became President has been gathered in the course of conversations and discussions with Olivetti designers and staff, notabl8 Paolo Viti, Antonio Macchi Cassia, Ettore Sottsass Jnr, Mario Bellini, and Hans von Klier. To them and to the many others who helped with the research for this book the author extends her thanks.

Bibliography

Books on Olivetti

Caizzi, Bruno, *Gli Olivetti*, Turin, 1962
Design Process Olivetti 1908-1983, intro. by Renzo Zorzi, Ivrea, 1983
Gregotti, Vittorio, *Il disegno del prodotto industriale, Italia 1960-1980*, Milan, 1980
Labò, Mario, *L'aspetto estetico dell'opera sociale di Adriano Olivetti*, Milan, 1955.
Olivetti 1908-1958, Ivrea, 1958
Olivetti: Design in Industry, Museum of Modern Art Bulletin, New York, 1952

Books by Adriano Olivetti

Society, State, Community, Milan, 1952,
The Factory and the Cummunity, Ivrea, 1956
A Development Plan for the Val d'Aosta, Ivrea, 1945,
Communal Political Life, Ivrea, 1945

Magazines and journals published by Olivetti

Communità, 1945 onwards
Notizie Olivetti, 1952 onwards
Rivista Olivetti, 1952 onwards
SeleArte, 1978 onwards
Tecnica ed Organizzazione, 1937 onwards

For the most recent listing of Olivetti sponsored publications, films, exhibitions, etc, the reader is referred to *Design Process Olivetti 1908-1983*, 1983.

Footnotes

1. Labò, Mario, (1955), p. 19
2. Caizzi, Bruno (1962) p. 9ff, Labò, Mario, (1955), pp 19-20, *Design Process Olivetti* (1983), p. 10ff
3. Labò, Mario, (1955), p. 22
4. Gregotti, Vittorio, (1980) p. 111
5. Caizzi, Bruno (1962) p. 171ff
6. Ochetto, Valerio, (1985), p. 53
7. See his articles 'Alcune note critiche al systema "Bedaux"', in *Organizzatione scientifica del lavoro*, Rome, June 1927, and 'Dirigenti e ideali dirretivi', in *Organizzazione scientifica del lavoro*, Rome, May 1931
8. This resulted in his later works, *A Development Plan for the Val d'Aosta*, Ivrea, 1945, and *Communal Political Life*, Ivrea, 1945
9. Caizzi, Bruno (1962) p. 201
10. Caizzi, Bruno (1962) p. 196-203 & Adriano Olivetti's articles on the organization and ethics of industry.
11. See his articles 'Alcune note critiche al systema "Bedaux"', in *Organizzatione scientifica del lavoro*, Rome, June 1927, and 'Scientific Aims and Industrial Trends', *Tecnica ed Organizzazione*, 1., Jan. 1937
12. Caizzi, Bruno (1962) p. 175
13. See below on design functions of the M1.
14. This ethical approach to economic activity is here described by the term 'common philiosophy'.
15. His main works are *Society, State, Community*, Milan, 1952, *The Factory and the Cummunity*, Ivrea, 1956 (both published by Communità) and numerous articles in journals and magazines.
16. See Adriano Olivetti *Society, State, Community*, Milan, 1952, p. 47ff
17. See Adriano Olivetti *Society, State, Community*, Milan, 1952, p. 47ff & Ochetto, Valerio, (1985), p. 123
18. See Adriano Olivetti *Society, State, Community*, Milan, 1952, p. 47ff & Ochetto, Valerio, (1985), p. 123
19. Especially Le Corbusier's *Vers Une Architecture*
20. See *A Development Scheme for the Val d'Aosta*, Ivrea, 1943
21. See Adriano Olivetti *Society, State, Community*, Milan, 1952, p. 47ff.
22. See Ochetto, Valerio, (1985), p. 65
23. See Vidari, *Figini e Pollini* (unpublished mss) pp 1-5
24. See Ochetto, Valerio, (1985), p. 85
25. See *Design Process Olivetti 1908-1983*, p. 26.
26. See Caizzi, Bruno (1962) p. 223
27. See *Design Process Olivetti 1908-1983*
28. See *Design Process Olivetti 1908-1983*, p. 19.
29. See Labò, Mario, (1955), p.20.
30. See Gregotti, Vittorio, (1980) p. 206
31. See Labò, Mario, (1955), p. 20
32. For example Nizzoli worked for many years with the gifted engineer Natale Capellaro.
33. See *Design Process Olivetti 1908-1983*, p. 40.
34. See *Design Process Olivetti 1908-1983*, p. 84.
35. See the introduction to the Museum of Modern Art catalogue, 1952.
36. See Sparke, Penny, *Design Consultants*, London, 1983, p. 22ff.
37. The influence of the Bauhaus only reached Italy after 1930 – see Labò, Mario, (1955), p. 20.
38. Pamplaoni uses the term *dirigismo estetico* to define Adriano's personal interventions in shaping the image of the company, in particular the way in which the company presented itself to the marketplace. This personal approach is in contrast to the cpnventional use of market research etc. See *Quaderni della Fondazione Olivetti*, Rome, 1984, p. 30.
39. See Tarantini, Domenico, 'Science into Technics', *Notizie Olivetti*, no. 68, 1960, pp. 46-49.
40. 39. See Tarantini, Domenico, in *Notizie Olivetti*, no. 68, 1960, pp. 46-49.
41. See Caizzi, Bruno (1962) p. 249.
42. See Sottsass, Ettore, 'Nuove Macchine Olivetti per la gestione contabile e scientifica', *Stile Industria*, no. 37, Milan 1962.
43. See Ochetto, Valerio (1955) p. 287 & Caizzi, Bruno (1962) p. 243 ff
44. Renzo Zorzi has written and spoken a great deal about Olivetti, but little of this important material has been published: sources include the introduction to *Design Process Olivetti 1908-1983*, the introduction to Barbacetto, G., *Design Interface*, Milan, 1987, and 'Product Design as Communication', *Domus*, Sept. 1987.